FLORIDA
SCIENCE
FUSION

fusion [FYOO • zhuhn] a combination of two or more things that releases energy

This **Interactive Student Edition** belongs to

_____

Teacher/Room

_____

HOLT McDOUGAL

 HOUGHTON MIFFLIN HARCOURT

Consulting Authors

Michael A. DiSpezio

Global Educator
North Falmouth, Massachusetts

Michael DiSpezio is a renaissance educator who moved from the research laboratory of a Nobel Prize winner to the K–12 science classroom. He has authored or co-authored numerous textbooks and written more than 25 trade books. For nearly a decade he worked with the JASON Project, under the auspices of the National Geographic Society, where he designed curriculum, wrote lessons, and hosted dozens of studio and location broadcasts. Over the past two decades, he has developed supplementary material for organizations and shows that include PBS *Scientific American Frontiers, Discover* magazine, and the Discovery Channel. He has extended his reach outside the United States and into topics of crucial importance today. To all his projects, he brings his extensive background in science and his expertise in classroom teaching at the elementary, middle, and high school levels.

Marjorie Frank

*Science Writer and
Content-Area Reading Specialist*
Brooklyn, New York

An educator and linguist by training, a writer and poet by nature, Marjorie Frank has authored and designed a generation of instructional materials in all subject areas, including past HMH Science programs. Her other credits include authoring science issues of an award-winning children's magazine; writing game-based digital assessments in math, reading, and language arts; and serving as instructional designer and co-author of pioneering school-to-work software for Classroom Inc., a nonprofit organization dedicated to improving reading and math skills for middle and high school learners. She wrote lyrics and music for *SCIENCE SONGS*, which was an American Library Association nominee for notable recording. In addition, she has served on the adjunct faculty of Hunter, Manhattan, and Brooklyn Colleges, teaching courses in science methods, literacy, and writing.

Acknowledgments for Covers

Front cover: *fiber optics* ©Dennis O'Clair/Stone/Getty Images; *Ferris wheel* ©Geoffrey George/Flickr/Getty Images; *snowboarder* ©Jonathan Nourok/Photographer's Choice/Getty Images; *water ripples* ©L. Clarke/Corbis; *molecule model* ©Stockbyte/Getty Images.

Back cover: *test tubes* ©PHOTOTAKE Inc./Alamy; *bat hitting ball* ©Tetra Images/Corbis; *fly* ©Gary Meszaros/Photo Researchers, Inc.; *ice cave* ©Tyler Stableford/Stone/Getty Images.

Printed in the U.S.A.

ISBN 978-0-547-39877-8

8 9 1421 14 13 12

4500395453   C D E F G

Michael R. Heithaus

Director, School of Environment and Society
Associate Professor, Department of Biological Sciences
Florida International University
North Miami, Florida

Mike Heithaus joined the Florida International University Biology Department in 2003. He has served as Director of the Marine Sciences Program and is now Director of the School of Environment and Society, which brings together the natural and social sciences and humanities to develop solutions to today's environmental challenges. While earning his doctorate, he began the research that grew into the Shark Bay Ecosystem Project in Western Australia, with which he still works. Back in the U.S., he served as a Research Fellow with National Geographic, using remote imaging in his research and hosting a 13-part *Crittercam* television series on the National Geographic Channel. His current research centers on predator-prey interactions among vertebrates, such as tiger sharks, dolphins, dugongs, sea turtles, and cormorants.

Donna M. Ogle

Professor of Reading and Language
National-Louis University
Chicago, Illinois

Creator of the well-known KWL strategy, Donna Ogle has directed many staff development projects translating theory and research into school practice in middle and secondary schools throughout the United States. She is a past president of the International Reading Association and has served as a consultant on literacy projects worldwide. Her extensive international experience includes coordinating the Reading and Writing for Critical Thinking Project in Eastern Europe, developing an integrated curriculum for a USAID Afghan Education Project, and speaking and consulting on projects in several Latin American countries and in Asia. Her books include *Coming Together as Readers; Reading Comprehension: Strategies for Independent Learners; All Children Read;* and *Literacy for a Democratic Society.*

Teacher Advisory Board

Lamica Caldwell
Tavares Middle School
Tavares, FL

Brad Carreker
Foundation Academy
Winter Garden, FL

Lisa J. Larson
Conway Middle School
Orlando, FL

Carolyn Levi
Kennedy Middle School
Rockledge, FL

Kerri McCullough
Windy Hill Middle School
Clermont, FL

Leyla Shaughnessy
Jones High School
Orlando, FL

Nancy Sneed Stitt
Meadowlawn Middle School
North St. Petersburg, FL

Sonia Watson
Tuskawilla Middle School
Oveido, FL

Antonio Young
Bay Point Middle School
St. Petersburg, FL

Program Advisors/Reviewers

Program Advisors

Rose Pringle, Ph.D.
Associate Professor
School of Teaching and Learning
College of Education
University of Florida
Gainesville, FL

Carolyn Staudt, M.Ed.
Curriculum Designer for Technology
KidSolve, Inc. / The Concord Consortium
Concord, MA

Content Reviewers

Paul D. Asimow, Ph.D.
Associate Professor of Geology and Geochemistry
Division of Geological and Planetary Sciences
California Institute of Technology
Pasadena, CA

Nigel S. Atkinson, Ph.D.
Professor of Neurobiology
Section of Neurobiology
The University of Texas at Austin
Austin, TX

Laura K. Baumgartner, Ph.D.
Postdoctoral Researcher
Pace Laboratory
Molecular, Cellular, and Developmental Biology
University of Colorado
Boulder, CO

Sonal Blumenthal, Ph.D.
Science Education Consultant
Austin, TX

Eileen Cashman, Ph.D.
Professor
Department of Environmental Resources Engineering
Humboldt State University
Arcata, CA

Wesley N. Colley, Ph.D.
Senior Research Scientist
Center for Modeling, Simulation, and Analysis
The University of Alabama in Huntsville
Huntsville, AL

Joe W. Crim, Ph.D.
Professor Emeritus
Department of Cellular Biology
The University of Georgia
Athens, GA

Elizabeth A. De Stasio, Ph.D.
Raymond H. Herzog Professor of Science
Professor of Biology
Department of Biology
Lawrence University
Appleton, WI

John E. Hoover, Ph.D.
Professor
Department of Biology
Millersville University
Millersville, PA

Charles W. Johnson, Ph.D.
Chairman, Division of Natural Sciences, Mathematics and Physical Education
Associate Professor of Physics
South Georgia College
Douglas, GA

Ping H. Johnson, Ph.D.
Associate Professor
Department of Health, Physical Education and Sport Science
Kennesaw State University
Kennesaw, GA

Tatiana A. Krivosheev, Ph.D.
Associate Professor of Physics
Department of Natural Sciences
Clayton State University
Morrow, GA

Louise McCullough, M.D., Ph.D.
Associate Professor of Neurology and Neuroscience
Director of Stroke Research and Education
University of Connecticut Health Center &
The Stroke Center at Hartford Hospital
Farmington, CT

Mark Moldwin, Ph.D.
Professor of Space Sciences
Atmospheric, Oceanic and Space Sciences
University of Michigan
Ann Arbor, MI

Hilary Clement Olson, Ph.D.
Research Scientist Associate V
Institute for Geophysics, Jackson School of Geosciences
The University of Texas at Austin
Austin, TX

Russell S. Patrick, Ph.D.
Professor of Physics
Department of Biology, Chemistry, and Physics
Southern Polytechnic State University
Marietta, GA

James L. Pazun, Ph.D.
Professor and Chairman
Chemistry and Physics
Pfeiffer University
Misenheimer, NC

L. Jeanne Perry, Ph.D.
Director (Retired)
Protein Expression Technology Center
Institute for Genomics and Proteomics
University of California, Los Angeles
Los Angeles, CA

Kenneth H. Rubin, Ph.D.
Professor
Department of Geology and Geophysics
University of Hawaii
Honolulu, HI

Michael J. Ryan, Ph.D.
Clark Hubbs Regents Professor in Zoology
Section of Integrative Biology
University of Texas
Austin, TX

Brandon E. Schwab, Ph.D.
Associate Professor
Department of Geology
Humboldt State University
Arcata, CA

Miles R. Silman, Ph.D.
Associate Professor
Department of Biology
Wake Forest University
Winston-Salem, NC

Marllin L. Simon, Ph.D.
Associate Professor
Department of Physics
Auburn University
Auburn, AL

Matt A. Wood, Ph.D.
Professor
Department of Physics & Space Sciences
Florida Institute of Technology
Melbourne, FL

Adam D. Woods, Ph.D.
Associate Professor
Department of Geological Sciences
California State University, Fullerton
Fullerton, CA

Teacher Reviewers

Lamica Caldwell
Tavares Middle School
Tavares, FL

Brad Carreker
Foundation Academy
Winter Garden, FL

Lynda L. Garrett, M.Ed.
Gamble Rogers Middle School
St. Augustine, FL

Barbara A. Humphreys
New River Middle School
Fort Lauderdale, FL

Lisa J. Larson
Conway Middle School
Orlando, FL

Sabine R. Laser
St. Cloud Middle School
St. Cloud, FL

Stacy Loeak
Rodgers Middle School
Riverview, FL

Susan McKinney
Nova Middle School
Davie, FL

Mindy N. Pearson, M.Ed. & NBCT
Van Buren Middle School
Tampa, FL

Kathleen M. Poe
Fletcher Middle School
Jacksonville Beach, FL

Barbara Riley
Science Education Consultant
Merritt Island, FL

Kimberly Scarola, M.Ed.
Pembroke Pines Charter Middle School
Pembroke Pines, FL

Leyla Shaughnessy, M.Ed.
Jones High School
Orlando, FL

Nancy Sneed Stitt, M.S.
Science Instructional Coach
Pinellas Park High School
Largo, FL

Contents in Brief

I've never seen gold in its natural form before!

It takes a change in temperature to pop popcorn!

© Houghton Mifflin Harcourt Publishing Company • Image Credits: (tr) ©Dan Suzio/Photo Researchers, Inc.; (b) ©foodfolio/Alamy

Contents

A thermal photograph can show the different heat levels in a volcano. This is Mount St. Helens.

Unit test date: _____

Assignments:

_____
_____
_____
_____
_____
_____

Luster is a physical property of metal that can make it beautiful and, therefore, valuable.

Contents (continued)

As a sound wave moves through the air, the air moves back and forth.

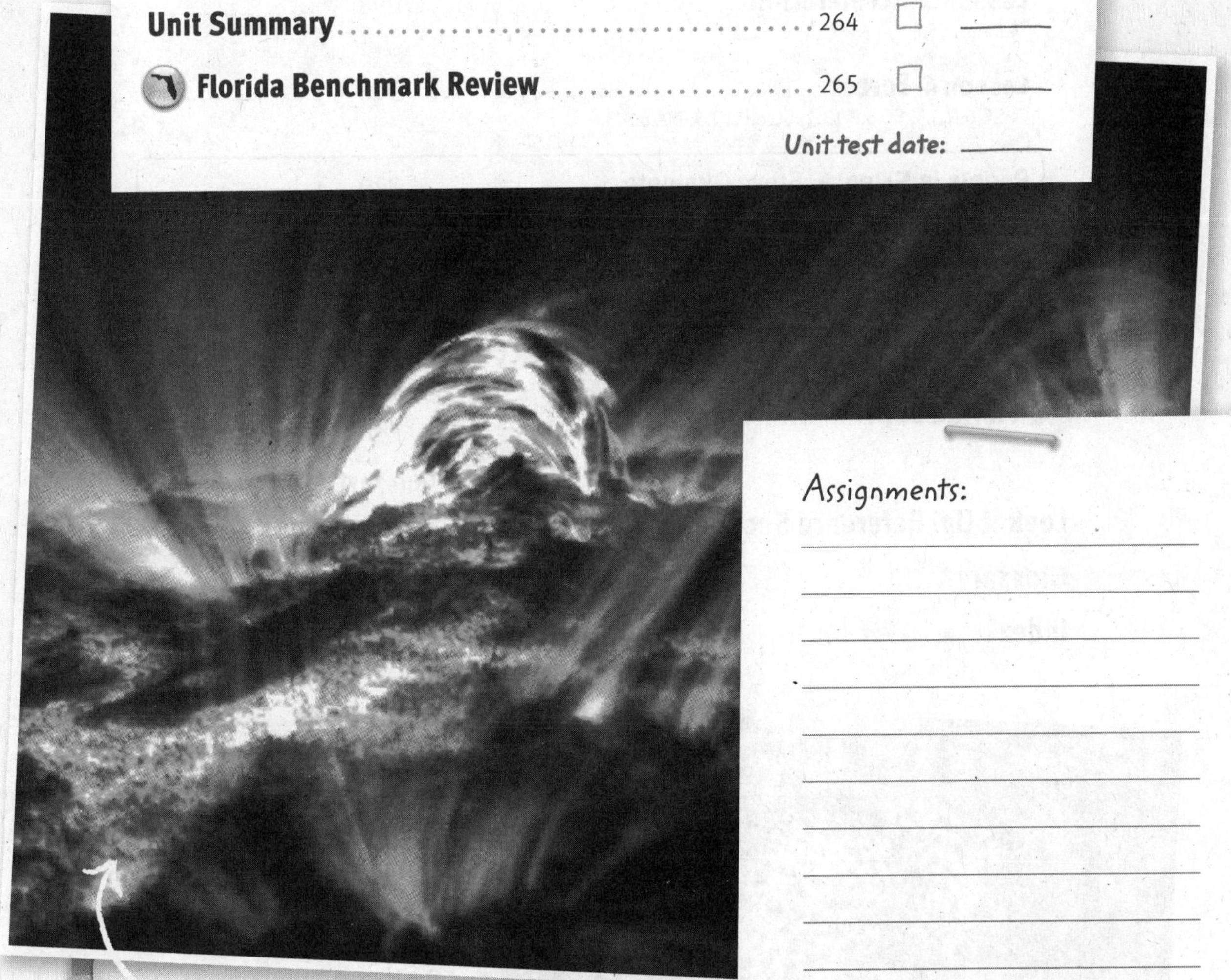

The nuclear energy of the sun is converted into the electromagnetic energy and thermal energy we need to live on Earth.

Assignments:
_____
_____
_____
_____
_____
_____
_____
_____
_____
_____

© Houghton Mifflin Harcourt Publishing Company • Image Credits: ©NASA

Contents *(continued)*

Kinetic energy depends on speed. So, a cheetah has more kinetic energy when it's running than when it's walking.

A roller coaster works by changing direction and speed to create a thrilling ride!

Assignments:

Power up with Science Fusion!

Your program fuses...

Online Virtual Experiences

Inquiry-Based Labs and Activities

Active Reading and Writing

... to generate energy for today's science learner — *you.*

Active Reading and Writing

Be an active reader and make this book your own!

You can answer questions, ask questions, create graphs, make notes, write your own ideas, and highlight information right in your book.

By the end of the school year, your book will become a record of the knowledge and skills you learned in science.

What causes objects to start moving? What causes objects to stop moving once they are in motion?

Active As you read these pages, draw circles around two words that name types of forces.

hat have you pushed or pulled today? Maybe you pushed open a pulled on your ... sh or a orce. Suppose you ... change mething is movi... object's speed or ...

Many forces act on you. Gravity is a ... that pulls objects down to Earth ... keeps you on th...
Friction is a fo... against the direc... slow things down ...

Gravity
Gravity is a force that ... on the ro...

Inquiry-Based Labs and Activities

ScienceFusion includes lots of exciting hands-on inquiry labs and activities, each one designed to bring science skills and concepts to life and get you involved.

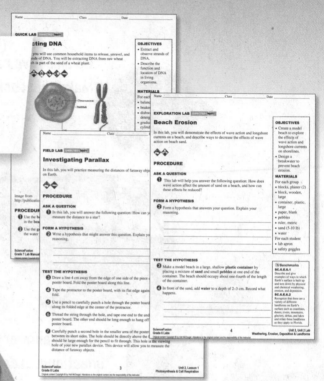

By asking questions, testing your ideas, organizing and analyzing data, drawing conclusions, and sharing what you learn...

You are the scientist!

Online Virtual Experiences

Unit 4 Lesson 1: The Water Cycle

Exploring the water cycle

Evaporation

Precipitation

Condensation

Explore cool labs, activities, interactive lessons, and videos in the virtual world—where science comes alive and you make it happen.

Unit 1 Lesson 1: How plants and animals get energy

Photosynthesis

Epidermis

Chloroplasts

Vein

Leaves

Stem

Roots

Burmese Python

See your science lessons from a completely different point of view—a digital point of view.

Science Fusion! is a new source of energy... just for YOU!

Sunshine State Standards

An Overview and What It Means to You

This book and this class are structured around the Next Generation Sunshine State Standards. As you read, experiment, and study, you will be learning what you need to know to take the tests with which educators measure your progress. You will also be continuing to build your science literacy, which makes you a more skillful person both in and out of school.

The test you'll take in eighth grade is intended to measure how well you learned scientific facts and procedures, and how well you can apply them to situations you might find in the real world. What you remember long after that test, called enduring understandings, will help you see, measure, interpret, and evaluate many more situations you encounter in life.

The Next Generation Sunshine State Standards grew out of 18 Big Ideas that describe major themes and overarching concepts in science. The Big Ideas and Benchmarks appear throughout your book. Look for them on the opening pages of each Unit and Lesson.

The next few pages address several questions, including:

- What are the standards underlying the instruction?
- Where is each Benchmark found in this book?
- What makes the Benchmarks relevant to you now?
- What kinds of questions will you be asked in the tests?

Notice the **Essential Question** on the Lesson opener. This question is a hint to the enduring understanding you may take away from this lesson, long after you've studied it and passed a test and perhaps forgotten some of the details.

Find the **Benchmarks** for each lesson on the Lesson opener.

Find the name and number of the **Big Ideas** for the unit on the Unit opener.

Nature of Science

Big Idea 1 The Practice of Science

What It Means to You

You have done science without knowing it. If you've ever tried to understand something new to you by drawing on what you already knew, you have thought scientifically. Science is more than a collection of facts or the following of one method. It is an attempt to understand the natural world in a way agreed upon by all.

Benchmarks

SC.6.N.1.1 Define a problem from the curriculum, use appropriate reference materials to support scientific understanding, plan and carry out scientific investigation of various types, such as systematic observations or experiments, identify variables, collect and organize data, interpret data in charts, tables, and graphics, analyze information, make predictions, and defend conclusions.
Where to Check It Out Unit 2, Lessons 2, 3, & 4

SC.6.N.1.2 Explain why scientific investigations should be replicable.
Where to Check It Out Unit 1, Lesson 3

SC.6.N.1.3 Explain the difference between an experiment and other types of scientific investigation, and explain the relative benefits and limitations of each.
Where to Check It Out Unit 1, Lesson 3

SC.6.N.1.4 Discuss, compare, and negotiate methods used, results obtained, and explanations among groups of students conducting the same investigation.
Where to Check It Out Unit 1, Lesson 3

SC.6.N.1.5 Recognize that science involves creativity, not just in designing experiments, but also in creating explanations that fit evidence.
Where to Check It Out Unit 1, Lesson 1

Sample Question Circle the correct answer.

1 Lee reads of a scientific study claiming drinking lots of water improves memory. The study used a large number of subjects, controlled all variables carefully, and shared results openly with other scientists. Lee, who feels he knows a lot about how science works, still isn't convinced. What else might convince him?

A. If he knew the study took place in a large lab.

B. If he knew it was done at a university.

C. If he knew elaborate equipment was used.

D. If others were able to replicate the findings.

Sunshine State Standards *(continued)*

Big Idea 2
The Characteristics of Scientific Knowledge

What It Means to You

Scientific knowledge is different from other forms of thought because it is based on empirical evidence, or evidence gained by the senses. Scientists gather a lot of empirical evidence before they try to form explanations from it. What this means is that scientific knowledge can be tested and measured. It can change when new evidence arises. Scientific knowledge is more than one person's opinion.

A scientist takes a water sample

Benchmarks

SC.6.N.2.1 Distinguish science from other activities involving thought.
Where to Check It Out Unit 1, Lesson 1

SC.6.N.2.2 Explain that scientific knowledge is durable because it is open to change as new evidence or interpretations are encountered.
Where to Check It Out Unit 1, Lesson 2

SC.6.N.2.3 Recognize that scientists who make contributions to scientific knowledge come from all kinds of backgrounds and possess varied talents, interests, and goals.
Where to Check It Out Unit 1, Lessons 1 & 5

Sample Question   Circle the correct answer.

2 Ryan made a list of activities he likes to do. Which activity would not be classified as scientific?

A. identifying rocks by color and texture

B. determining how fast his plant is growing by measuring the height of it every day

C. drawing pictures of superheroes he's created

D. making notes about how many hours the sun shines each day

Nature of Science

Big Idea 3 The Role of Theories, Laws, Hypotheses, and Models

What It Means to You

Learning science is like learning a language. Terms like *theory*, *model*, and *law*, while used loosely in everyday language, have specific meanings in science.

Benchmarks

SC.6.N.3.1 Recognize and explain that a scientific theory is a well-supported and widely accepted explanation of nature and is not simply a claim posed by an individual. Thus, the use of the term theory in science is very different than how it is used in everyday life.

Where to Check It Out Unit 1, Lesson 2

SC.6.N.3.2 Recognize and explain that a scientific law is a description of a specific relationship under given conditions in the natural world. Thus, scientific laws are different from societal laws.

Where to Check It Out Unit 1, Lesson 2

SC.6.N.3.3 Give several examples of scientific laws.

Where to Check It Out Unit 1, Lesson 2

SC.6.N.3.4 Identify the role of models in the context of the sixth grade science benchmarks.

Where to Check It Out Unit 1, Lesson 4

Sample Question Circle the correct answer.

3 Brianna observes that the air inside a balloon always seems to get smaller the colder the temperature gets. Which of the following is a scientific law that would describe this observation?

  A. As temperature decreases, a gas's volume decreases.

  B. Gases are made of tiny particles that move.

  C. Balloons can only hold so much gas.

  D. As temperature decreases, a gas's volume increases.

Physical Science

Big Idea 8 Properties of Matter

What It Means to You

We describe matter by its physical and chemical properties. Mass and volume are examples of physical properties. The ability to burn, or flammability, is an example of a chemical property. Mass is one physical property common to all matter. While related, mass and weight are not the same. Mass is a measure of the amount of matter. Weight is a measure of the force of attraction between an object and Earth.

Oil and vinegar don't mix.

Benchmarks

SC.8.P.8.1 Explore the scientific theory of atoms (also known as atomic theory) by using models to explain the motion of particles in solids, liquids, and gases.
Where to Check It Out Unit 2, Lesson 4

SC.8.P.8.2 Differentiate between weight and mass recognizing that weight is the amount of gravitational pull on an object and is distinct from, though proportional to, mass.
Where to Check It Out Unit 2, Lesson 1

SC.8.P.8.3 Explore and describe the densities of various materials through measurement of their masses and volumes.
Where to Check It Out Unit 2, Lesson 1

SC.8.P.8.4 Classify and compare substances on the basis of characteristic physical properties that can be demonstrated or measured; for example, density, thermal or electrical conductivity, solubility, magnetic properties, melting and boiling points, and know that these properties are independent of the amount of the sample.
Where to Check It Out Unit 2, Lesson 2

SC.8.P.8.5 Recognize that there are a finite number of elements and that their atoms combine in a multitude of ways to produce compounds that make up all of the living and nonliving things that we encounter.
Where to Check It Out Unit 2, Lesson 5

SC.8.P.8.6 Recognize that elements are grouped in the periodic table according to similarities of their properties.
Where to Check It Out Unit 2, Lesson 7

SC.8.P.8.7 Explore the scientific theory of atoms (also known as atomic theory) by recognizing that atoms are the smallest unit of an element and are composed of sub-atomic particles (electrons surrounding a nucleus containing protons and neutrons).
Where to Check It Out Unit 2, Lesson 6

SC.8.P.8.8 Identify basic examples of and compare and classify the properties of compounds, including acids, bases, and salts.
Where to Check It Out Unit 2, Lesson 5

SC.8.P.8.9 Distinguish among mixtures (including solutions) and pure substances.
Where to Check It Out Unit 2, Lesson 5

Sample Question Circle the correct answer.

4 An space alien arrives on Earth. He says he comes from a planet larger than Earth and that, on his planet, he weighs 150 "Earth" pounds. When he's weighed on Earth, he's told he weighs only 125 pounds. The alien can't believe it, because he felt he ate a lot on the ride over and should weigh more. Can you explain this?

A. All aliens lose weight as they eat.

B. Space travel causes weight loss.

C. The alien only thought he ate a lot.

D. Earth is lesser and so the alien will weigh less, because of the lesser force between him and the planet.

Big Idea 9 Changes in Matter

What It Means to You

Matter can undergo two types of changes. In a physical change, such as when water turns to ice, a substance does not change its identity. The ice is just solid water. In a chemical change, a substance does change its identity. For example, the ashes left after a pile of wood burns are a different substance than the wood.

Benchmarks

SC.8.P.9.1 Explore the Law of Conservation of Mass by demonstrating and concluding that mass is conserved when substances undergo physical and chemical changes.
Where to Check It Out Unit 2, Lesson 3

SC.8.P.9.2 Differentiate between physical changes and chemical changes.
Where to Check It Out Unit 2, Lesson 3

SC.8.P.9.3 Investigate and describe how temperature influences chemical changes.
Where to Check It Out Unit 2, Lesson 3

Sample Question Circle the correct answer.

5 Rita wants to make some toast for breakfast. She puts a slice of bread into the toaster. After three minutes, Rita notices that the sides of the bread are black. What has happened?

A. The bread has undergone a change of state.

B. The bread has udergone a change in density.

C. Some of the matter in the bread was destroyed.

D. A new substance has fomed as a result of a chemical change.

Water freezing on the oranges helps to protect them from cooler temperatures.

Physical Science

Big Idea 10 Forms of Energy

What It Means to You

Every change you see occuring is the result of energy. Energy is the ability to cause change. Earth receives most of its energy from the sun. It arrives as radiation of different wavelengths. These waves move through the vacuum of space to provide the power for life on Earth. Some of this energy you can see, like visible light. Others you cannot, but you can feel the effects. Ultraviolet radiation from the sun provides the energy to drive the chemical changes that produce vitamin D in your skin. It can also burn the skin if exposed to it for too long. Accounting for the energy we use on Earth is in large part understanding what happens to the energy we get from the sun.

Energy from the sun on a highway causes the temperature of the pavement to increase.

Benchmarks

SC.7.P.10.1 Illustrate that the sun's energy arrives as radiation with a wide range of wavelengths, including infrared, visible, and ultraviolet, and that white light is made up of a spectrum of many different colors.
Where to Check It Out Unit 3, Lesson 3

SC.7.P.10.2 Observe and explain that light can be reflected, refracted, and/or absorbed.
Where to Check It Out Unit 3, Lesson 4

SC.7.P.10.3 Recognize that light waves, sound waves, and other waves move at different speeds in different materials.
Where to Check It Out Unit 3, Lessons 1, 2, & 4

Sample Question Circle the correct answer.

6 Energy from the sun arrives to Earth as electromagnetic waves with a variety of wavelengths. Which statement describes an electromagnetic wave with a long wavelength?

A. It has a high frequency and high energy.

B. It has a high frequency and low energy.

C. It has a low frequency and low energy.

D. It has a low frequency and high energy.

Physical Science

Big Idea 11 Energy Transfer and Transformations

What It Means to You

Energy is never gained or lost. It is only transformed. This is a fundamental law of nature, the Law of Conservation of Energy. You see energy being transformed all around you. When a book falls off a table, the energy it has from being above the gound, potential energy, gets transformed into the energy of motion that carries it to the ground, kinetic energy. In a microwave oven, the radiant energy from microwaves gets turned into heat energy that raises the temperature of the food. When we speak of "saving energy," what we really mean is trying to transform as much unusable energy as possible into usable forms.

Older refrigerators were poor transformers of energy.

Benchmarks

SC.6.P.11.1 Explore the Law of Conservation of Energy by differentiating between potential and kinetic energy. Identify situations where kinetic energy is transformed into potential energy and vice versa.

Where to Check It Out Unit 5, Lesson 1

SC.7.P.11.1 Recognize that adding heat to or removing heat from a system may result in a temperature change and possibly a change of state.

Where to Check It Out Unit 4, Lessons 2 & 3

SC.7.P.11.2 Investigate and describe the transformation of energy from one form to another.

Where to Check It Out Unit 4, Lesson 1

SC.7.P.11.3 Cite evidence to explain that energy cannot be created nor destroyed, only changed from one form to another.

Where to Check It Out Unit 4, Lesson 1

SC.7.P.11.4 Observe and describe that heat flows in predictable ways, moving from warmer objects to cooler ones until they reach the same temperature.

Where to Check It Out Unit 4, Lessons 2 & 3

Sample Question Circle the correct answer.

7 Gordon throws a baseball into the air. It rises, stops when it reaches a certain height, and then falls back into his hand. When does the ball have its most potential energy?

A. when it is in Gordon's hands

B. as it travels up from Gordon's hands

C. at its highest point in the air

D. as it travels back to Gordon's hands

Physical Science

Big Idea 12 Motion of Objects

What It Means to You

Sometimes, the tiniest push or pull can start an object into motion. Objects in motion are all around us. They may move towards or away from us. They may circle around us or fly by us. The motions of all objects, however, can be described as the distance the object travels over a certain amount of time. We say the objects that move most quickly are the ones that travel the greatest distance in the least time.

Benchmark

SC.6.P.12.1 Measure and graph distance versus time for an object moving at a constant speed. Interpret this relationship.
Where to Check It Out Unit 5, Lesson 2

Sample Question Circle the correct answer.

8 A weather station records that the wind is moving at a velocity of 12 km/h northeast. Why is this a velocity and not a speed?

A. because it's given in SI units

B. because it's an average value for a given time

C. because it's a constant value

D. because both speed and direction are given

Physical Science

Big Idea 13 Forces and Changes in Motion

What It Means to You

Forces are what starts and stops all motion. Some forces, like friction between a bicycle and the pavement, act when objects are in contact. Other forces, like the gravitational pull of the sun on the Earth, act at a distance.

Benchmarks

SC.6.P.13.1 Investigate and describe types of forces including contact forces and forces acting at a distance, such as electrical, magnetic, and gravitational.
Where to Check It Out Unit 5, Lessons 4 & 5

SC.6.P.13.2 Explore the Law of Gravity by recognizing that every object exerts gravitational force on every other object and that the force depends on how much mass the objects have and how far apart they are.
Where to Check It Out Unit 5, Lesson 5

SC.6.P.13.3 Investigate and describe that an unbalanced force acting on an object changes its speed, or direction of motion, or both.
Where to Check It Out Unit 5, Lesson 4

Sample Question Circle the correct answer.

9 Ignacio uses a hammer to hit a nail into a board on the wall. Later, he hits a nail into a board on the floor. How does gravity make it easier to hammer the nail in the second case?

A. Gravity pushes the board up to help the nail go in.

B. Gravity pulls the board and the nail toward each other.

C. Gravity pulls the hammer down so that it pushes on the nail.

D. Gravity pulls the nail down but does not pull on the hammer.

The following standards from math and language arts are part of this year's science curriculum. You will find them throughout the book, in the lessons where they best align.

Benchmarks

MA.6.S.6.2 Select and analyze the measures of central tendency or variability to represent, describe, analyze, and/or summarize a data set for the purposes of answering questions appropriately.

MA.6.A.3.6 Construct and analyze tables, graphs, and equations to describe linear functions and other simple relations using both common language and algebraic notation.

LA.6.4.2.2 The student will record information (e.g., observations, notes, lists, charts, legends) related to a topic, including visual aids to organize and record information and include a list of sources used;

LA.6.2.2.3 The student will organize information to show understanding (e.g., representing main ideas within text through charting, mapping, paraphrasing, summarizing, or comparing/contrasting).

Nature of Science

People used to think that because Earth was flat, you would fall off the edge if you got too close.

Big Idea 1

The Practice of Science

Big Idea 2

The Characteristics of Scientific Knowledge

Big Idea 3

The Role of Theories, Laws, Hypotheses, and Models

What do you think?

Careful observations and experiments provide us with new information that may change or confirm what we know about the world we live in. What is one way in which science has changed your view of the world?

Today, we know that Earth is a sphere.

Unit 1
Nature of Science

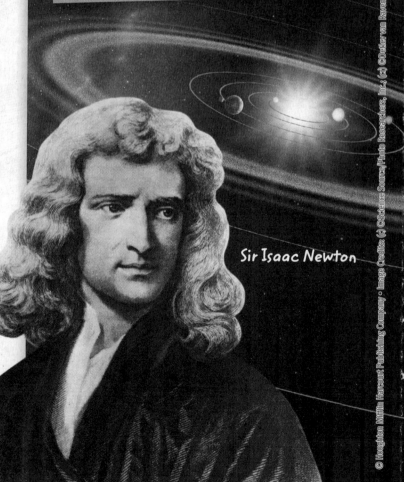

CITIZEN SCIENCE
Things Change

People used to have strange ideas about the world that they lived in. How science has changed some of those ideas is shown here.

1687
People used to think that the sun and planets revolved around Earth. In 1687, Newton described gravity and how it affects objects. His work explained why all of the planets, including Earth, must revolve around the much larger sun. Newton's work finally convinced people that the sun and not Earth was at the center of the solar system.

Sir Isaac Newton

Louis Pasteur

1950s

In 1915, people didn't believe Alfred Wegener when he proposed that the continents were moving slowly. It wasn't until the 1950s that advances in technology provided four different lines of evidence, which proved that continents do move. Wegener was right.

Water ice on Mars

1861

People used to think that living things could come from nonliving things, such as flies and beetles from rotting meat. This idea was called *spontaneous generation*. It was Pasteur's experiments that finally disproved this idea.

EURASIA
NORTH AMERICA
PANGAEA
SOUTH AMERICA
AFRICA
INDIA
AUSTRALIA
ANTARCTICA
Equator

Modern continents used to be a part of Pangaea.

2008

People used to think that there were Martians on Mars. However, probes and landers have replaced ideas of little green men with real information about the planet. In 2008, we discovered water ice there.

Create Your Own Timeline

① Think About It

Choose a favorite science topic and write it down below.

_____

② Conduct Research

Here are some questions to ask as you research your topic:

• What famous people contributed to the development of your topic and when?

_____

_____

_____

• What images can you use to illustrate the changes that occurred to your topic over time?

_____

_____

③ Make A Plan

Sketch out how you would like to organize your information in the space below, including time, people involved, pictures, and brief passages showing the changes in your topic.

Take It Home

Describe what you have learned to adults at home. Then have them help you create a poster of how your topic has changed over time.

What Is Science?

ESSENTIAL QUESTION

How is science different from other fields of study?

By the end of this lesson, you should be able to distinguish what characterizes science and scientific explanations from other forms of knowledge and recognize creativity in science.

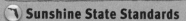

Sunshine State Standards

SC.6.N.1.5 Recognize that science involves creativity, not just in designing experiments, but also in creating explanations that fit evidence.

SC.6.N.2.1 Distinguish science from other activities involving thought.

SC.6.N.2.3 Recognize that scientists who make contributions to scientific knowledge come from all kinds of backgrounds and possess varied talents, interests, and goals.

A scientist studies the genetic code. To most people, this looks impossible to understand. To her eyes, it's a wealth of information.

Engage Your Brain

1 Predict Check T or F to show which statement is true or false.

T F

☐ ☐ Science can determine what book you will enjoy.

☐ ☐ Scientists can often be creative when designing experiments.

☐ ☐ Because they are well educated, scientists do not need to make many observations before coming to a conclusion.

☐ ☐ Scientific results can be proven incorrect.

2 Contrast The pottery in the photo is known for its unique appearance. This is partly because of the glaze used on it. What is one question a scientist might ask about this pottery and one question a nonscientist might ask?

_____

_____

_____

_____

_____

_____

Active Reading

3 Apply Use context clues to write your own definition for the underlined word.

Example sentence
Having watched frogs in ponds her whole childhood, Reilley had a lot of <u>empirical</u> evidence about how they behaved.

empirical

_____

_____

_____

Vocabulary Terms
- science
- empirical evidence

4 Identify As you read, place a question mark next to any words that you don't understand. When you finish reading the lesson, go back and review the text that you marked. If the information is still confusing, consult a classmate or teacher.

Science Is Everywhere

What does science study?

One way to define **science** is as the systematic study of natural events and conditions. It is a logical, structured way of thinking about the world. Scientists ask questions about nature. They try to give explanations to describe what they observe. Any explanation a scientist gives must rely on information available to everyone. It must be an explanation others can test.

You probably have done science yourself without knowing it. If you have looked around you and tried to explain what you saw in a way that could be tested, you have done science.

Active Reading

5 Apply As you read, underline examples of subjects that can be studied by science.

The Natural World

Science is subdivided into different branches. Each branch considers a different part of the world. Each branch, however, studies the world in the same logical and structured way.

Biology, or life science, is the study of all living things, from the smallest, one-celled organisms to mammals. Geology, or earth science, studies Earth, from the materials that make it up to the processes that shape it. Astronomy, the study of objects in outer space, often is included under Earth science. Physical science is the study of energy and all nonliving matter. Physical science includes both physics and chemistry.

These branches of science can and often do overlap. You might hear a scientist called a *biochemist* or *geophysicist*. Such terms refer to those whose work falls a little in each branch.

Think Outside the Book Inquiry

6 Infer List three questions you would like to have answered. Categorize them as scientific or nonscientific. For the nonscientific questions, can you rephrase them in a scientific way? Do you think you can answer every question scientifically?

Testable Ideas

What are types of questions scientists ask? Scientists ask questions that can be tested. They ask questions that have answers they can measure in some way. An explanation in science is usually agreed upon by many people and not just someone's opinion.

One way to understand how scientific thinking differs from other activities is to think of a sculptor making a piece of art. For example, consider the ice sculptor on the next page. Different people can have different ideas of the value of the art. Some may think it is beautiful. Others may find it ugly. Still another may think it's beautiful one day and ugly the next. These are all opinions. No one's opinion is more correct than another's. The types of books you like, the clothes you like to wear, or the foods you like to eat are not questions science normally addresses.

However, now think of other things the sculptor or onlooker might wonder about the piece. How long will an ice sculpture like this last before it melts? Might the sculpture stay frozen longer if something is used to treat the ice? Would using warmer tools make sculpting ice easier? Questions like these have testable answers. The results can be measured and compared. More important, they can be proved false. This is what distinguishes scientific questions from other kinds.

7 Apply This sculptor wonders whether the piece may start to melt before it's finished. Is this a question he can investigate scientifically? Explain.

_____
_____
_____
_____
_____
_____

Tools like this thermometer help scientists make measurements.

8 Explain This sculptor wonders if making the wings thinner would make the sculpture look more graceful. Is this a question that could be tested by science? Explain.

_____
_____
_____
_____
_____

9 Discriminate What other testable questions might one ask about the statue?

_____
_____

"Give me an explanation..."

EVIDENCE

What is a scientific explanation?

A scientific explanation describes a natural process. It relies heavily on evidence gained from direct observation and testing. It is an explanation that others can test and refute.

Evidence gained from observation is empirical evidence. **Empirical evidence** includes observations, measurements, and other types of data scientists gather. Scientists use these data to support scientific explanations. Personal feelings and opinions are not empirical evidence.

A scientist never should hide any evidence he or she claims supports a scientific explanation. Whatever that evidence might be, the scientist must disclose all of it, if he or she wants to be taken seriously. If one scientist does an experiment, other scientists must be able to do the same experiment and get the same results. This openness is what makes scientific explanations strong.

LOGIC

Scientific explanation can be complex and, perhaps, even unintelligible to nonscientists. This should not discourage you from at least trying to evaluate explanations you hear like a scientist would.

For example, what makes popcorn pop? You most likely have seen it pop. You probably even have some idea as to how it happens. Here is a scientific explanation for it you can evaluate.

The corn pops because of a change in temperature. All plants contain water. Maybe the rise in temperature causes that water in the shell to boil. When the water turns into a gas, it pushes the kernel apart. The popcorn "pops" when the hard outer shell explodes. This is an explanation you can evaluate.

Active Reading 10 **List** Give two examples of things that are not empirical evidence.

_____

_____

TESTS

How is a scientific explanation evaluated?

Now that you have an explanation for what makes popcorn pop, you can try to evaluate it as a scientist might. Here is how you might proceed. For each step, some sample responses are provided. Try to think of others.

First, look at any empirical evidence. Think of all the evidence that might support the explanation. Think of the times you've seen popcorn pop. What have you noticed?

Second, consider if the explanation is logical. Does it contradict anything else you know? What about it don't you understand? What else might you also wish to know?

Third, think of other tests you could do to support your ideas. Could you think of a test that might contradict the explanation?

Last, evaluate the explanation. Do you think it has stood up to logic and testing? What about it might be improved?

> **The Scientific Explanation:**
> Popcorn pops because the rise in temperature causes the water in it to expand and "pop" the kernel outward.

The Evidence

For the first step, identify all the evidence you can think of for what causes popcorn to pop.

11 Identify What have you observed about how and when popcorn pops?

• Pops when placed in a microwave

• Pops on a stove top

_____

_____

_____

_____

_____

_____

Inquiry

The Logic

Second, consider if the explanation is consistent with other evidence you have seen.

12 Infer Describe how well your explanation agrees with all of the evidence you have and with all that you know.

• See that water does turn to a gas when heated

• Other things expand when heated

_____

_____

_____

_____

The Tests

Think of other tests you could do that would support the explanation.

13 Predict What other ways might you pop popcorn if this explanation is correct?

• Could pop it in a solar cooker

• Could pop it using hot air

_____

_____

_____

_____

The Conclusion

Last, evaluate the explanation. Describe its strong points. Describe how it might be improved.

14 Evaluate How strong do you think the explanation is? How might it be improved?

_____

_____

_____

_____

Creative Expression

How do scientists show creativity?

Scientists must rely only on what they can observe. They must always try to think logically. Indeed, this might seem dull. However, the best scientists are very creative. They can be creative both in the experiments they design and in the explanations they draw from them.

In Designing Experiments

How might creativity help in designing experiments? In one case, environmental scientists in the Washington, DC, area were looking for a method to detect harmful substances in drinking water. It would be too dangerous to have people drink the water directly, so they had to be creative.

Scientists knew bluegills are very sensitive to some contaminants. The fish "cough" to expel dirty water from their gills. Some scientists thought to use the fish coughing to identify contaminated water. They set bluegills in tanks in different locations. Sensors hooked up to the tanks detected the fishes' coughing and alerted monitors to potential harm. To ensure each fish's safety, a fish stayed in the tank only a short time.

Active Reading

15 Apply Underline examples of creative solutions used by scientists to solve problems.

The bluegill's "coughing" expels contaminants from its gills.

16 Infer How does the bluegill example illustrate creativity in designing experiments?

_____

_____

_____

_____

Newton claimed he got the idea for gravity when he saw an apple fall from a tree.

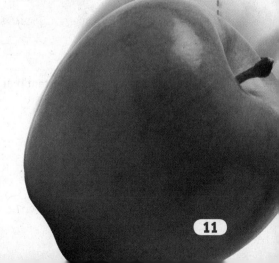

In Explaining Observations

Sometimes, a creative mind can put old evidence together in a new way. New explanations can often be as important as new observations.

Isaac Newton claimed the law of gravity came to him when he saw an apple fall. He reasoned that some force, gravity, pulled the apple to the ground. The question was why didn't gravity pull the moon to the ground as well?

Newton claimed it did. He explained the moon just didn't reach the Earth because it was moving too fast. To understand the idea, think of what would happen if you threw an apple as hard as you could. The harder you throw it, the farther it goes before gravity pulls it to the ground. What if you threw it so hard that it would travel once around the Earth before it reached the ground? This is what is happening to the moon. As it moves, Earth's gravity attracts it. It just moves too fast to fall to the ground.

Newton's explanation changed the understanding of motion forever. He had taken something many had seen, the fall of an apple, and explained it in a new way.

17 Devise Write a caption for this figure explaining how Newton related the moon to an apple falling to the ground.

_____

_____

_____

_____

Visual Summary

To complete this summary, circle the correct word or phrase. Then use the key below to check your answers. You can use this page to review the main concepts of the lesson.

What Is Science?

Science is the systematic study of the natural world.

18 The natural sciences are normally divided into the life, earth, and physical / behavioral branches.

19 Science can / can't explain why you think a particular sculpture looks good.

Scientific explanations are supported by empirical evidence.

20 Empirical evidence includes observations / personal beliefs.

21 Scientific explanations are / are not able to be proved false.

Science can seem to be very dull work, but scientists are often very creative people.

22 Scientists are often creative in designing / comparing experiments.

23 Creative explanations must / need not rely on new observations.

Answers: 18 physical; 19 can't; 20 observations; 21 are; 22 designing; 23 need not

24 Hypothesize Why is it important that a scientist be both very logical and very creative?

Lesson Review

Vocabulary

Fill in the blanks with the term that best completes the following sentences.

1 The study of _____ involves the study of the natural world.

2 Science uses _____ to support its explanations.

Key Concepts

3 Distinguish You just bought a book titled *The Most Beautiful Artworks of the Century*. Is this likely to be a science book? Explain.

_____

_____

_____

4 Determine A manufacturer claims its cleanser works twice as fast as any other. Could tests be performed to support the claim? Explain.

_____

_____

_____

5 Contrast What is empirical evidence and what is it not?

_____

_____

_____

_____

6 Identify What are two ways in which scientists can show creativity?

_____

_____

_____

_____

Critical Thinking

Use this table to answer the following questions.

Color of flower	Number of butterfly visits	Number of moth visits
Red	11	0
Yellow	13	1
White	0	24

7 Distinguish For a science fair project, Ina wanted to investigate if flower color influenced the attraction of butterflies and moths. She made the table after observing the visits of butterflies and moths over a one-day period. Did she collect empirical evidence? Explain.

_____

_____

_____

_____

8 Infer Ina concludes that color does influence the attraction of butterflies and moths. Do you think this was a logical conclusion? Explain.

_____

_____

_____

_____

9 Judge Does being creative in doing science mean that a scientist should make things up? Why?

_____

_____

_____

_____

_____

Scientific Knowledge

This scientist is a paleontologist. She is very carefully removing small pieces of rock from fossilized bones. She is trying to uncover the fossil without damaging it.

ESSENTIAL QUESTION

How do we know about the world we live in?

By the end of this lesson, you should be able to identify examples of scientific knowledge and describe how they may change with new evidence.

Sunshine State Standards

SC.6.N.2.2 Explain that scientific knowledge is durable because it is open to change as new evidence or interpretations are encountered.

SC.6.N.3.1 Recognize and explain that a scientific theory is a well-supported and widely accepted explanation of nature and is not simply a claim posed by an individual. Thus, the use of the term theory in science is very different than how it is used in everyday life.

SC.6.N.3.2 Recongnize and explain that a scientific law is a description of a specific relationship under given conditions in the natural world. Thus, scientific laws are different from societal laws.

SC.6.N.3.3 Give several examples of scientific laws.

LA.6.4.2.2 The student will record information (e.g., observations, notes, lists, charts, legends) related to a topic, including visual aids to organize and record information and include a list of sources used.

© Houghton Mifflin Harcourt Publishing Company • Image Credits: ©Richard T. Nowitz/Photo Researchers, Inc.

Engage Your Brain

1 Conclude Fill in the blank with the word or phrase that you think correctly completes the following sentences.

A scientific _____ describes a basic principle of nature that always occurs under certain conditions.

A scientific model doesn't need to be something physical. It can also be a mathematical

_____

A good scientific theory is one that

_____ the most evidence.

2 Predict Look at the two plants in the photo. What is different about the plant on the left? What do you think may have happened to it? How do you know this?

_____

_____

_____

_____

_____

 Active Reading

3 Apply Many scientific words, such as *model*, also have everyday meanings. Use context clues to write your own definition of the word *model*.

Example sentence

The **model** introduced by the automaker this

year was a great improvement.

_____

_____

Example sentence

Rita was a **model** student.

_____

_____

_____

Vocabulary Terms

- theory
- model
- law

4 Identify This list contains the vocabulary terms you'll learn in this lesson. As you read, circle the definition of each term.

Explain That!

What are some types of scientific explanations?

Active Reading 5 **Identify** As you read, underline examples of scientific theories and models.

Science attempts to explain the world around us. Scientists make observations to collect information about the world. They then develop explanations for the things we see around us. Examples of scientific explanations are theories, models, and laws.

Theories

A scientific **theory** is a well-supported explanation about the natural world. Scientific theories have survived a great deal of testing. Theories explain the observations scientists have made. Scientists also use theories to make predictions about what they may not have seen yet. Theories are powerful things in science. They are much stronger than a hunch made by only one person.

Plate tectonics (playt tek•TAHN•ikz) is an example of a scientific theory. It states that Earth's outer layer is divided into individual plates. The plates move over Earth's surface and carry the landmasses with them.

The theory changed the study of Earth science greatly. Scientists found it could explain many things about the forces that shape Earth's surface. For example, they observed that most major earthquakes occur close to where plates meet and press against each other. In fact, scientists have yet to observe anything that opposes the theory. Plate tectonics helped scientists understand many natural events, such as mountain formation, volcanic eruption, and earthquake activity. It is a powerful scientific theory.

At this plate boundary in northeast Iceland, you can see the ground splitting.

Models

A scientific **model** is a representation of something in the natural world. Models allow scientists to study things that may be too large, too small, or in some way too difficult to study.

Again, be careful of how you think of a model. In science, models do not need to be physical things. A model can be a computer program or a mathematical equation. A model is anything familiar that helps scientists understand anything not familiar. Scientists use models to help them understand past, present, and even future events.

For example, if the land masses on Earth are moving, Earth's surface would not have looked the same millions of years ago. Scientists cannot know for sure what Earth's surface looked like. They can, however, attempt to make a model of it.

Maps are one example of a scientific model. Below are maps of what Earth's surface looks like today and what scientists think it looked like about 225 million years ago. The model shows that all land was once one big mega-continent. Scientists refer to this continent as *Pangaea* (pan•JEE•uh). The model shows how today's continents once formed Pangaea. Of course, the model of Pangaea does have its limitations. It does not allow scientists to study the "real thing," but it can give them a better sense of what Pangaea was like.

Active Reading

6 Infer What is the theory that can explain the model of Pangaea?

_____

_____

_____

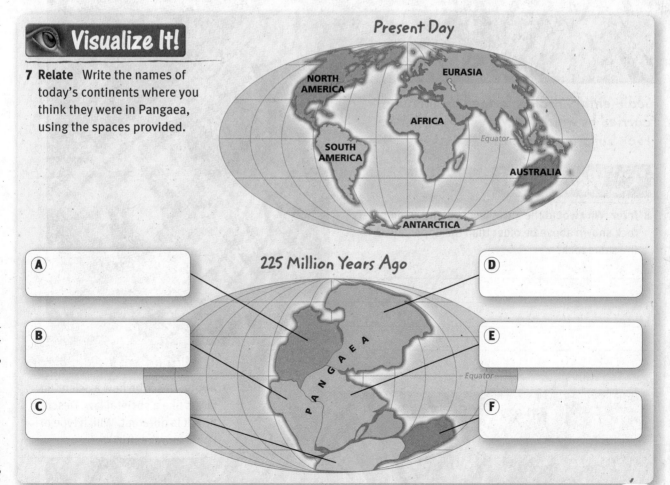

Visualize It!

7 Relate Write the names of today's continents where you think they were in Pangaea, using the spaces provided.

Present Day

NORTH AMERICA

EURASIA

AFRICA

SOUTH AMERICA

Equator

AUSTRALIA

ANTARCTICA

A

B

C

225 Million Years Ago

PANGAEA

Equator

D

E

F

Laws

Theories and models often are modified as we learn more about the natural world. A scientific **law** describes a basic principle of nature that always occurs under certain conditions.

There are many scientific laws. The law of inertia states that an object in motion or at rest will stay in motion or at rest unless a force acts on it. Charles' law states that, at a constant pressure, as the temperature of a gas increases, its volume increases. Notice that laws simply tell you what to expect. For example, from the law of inertia, you can expect that an object at rest will stay at rest. Unlike a law in society, which is established, enforced, and sometimes changed, scientific laws are eternal and unchangeable.

Laws can be expressed in different ways. A law can be a statement or a mathematical equation. For example, Charles' law can be expressed mathematically as $V_1 T_2 = V_2 T_1$. This is just another way of showing the relationship between the volume and the temperature of a gas at a constant pressure.

Every branch of science has its scientific laws. In geology, the law of superposition states that any one layer of rock is always younger than the layer below it. Therefore, younger layers of rock will always overlie older layers. Again, the law is simply a description of what is seen.

Sedimentary rock is formed by particles carried by wind and water. Layers in the rock build up over time.

Visualize It!

8 Infer Why would the lower layers in the sedimentary rock shown above be older than the upper layers in the same rock?

_____

_____

_____

_____

_____

Think Outside the Book Inquiry

9 Apply Describe how a scientific law is like a societal law. Describe how it is different. Which type of law is more restrictive?

Bending the Law

Mutual Attraction

The law of gravity is a well-known scientific law. It states that the attraction of two masses to each other gets greater the larger the masses are and the closer they are. Isaac Newton first stated the law in the 1600s. He did not give a theory to explain gravity. He just described it.

Over 200 years later, Albert Einstein gave a theory that might explain how gravity works. He suggested that space curved around large masses. You can imagine the effect as similar to putting a heavy ball atop a tightly-stretched blanket. The more massive the ball, the more the blanket will curve. Large objects like stars curve space a great deal.

Bending Space

Scientists have proposed that vast amounts of unseen dark matter exist in outer space based on how its gravity affects the light from distant galaxies. The light appears to curve.

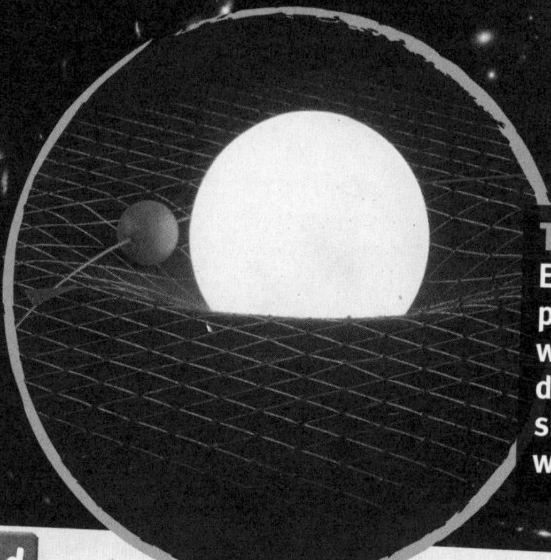

Throw a Curve!

Einstein proposed that large objects, like planets and stars, warped space. Gravity was the result of smaller objects "falling" down this warped space. The illustration shows how a large object, like the sun, warps space.

Extend

Inquiry

10 Identify How was Newton's description of gravity a law and not a theory?

11 Describe Describe a way you might try demonstrating Einstein's theory of gravity to a friend.

12 Infer Using Einstein's theory of gravity, explain why it's hard to notice the attraction of the small things on Earth to each other.

Consider the *Source*

What makes good scientific knowledge?

What makes a good scientific theory or model? Good scientific knowledge does not always last forever. Theories and models often change with new evidence. The best scientific theories and models are those that are able to adapt to explain new observations.

The theory of light is an interesting example of how scientific knowledge can adapt and change. Scientists debated the theory of light for some time. At one time, scientists saw light as particles, and later as waves. The wave theory, however, seemed to explain more about light. For a long time, scientists accepted it. Light is still often depicted as waves.

Today, however, scientists view light as having both a particle nature and a wave nature. In a sense, the particle theory of light did not die. It was good scientific knowledge. It was just incomplete.

Most scientists today probably would agree that all scientific knowledge is incomplete. Even the best theories do not explain everything. Indeed, this is the reason science continues. The goal of science is best described as the attempt to explain as much as possible and to be open to change as new evidence arises. As you study science, perhaps the best advice to remember is that everything we know about the world is simply the best guesses we have made. The best scientists are those that are open to change.

✎ Active Reading

13 Identify As you read, underline two different theories for light.

◉ Visualize It!

14 Apply The figures below model reflection in both the particle and wave theories of light. How might the particle theory have explained light passing through some objects and not others?

_____

_____

_____

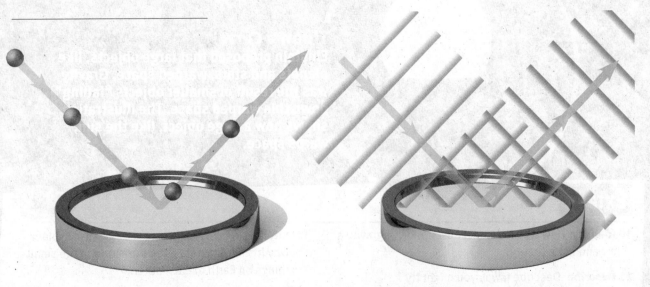

Reflection in the particle theory of light.   Reflection in the wave theory of light.

Information from places like NASA is reliable. Using our modern theory of light, NASA scientists can tell a lot about distant galaxies just by studying the light they see from them.

What makes a good source?

Where can you find good scientific knowledge? Because information can easily be sent across the world, you need to be able to separate reliable sources from the unreliable.

In general, you can trust information that comes from a government or university source. Nationally recognized research institutions, such as NASA, the Mayo Clinic, or Salk Institute, are also good sources. These institutions rely on their reputations. They would suffer if their information was found to be not accurate.

You should be cautious with publications more than a few years old. Remember, scientific knowledge changes. You should also be cautious of information made by those trying to sell a product. More often, their motivation is to use science to make money, not to instruct.

15 Evaluate In the table below, check the appropriate box indicating whether information from each source would be reliable, somewhat reliable, or not very reliable. Discuss your choices with others.

Government science agency (.gov site)	☐ reliable ☐ somewhat reliable ☐ not very reliable
Advertising agency	☐ reliable ☐ somewhat reliable ☐ not very reliable
Science textbook from 1985	☐ reliable ☐ somewhat reliable ☐ not very reliable
University (.edu site)	☐ reliable ☐ somewhat reliable ☐ not very reliable
Personal webpage	☐ reliable ☐ somewhat reliable ☐ not very reliable

Visual Summary

To complete this summary, check *true* or *false* below each statement. Then, use the key below to check your answers. You can use this page to review the main concepts of the lesson.

Scientific Knowledge

Models, Theories, and Laws
Models, theories, and laws are three types of scientific knowledge.

16 Any hunch you have is as good as a scientific theory.

☐ True ☐ False

17 Models can represent things that are too far away or too small to see.

☐ True ☐ False

18 Scientific laws can be thought of as general descriptions of what we see happening around us.

☐ True ☐ False

Adaptability of Scientific Knowledge
Scientific knowledge is durable, because it is open to change.

19 Scientific theories can change when new evidence is found.

☐ True ☐ False

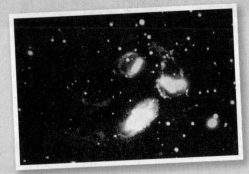

Reliable Sources
Sources for reliable scientific information include government agencies and research institutions, like NASA.

20 You can trust scientific information from advertisers, because they are selling a product.

☐ True ☐ False

Answers: 16 False; 17 True; 18 True; 19 True; 20 False

21 Relate Laws can be explained by theories. If a theory changes, does it mean the law must change? Explain.

Lesson Review

Vocabulary

Fill in the blank with the term or phrase that best completes the following sentences.

1 A(n) _____ is a representation of something in the natural world.

2 Unlike in society, a scientific _____ is simply a description of what we see.

3 A scientific _____ has a lot of support and is more than just a "hunch."

Key Concepts

4 Differentiate How might a theory relate to a model?

_____

_____

_____

5 Discriminate Where might you look on the Internet to find good scientific information about an illness?

_____

_____

6 Identify What two types of scientific knowledge can be expressed as mathematical equations?

_____

_____

7 Analyze Scientific theories can change over time as new information is discovered. If a scientific theory changes, does this mean that it was not a good theory to begin with?

_____

_____

_____

_____

_____

Critical Thinking

The gravity of the sun and the moon affects tides on Earth. The model below shows the positions of the sun, the moon, and Earth during a spring tide. Use it to answer questions 8 and 9.

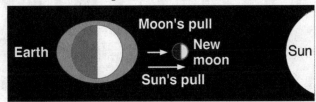

8 Analyze How does this model make it easier for someone to understand the sun's and the moon's influences on the tides?

_____

_____

_____

9 Evaluate What do you think are the limitations of this model?

_____

_____

_____

_____

_____

10 Evaluate Do you agree or disagree with the following statement? Explain your answer. Both theories and laws can be used to predict what will happen in a situation that has not already been tested.

_____

_____

_____

_____

_____

_____

_____

Scientific Investigations

ESSENTIAL QUESTION

How do scientists work?

By the end of this lesson, you should be able to summarize the processes and characteristics of different kinds of scientific investigations.

🌀 Sunshine State Standards

SC.6.N.1.1 Define a problem from the sixth grade curriculum, use appropriate reference materials to support scientific understanding, plan and carry out scientific investigation of various types, such as systematic observations or experiments, identify variables, collect and organize data, interpret data in charts, tables, and graphics, analyze information, make predictions, and defend conclusions.

SC.6.N.1.2 Explain why scientific investigations should be replicable.

SC.6.N.1.3 Explain the difference between an experiment and other types of scientific investigation, and explain the relative benefits and limitations of each.

SC.6.N.1.4 Discuss, compare, and negotiate methods used, results obtained, and explanations among groups of students conducting the same investigation.

LA.6.4.2.2 The student will record information (e.g., observations, notes, lists, charts, legends) related to a topic, including visual aids to organize and record information and include a list of sources used.

Particle accelerators such as the one shown here cause the particles that make up atoms to move at almost the speed of light. They allow scientists to investigate the nature of matter.

Engage Your Brain

1 Evaluate Check T or F to show whether you think each statement is true or false.

T F

☐ ☐ Every scientific investigation is an experiment.

☐ ☐ You could do an experiment to see if eating breakfast helps students raise their grades.

☐ ☐ Scientists need fancy instruments to do experiments.

☐ ☐ Scientists must repeat an experiment for it to be useful.

2 Infer What do you think the scientists who gathered the data for this graph were studying?

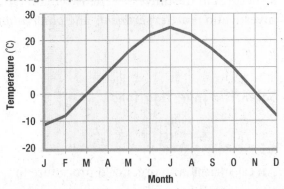

Average Temperature in Minneapolis

_____

_____

_____

_____

Active Reading

3 Synthesize The word *experiment* comes from the Latin word *experiri*, meaning "to try." What do you think the meaning of the word *experiment* is?

_____

_____

_____

_____

Vocabulary Terms

- experiment
- observation
- hypothesis
- variable
- data

4 Apply As you learn the meaning of each vocabulary term in this lesson, write a sentence of your own using the term.

Scientists at Work!

What are some types of scientific investigations?

Scientists carry out investigations to learn about the natural world—everything from the smallest particles to the largest structures in the universe. The two main types of scientific investigations are *experiments* and *observations*.

Scientific Investigations

Experiments

An **experiment** is an organized procedure to study something under controlled conditions. Experiments are often done in a laboratory. This makes it easier to control factors that can influence a result. For example, a scientist notices that a particular kind of fish is becoming less common in a lake near his home. He knows that some fish need more oxygen than others. To find out if this local fish species is being harmed by decreased oxygen levels, he might do the following experiment. First, he measures oxygen levels in the lake. Then, he sets up three tanks of water in a laboratory. The water in each tank has a different level of oxygen. Other factors that might affect fish, such as temperature, are the same in all three tanks. The scientist places the same number of fish in each tank. Then he collects information on the health of the fish.

Active Reading **5 Infer** Why would the scientist in the example want the temperature to be the same in all three tanks?

_____

_____

_____

_____

_____

This scientist is studying salmon in a controlled laboratory experiment.

Visualize It!

6 Analyze List the factors that the scientists cannot control in the field investigation shown in this picture.

_____

_____

_____

_____

_____

This scientist is observing salmon in their natural environment in Mongolia.

Active Reading

7 Identify As you read, underline reasons why a scientist might choose to do observations that do not involve experiments.

Other Types of Investigations

Observation is the process of obtaining information by using the senses. The word can also refer to the information obtained by using the senses. Although scientists make observations while conducting experiments, many things cannot be studied under controlled conditions. For example, it is impossible to create or manipulate a star. But astronomers can observe stars through telescopes.

Observations of the natural world are generally less precise than experiments because they involve factors that are not controlled by scientists. However, they may give a better description of what is actually happening in nature.

Important scientific observations can be made anywhere. The scientist who experiments with fish and oxygen levels in the example you read on the opposite page might observe a lake to find out which animals and plants live in it. His observations may or may not support the findings of the laboratory experiment.

Another type of investigation is the creation of models, which are representations of an object or system. Models are useful for studying things that are very small, large, or complex. For example, computer models of Earth's atmosphere can help scientists forecast the weather.

Why Ask Why?

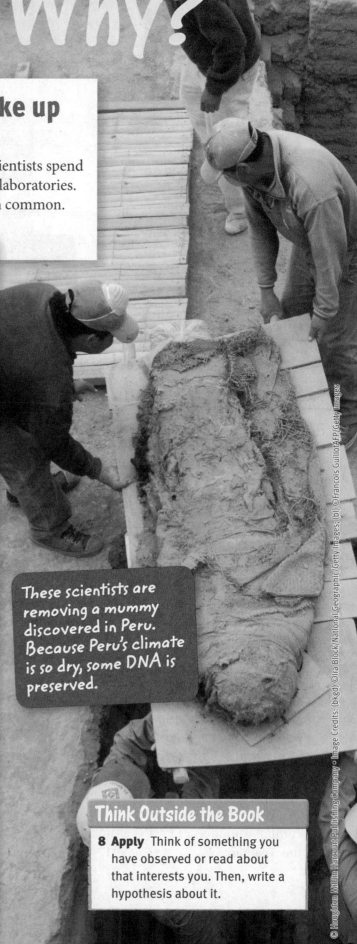

What are some parts that make up scientific investigations?

The work that scientists do can vary greatly. Some scientists spend much of their time outdoors. Others mostly work in laboratories. Yet scientific investigations have some basic things in common.

Hypothesis

A **hypothesis** (hy•PAHTH•ih•sis) is a testable idea or explanation that leads to scientific investigation. A scientist may think of a hypothesis after making observations or after reading findings from other scientists' investigations. The hypothesis can be tested by experiment or observation.

For example, imagine that while outside after a snowstorm, you notice that plant leaves seem to be healthy. You wonder how the leaves stayed alive because the temperature was below freezing during the storm. You also know that heat does not pass as easily through snow as it does through air. With this information, you could make the following hypothesis: "The leaves on the plants stayed healthy because the snow cover slowed their loss of heat." This is a hypothesis that could be tested by an experiment.

These scientists are removing a mummy discovered in Peru. Because Peru's climate is so dry, some DNA is preserved.

Mummies such as this one have been preserved by the cold, dry climate of the Andes Mountains in Peru.

Think Outside the Book

8 Apply Think of something you have observed or read about that interests you. Then, write a hypothesis about it.

This scientist is analyzing DNA found in a mummy from Peru.

Elements of Investigations

Variables

A **variable** is any factor that can change in an experiment, observation, or model. When scientists plan experiments, they try to change only one variable and keep the other variables constant, or unchanged. However, it may not be possible to control all the variables that can affect the results.

Suppose you decide to test the hypothesis that snow protects leaves from below-freezing temperatures. If you did the experiment in the field, you would not be able to control many variables. But you could set up a laboratory experiment to test your hypothesis. First, you would put similar plants in two chambers. Both chambers would be cooled to the same temperature. You would cover the plants in one chamber with snow and leave the plants in the other chamber without a snow cover. The snow cover is the variable you want to test. You would try to keep all the other variables the same in both chambers. For example, when you open one chamber to pour snow on the plants, you would keep the other chamber open for the same amount of time.

Observations and Data

Data are information gathered by observation or experimentation that can be used in calculating or reasoning. Everything a scientist observes in an investigation must be recorded. The setup and procedure of an experiment also need to be recorded. By carefully recording this information, scientists make sure that they will not forget important details.

The biologist shown in the photo above would record the results of her analysis of mummy DNA. In addition, she would identify the type of tissue that was examined—whether it came from a tooth or bone, for example. She would also record the type of instrument used to examine the tissue and the procedures that she followed. All of these details may be important when she reports her findings. The information will also help other scientists evaluate her work.

9 Identify What kind of data would you record for an experiment testing whether snow protects leaves from cold temperatures?

_____

_____

_____

Many Methods

What are some scientific methods?

Scientific methods are the ways in which scientists answer questions and solve problems. There is no single formula for an investigation. Scientists do not all use the same steps in every investigation or use steps in the same order. They may even repeat some of the steps. The following graphic shows one path a scientist might follow when conducting an experiment.

Visualize It!

10 Diagram Using a different color, draw arrows showing another path a scientist might follow if he or she were observing animals in the wild.

Defining a Problem

After making observations or reading scientific reports, a scientist might be curious about some unexplained aspect of a topic. A scientific problem is a specific question that a scientist wants to answer. The problem must be well-defined, or precisely stated, so that it can be investigated.

Planning an Investigation

A scientific investigation must be carefully planned so that it tests a hypothesis in a meaningful way. Scientists need to decide whether an investigation should be done in the field or in a laboratory. They must also determine what equipment and technology are required and how materials for the investigation will be obtained.

Forming a Hypothesis and Making Predictions

When scientists form a hypothesis, they are making an educated guess about a problem. A hypothesis must be tested to see if it is true. Before testing a hypothesis, scientists often make predictions about what will happen in an investigation.

© Houghton Mifflin Harcourt Publishing Company • Image Credits: ©Hill Street Studios/Blend Images/Corbis

Identifying Variables

Before conducting a controlled experiment, scientists identify all the variables that can affect the results. Then they decide which variable should change and which ones should stay constant. Some variables may be impossible to control.

Collecting and Organizing Data

The data collected in an investigation must be recorded and properly organized so that they can be analyzed. Data such as measurements and numbers are often organized into tables, spreadsheets, or graphs.

Interpreting Data and Analyzing Information

After they finish collecting data, scientists must analyze this information. Their analysis will help them draw conclusions about the results. Scientists may have different interpretations of the same data because they analyze it using different methods.

Defending Conclusions

Scientists conclude whether the results of their investigation support the hypothesis. If the hypothesis is not supported, scientists may think about the problem some more and try to come up with a new hypothesis to test. When they publish the results of their investigation, scientists must be prepared to defend their conclusions if they are challenged by other scientists.

Use It or Lose It

How are scientific methods used?

Scientific methods are used to study any aspect of the natural world. They can also be used in the social sciences, which focus on human society. It is often harder to control variables in the social sciences. Nevertheless, these fields are made stronger by the methods developed for physical, life, and earth science.

Think Outside the Book Inquiry

11 **Plan** Suppose that you want to investigate something using scientific methods. First, define a problem. Then, plan a scientific investigation using the methods discussed in the previous pages.

Use of Scientific Methods

Different Situations Require Different Methods

After forming a hypothesis, scientists decide how they will test it. Some hypotheses can be tested only through observation. Others must be tested in laboratory experiments. However, observation and experiments are often used together to build scientific knowledge. For example, if you want to test the strength of a metal used in airplane construction, you may study it in a laboratory experiment. But after conducting the experiment, you may want to inspect airplanes that have flown for a period of time to see how the metal holds up under actual flight conditions.

If an investigation does not support a hypothesis, it is still useful. The data from the investigation can help scientists form a better hypothesis. Scientists may go through many cycles of testing and data analysis before they arrive at a hypothesis that is supported.

12 **Apply** Give another example of a scientific investigation that would require both observation and experiments.

_____

_____

_____

_____

Scientific Methods Are Used in Physical Science

Physical science includes the study of physics and chemistry. Scientists have used physics to figure out how gecko lizards stick to walls and ceilings.

Various explanations of the gecko's unique ability have been developed. Some scientists thought that static electricity helps geckos stick to walls. Others thought that the gecko produces a kind of glue from its feet. But experiments and observations did not support these hypotheses.

When a team of researchers studied the gecko's feet with a microscope, they found that each foot was covered with hundreds of thousands of tiny hairs. After measuring the force exerted by each hair against a surface, they came up with two possible hypotheses. One hypothesis was that geckos stick to walls because the hairs interact with a thin film of water. The other hypothesis was that the weak forces between the hairs and a surface combine to produce a force great enough to hold the gecko to the surface.

The team designed an experiment to test both hypotheses. The experiment showed that the force of a gecko's hair against a surface was the same whether or not the surface had any water on it. The scientists concluded that the gecko sticks to walls because of the combined forces of the hairs on its feet.

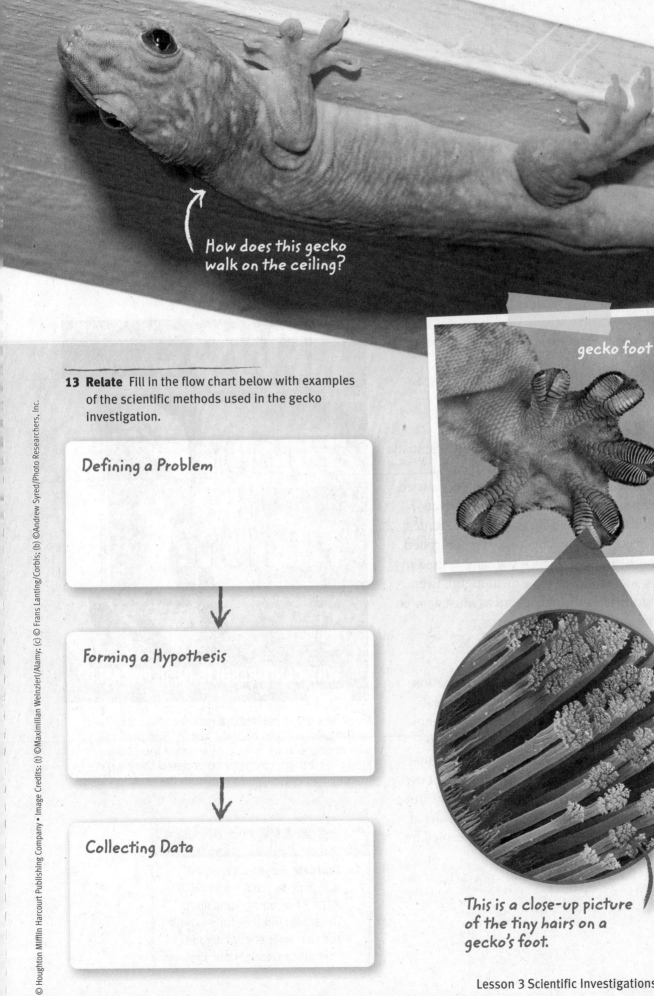

How does this gecko walk on the ceiling?

13 Relate Fill in the flow chart below with examples of the scientific methods used in the gecko investigation.

Defining a Problem

↓

Forming a Hypothesis

↓

Collecting Data

gecko foot

This is a close-up picture of the tiny hairs on a gecko's foot.

Getting It Right

What are some ways to confirm that an investigation is valid?

Scientific investigations should be carried out with great care. But scientists are only human. Sometimes they fail to plan properly. They may make mistakes in collecting or analyzing data because they are in a hurry. On rare occasions, irresponsible scientists produce false results on purpose. Fortunately, there are procedures that help expose flawed investigations.

Evaluating Investigations

Peer Review

Before a study is published, it is read by scientists who were not involved in the investigation. These peer reviewers evaluate the methods used in a study and the conclusions reached by its authors. For example, a reviewer could decide that an experiment was not properly controlled. Or a reviewer might say that the sample used in a survey was too small to be meaningful. Even after a study is published, scientists must answer questions raised by other scientists.

Replication

An important way to confirm an investigation is for other scientists to replicate it, or repeat the investigation and obtain the same findings. To make this possible, scientists must disclose the methods and materials used in the original study when they publish their findings. Not every investigation needs to be replicated exactly. But if a study cannot be supported by the results of similar investigations, it will not be accepted by the scientific community.

WEEKLY

NEWS *Special Edition*

FUSION OR FICTION?

Was this experiment flawed?

WHY CAN'T RESULTS BE REPLICATED?

In 1989 a pair of scientists reported that they had accomplished cold nuclear fusion. The possibility of a cheap source of energy excited the public. However, other scientists considered the claim impossible. Attempts to replicate the findings failed.

Think Outside the Book

14 Evaluate Research the cold fusion news reported in 1989. Write a few paragraphs about the study. Did the study exhibit the characteristics of a good scientific investigation? Explain.

How can you evaluate the quality of scientific information?

Scientific information can be found on the Internet, in magazines, and in newspapers. It can be difficult to decide which information should be trusted. The most reliable scientific information is published in scientific journals.

The most reliable information on the Internet is on government or academic webpages. Other sites should be examined closely for errors, especially if they are selling things.

Although the lab reports that you prepare for school might not be published, you should try to meet the same standards of published studies. For example, you should provide enough information so that other students can replicate your results.

Visualize It!

15 Apply List two examples of poor scientific methodology found in this student's lab report.

_____

_____

_____

Problem: How does the amount of sunlight affect the growth of plants?

Hypothesis: Plants that spend more time in the sunlight will grow taller because plants grow taller in warm conditions.

Changed variables: amount of time in the sunlight and type of plant

Constant variables: amount of water

Materials: plants, water, sunlamp, ruler

Procedure: Take the plants and put them under the sunlamp. Leave some of them under the lamp for longer amounts of time than others.

Data Table:

Plant number	Length of time in sunlight per day	Height after 2 weeks
1	5 hours	8 inches
2	8 hours	12 inches

16 Assess Would you believe this result or would you be skeptical of it? Explain your answer.

_____

_____

_____

_____

_____

Visual Summary

To complete this summary, circle the correct word from each set of words. Then, use the key below to check your answers. You can use this page to review the main concepts of the lesson.

Scientific Methods
Scientists use scientific methods to answer questions and solve problems.

19 A problem / hypothesis / variable must be tested to see if it is supported.

20 Scientists must decide which data / hypotheses / variables will stay constant in an experiment.

Types of Scientific Investigations
Scientists carry out investigations through experiments and observation.

17 Scientific investigations that involve testing a single variable are called models / experiments / theories.

18 Hypotheses / Models / Observations are often made before other types of investigations are done.

Scientific Investigations

Characteristics of Good Scientific Investigations
There are procedures that separate good scientific investigations from flawed ones.

21 The findings of experiments are generally not accepted until they are published / proven / replicated.

22 The most reliable scientific information comes from reporters / scientists / companies working in a particular field.

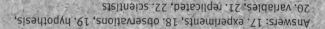

Answers: 17. experiments, 18. observations, 19. hypothesis, 20. variables, 21. replicated, 22. scientists

23 Relate What is the relationship between a scientific problem and a hypothesis?

Lesson Review

Vocabulary

Fill in the blank with the term that best completes the following sentences.

1 A(n) _____ determines what will be tested in a scientific experiment.

2 All of the _____ gathered in an investigation must be recorded.

3 A good scientific _____ can be repeated by someone else and the same results will be found.

Key Concepts

Example	Scientific Method
4 Identify Scientists use instruments to record the strength of earthquakes in an area.	
5 Identify Scientists decide that in an experiment on fish, all the fish will be fed the same amount of food.	

6 Identify What are two key characteristics of a good scientific investigation?

_____

_____

_____

_____

7 Explain Why is it important for scientists to share information from their investigations?

_____

_____

_____

_____

Critical Thinking

Use this drawing to answer the following questions.

water   salt water

8 Analyze Which variable changes in the investigation depicted in the drawing?

_____

_____

9 Conclude Identify one variable that is kept constant for both groups in this experiment.

_____

_____

10 Infer What kind of data might be collected for this experiment?

_____

_____

_____

11 Evaluate Which is less likely to be a reliable source of information, the webpage of a university or the webpage of a scientist who is trying to sell a new invention? Explain.

_____

_____

_____

_____

_____

_____

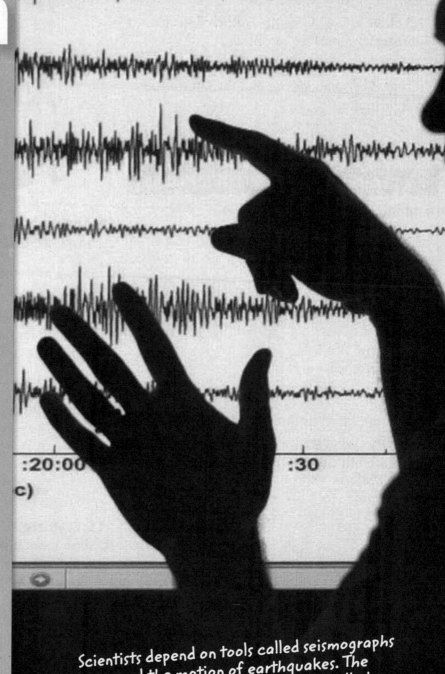

Representing Data

ESSENTIAL QUESTION

In what ways can you organize data to fully understand them?

By the end of this lesson, you should be able to use tables, graphs, and models to display and analyze scientific data.

Sunshine State Standards

SC.6.N.3.4 Identify the role of models in the context of the sixth grade science benchmarks.

MA.6.S.6.2 Select and analyze the measures of central tendency or variability to represent, describe, analyze, and/or summarize a data set for the purposes of answering questions appropriately.

MA.6.A.3.6 Construct and analyze tables, graphs, and equations to describe linear functions and other simple relations using both common language and algebraic notation.

LA.6.4.2.2 The student will record information (e.g., observations, notes, lists, charts, legends) related to a topic, including visual aids to organize and record information and include a list of sources used.

Scientists depend on tools called seismographs to record the motion of earthquakes. The graph produced by a seismograph is called a seismogram. This seismogram shows the ground motion of an earthquake that hit the United Kingdom in 2007.

Engage Your Brain

1 Predict Check T or F to show whether you think each statement is true or false.

T	F	
☐	☐	Scientific models have been used to show results of scientific experiments.
☐	☐	Certain types of graphs are better than others for displaying specific types of data.
☐	☐	Most graphs are confusing and unnecessary.
☐	☐	If something can be shown in a table, then it should not be shown in a graph.

2 Evaluate Name two things about the model shown that are similar to the object that the model represents. Then name two things about the model that are different.

_____

_____

_____

_____

_____

_____

Active Reading

3 Apply Many words, such as *model*, have multiple meanings. Use context clues to write your own definition for each meaning of the word *model*.

Example sentence
After getting an *A* on another test, Julio's teacher told him he was a <u>model</u> student.

model:

_____

_____

Example sentence
For her science project, Samantha created a <u>model</u> of the solar system.

model:

_____

_____

Vocabulary Term
• model

4 Identify As you read this lesson, underline examples of models.

Crunching Data!

How do scientists make sense of data?

Before scientists begin an experiment, they often create a data table for recording their data. *Data* are the facts, figures, and other evidence gathered through observations and experimentation. The more data a scientist collects, the greater is the need for the data to be organized in some way. Data tables are one easy way to organize a lot of scientific data.

Scientists Organize the Data

A data table provides an organized way for scientists to record the data that they collect. Information that might be recorded in data tables are times, amounts, and *frequencies,* or the number of times something happens.

When creating a data table, scientists must decide how to organize the table into columns and rows. Any units of measurement, such as seconds or degrees, should be included in the column headings and not in the individual cells. Finally, a title must always be added to describe the data in the table.

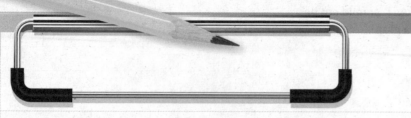

The data table below shows the number of movie tickets sold each month at a small theater.

Movie Tickets Sold Monthly	
Month	Number of tickets
January	15,487
February	12,654
March	15,721
April	10,597
May	10,916
June	11,797
July	18,687
August	18,302
September	16,978
October	10,460
November	11,807
December	17,497

Do the Math — You Try It

5 Extend Circle the row in the table that shows the month when the greatest number of tickets were sold. Then circle the row that shows the month when the least number of tickets were sold. Finally, subtract the least number from the greatest number to find the range of the number of tickets sold.

_____ − _____ = _____

greatest number of tickets   least number of tickets   range

Scientists Graph and Analyze the Data

In order to analyze their collected data for patterns, it is often helpful for scientists to construct a graph of their data. The type of graph they use depends upon the data they collect and what they want to show.

A *bar graph* is used to display and compare data in a number of separate categories. The length, or height, of each bar represents the number in each category. For example, in the movie theater data, the months are the categories. The lengths of the bars represent the number of tickets sold each month.

Other types of graphs include line graphs and circle graphs. A *line graph* is often used to show continuous change over time. A *circle graph,* or pie chart, is used when you are showing how each group of data relates to all of the data. For example, you could use a circle graph to depict the number of boys and girls in your class.

Active Reading

5 Interpret What kind of data would you display in a bar graph?

_____

_____

_____

_____

Visualize It!

7 Analyze The data in the graph below are the same as the data in the table at the left. During what three months are the most movie theater tickets sold?

_____

_____

_____

Movie Tickets Sold Monthly

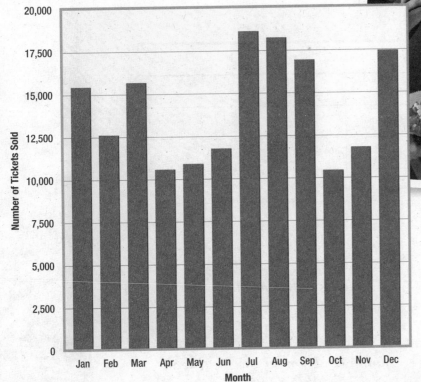

8 Extend What other kind of data could you collect at home that might show differences over the course of a year?

_____

_____

_____

Graph It!

What do graphs show?

Graphs are visual representations of data. They show information in a way that is often easier to understand than data shown in tables. All graphs should have a title explaining the graph.

In certain types of graphs, the data displayed on the horizontal axis are the values of the *independent variable*. This is the variable that is deliberately manipulated in an investigation. For example, if you collect rainfall data over four weeks, the week number is the independent variable because you have chosen to collect data once a week. You have manipulated the time interval between data collections.

The data displayed on the vertical axis are the values of the *dependent variable*. This is the variable that changes as a result of the manipulation of one or more independent variables. For example, the inches of rainfall per week is the dependent variable.

Visualize It!

9 Complete The data at the right show the amount of rain, in inches, that fell in each of four weeks at a school. Use the empty table below to organize the data. Include a title for the table, the column headings, and all of the data.

Week 1: 0.62 in.
Week 2: 0.40 in.
Week 3: 1.12 in.
Week 4: 0.23 in.

Title

Headings

Data

Do the Math You Try It

10 Extend The average, or mean, of the rainfall data is the sum of the data values divided by the number of data values. Calculate the mean of the rainfall data. Round your answer to the nearest hundredth.

$$\underline{\quad} + \underline{\quad} + \underline{\quad} + \underline{\quad} = \underline{\quad}$$

Weeks 1 through 4   Sum

$$\underline{\quad} \div \underline{\quad} \approx \underline{\quad}$$

Sum   Number of   Mean
data values

How are graphs constructed?

To make a bar graph of the rainfall data at the left, first draw a horizontal axis and a vertical axis. Next, write the names of the categories to be graphed along the horizontal axis. Include an overall label for the axis as well. Next, label the vertical axis with the name of the dependent variable. Be sure to include the units of measurement. Then create a scale along the axis by marking off equally spaced numbers that cover the range of the data collected. For each category, draw a solid bar using the scale on the vertical axis to determine the height. Make all the bars the same width. Finally, add a title that describes the graph.

11 Identify As you read, number the steps used to construct a graph. You may want to rely on signal words that indicate a new step, such as *then* or *next*.

12 Graph Construct a bar graph of the rainfall data at the left. On the lines provided, include a title for the graph and axis labels. Use a scale of 0.20 in. for the horizontal axis, and label the bars on the vertical axis.

Visualize It!

13 Analyze During which week was the rainfall amount approximately twice what it was during week 4? Use your graph to explain.

_____

_____

_____

_____

_____

Title: _____

Amount of Rainfall (in.)

0.0

Week 1 ____ ____ ____

_____

This rain gauge is used to gather and measure liquid precipitation.

Model It!

What types of models can be used to represent data?

A crash-test dummy, a mathematical equation, and a road map are all models that represent real things. A **model** is a representation of an object or a process that allows scientists to study something in greater detail. A model uses something familiar to help you understand something that is not familiar.

Models can represent things that are too small to see, such as atoms. They can also represent things that are too large to see fully, such as Earth. Models can be used to explain the past and the present. They can even be used to predict future events. Two common kinds of scientific models are physical models and mathematical models.

Active Reading

14 Apply As you read, underline different ways that scientists use models.

Physical Models

Physical models are models that you can touch. Toy cars, models of buildings, maps, and globes are all physical models. Physical models often look like the things they represent. For example, this model of Earth shows that Earth is divided into three layers— the crust, the mantle, and the core. The table below shows the estimated densities of each of Earth's layers.

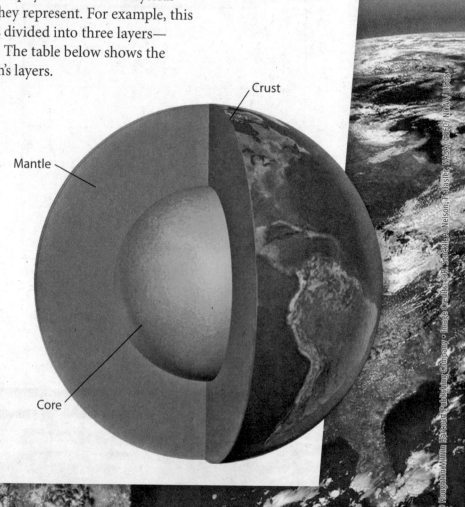

Crust
Mantle
Core

Density of Earth's Layers

Layer	Density (g/cm³)
crust	2.7–3.3
mantle	3.3–5.7
core	9.9–13.1

Visualize It!

15 Analyze The table shows the estimated densities of Earth's layers. Write the layers of Earth in order of most dense to least dense.

_____

_____

Mathematical Models

Every day, people try to predict the weather. One way to predict the weather is to use mathematical models. A *mathematical model* is made up of mathematical equations and data. Some mathematical models are simple. These models allow you to calculate things such as how far a car will travel in an hour or how much you would weigh on the moon.

Other mathematical models are so complex that computers are needed to process them. Some of these very complex models, such as population growth, have many variables. Sometimes, certain variables that no one thought of exist in the model. A change in any variable could cause the model to fail.

What are some benefits and limitations of models?

Just as models can represent things that are too small or too large to see, models benefit scientists in other ways. They allow scientists to change variables without affecting or harming the subject that they are studying. For example, scientists use crash-test dummies to study the effects of car accidents on people.

All models are limited because they are simplified versions of the systems that they try to explain. Simplification makes a model easy to understand and use. However, information is left out when a model is made.

Additionally, all models can change. Models can change if a scientist finds new data or thinks about concepts in a new way. Sometimes, new technology challenges existing models. Or, technology may help create new models that allow us to understand the world differently.

© Houghton Mifflin Harcourt Publishing Company • Image Credits: ©R. Stockli, A. Nelson, F. Hasler, NASA/ GSFC/ NOAA/ USGS

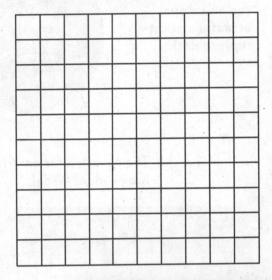

Do the Math **You Try It**

16 **Calculate** The air we breathe is made up of 78% nitrogen, 21% oxygen, and 1% other gases. Use three different colored pencils to color the appropriate number of squares in the grid for each of these percentages.

Think Outside the Book Inquiry

17 **Apply** With a classmate, discuss the benefits and limitations of globes and maps as physical models.

Visual Summary

To complete this summary, check the box that indicates true or false. Then, use the key below to check your answers. You can use this page to review the main concepts of the lesson.

Representing Data

A scientific model can be a visual or mathematical representation.

T F
☐ ☐ **18** The equation for density is a physical model.

A table can be used to record and organize data as it is being collected.

Density of Earth's Layers	
Layer	Density (g/cm³)
crust	2.7–3.3
mantle	3.3–5.7
core	9.9–13.1

T F
☐ ☐ **19** Units of measurement should be placed with the column or row headings in tables.

Answers: 18 F; 19 T; 20 F

A graph is a visual display of data that shows relationships between the data.

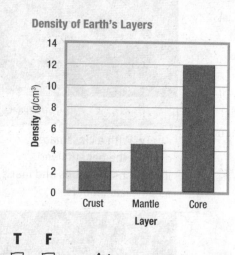

T F
☐ ☐ **20** A bar graph is used to show continuous data.

21 Synthesize Provide an example of something in the natural world that could be depicted in each of the following ways: a table, a graph, and a model. (Use examples not given in this lesson.)

Lesson Review

Vocabulary

Fill in the blank with the term that best completes the following sentences.

1 A(n) _____ can be a visual or mathematical representation of an object or a process.

2 After data are collected, they are often arranged in a(n) _____.

3 Data can be arranged in visual displays called _____ to make identifying trends easier.

Key Concepts

4 Differentiate How is a physical model different from a mathematical model?

_____

_____

_____

5 Identify A data table shows the height of a person on his birthday each year for ten years. What is the dependent variable?

_____

_____

_____

6 Judge Which kind of graph would be best for depicting data collected on the weight of a baby every month for six months?

_____

_____

_____

_____

7 Apply What kind of model would you use to represent the human heart?

_____

_____

_____

Critical Thinking

Use this graph to answer the following questions.

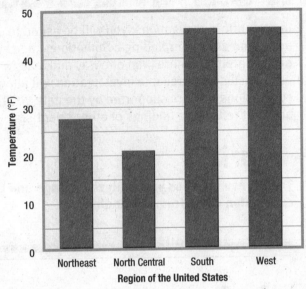

Average January Temperatures

8 Identify Which region of the country has the coldest January temperatures?

_____

9 Estimate How can you use the graph to determine the range of the temperature data? Write the range to the nearest degree.

_____

_____

_____

_____

_____

10 Apply Give an example of a physical model and explain one limitation of the model. Then give an example of a mathematical model and explain one limitation.

_____

_____

_____

_____

_____

Making Conclusions from Evidence

In scientific investigations, you will be asked to collect data and summarize your findings. Sometimes, a set of data can be interpreted in more than one way and lead to more than one conclusion. A reliable investigation will allow you to make conclusions that are supported by the data you have collected, and that reflect the findings of other scientists.

Tutorial

Take these steps as you analyze findings and evaluate a conclusion made from the findings.

Flu Prevention Breakthrough

A medical study has shown that a new drug, Compound Z, protected children from the flu. The results of the study that was conducted last year showed that only 5% of students who were taking Compound Z were affected by the flu. During the same period of time, 20% of the general population was affected by the flu.

Researchers do not know exactly how Compound Z protects children from the flu.

Other data should be considered before the conclusion above can be supported. For example, data should be gathered to determine the percentage of children who were not taking Compound Z and got the flu. And, within the 20% of the general population who got the flu, what percentage were children?

1 What conclusion is made by the study? Identify the conclusion or interpretation of the data that is being made in the study.

2 What evidence or data is given and does the data support the conclusion? Identify all the observations and findings that are presented to support the conclusion. Decide whether the findings support the conclusion. Look for information and data in other studies that replicate the experiments and verify the conclusion.

3 Should other data be considered before accepting the conclusion as true? There may be more than one way to interpret findings of scientific work, and important questions left unanswered. When this happens, plan to make observations, look for more information, or do further experiments that could eliminate one explanation as a possibility.

Sunshine State Standards

SC.6.N.1.1 Define a problem from the sixth grade curriculum, use appropriate reference materials to support scientific understanding, plan and carry out scientific investigation of various types, such as systematic observations or experiments, identify variables, collect and organize data, interpret data in charts, tables, and graphics, analyze information, make predictions, and defend conclusions.

LA.6.4.2.2 The student will record information (e.g., observations, notes, lists, charts, legends) related to a topic, including visual aids to organize and record information and include a list of sources used.

You Try It!

Climate change is one of the most debated issues in modern science.

In the past 100 years, Earth's average global temperature has risen more than 0.74 °C. In 2008, the cold La Niña current in the Pacific caused the average global temperature to drop, but the global average was still warmer than any year from 1880 to 1996. The concentration of the greenhouse gas carbon dioxide (CO_2), rose from by about 76 parts per million from 1958 to 2008. Many people interpret this to mean that human activity is causing global climate change. However, evidence from the geologic record shows that Earth's climate has experienced even larger climate changes in the past.

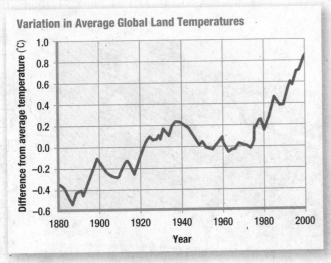

Variation in Average Global Land Temperatures

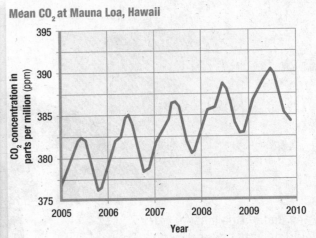

Mean CO_2 at Mauna Loa, Hawaii

1 Gathering Data The graphs shown above are taken from a study on climate change. Identify trends or patterns that you observe in the graphs.

_____

_____

_____

_____

2 Making a Conclusion Draw a conclusion that is supported by the data you describe. Summarize your conclusion in a single paragraph.

_____

_____

_____

_____

_____

_____

3 Analyzing Data Which conclusions are supported by the data in the graphs? Which conclusions are not supported by the data?

_____

_____

_____

_____

4 Making Predictions What other data do you need to further support your conclusion?

_____

_____

_____

_____

Take It Home

Find an article that makes a conclusion based on a scientific study. Evaluate the conclusion and determine whether the evidence given supports the conclusion. Bring the article to class and be prepared to discuss.

Science
and Society

ESSENTIAL QUESTION

How does science affect our lives?

By the end of this lesson, you should be able to describe the impact that science has had on society and the role of scientists throughout history and today.

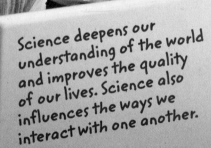

Science deepens our understanding of the world and improves the quality of our lives. Science also influences the ways we interact with one another.

Sunshine State Standards

SC.6.N.2.3 Recognize that scientists who make contributions to scientific knowledge come from all kinds of backgrounds and possess varied talents, interests, and goals.

Engage Your Brain

1 Predict Check T or F to show whether you think each statement is true or false.

T F

☐ ☑ Science has very few career opportunities and does not impact our lives.

☐ ☐ Good scientists are creative, logical thinkers and keen observers.

☐ ☐ Only scientists are capable of scientific thinking.

2 Identify List the first five things you did this morning after you woke up. Put a checkmark next to any of these things that were made possible by the work of scientists.

_____

_____

_____

_____

_____

Active Reading

3 Derive Many English words have their roots in other languages. Use the Latin word below to make an educated guess about the meaning of the word *scientific*.

Latin word	Meaning
scientia	knowledge

Example sentence
After years of <u>scientific</u> experimentation and observation, the researcher reported a major discovery.

scientific:

_____

_____

Vocabulary

4 Identify As you read, place a question mark next to any words you don't understand. When you finish reading the lesson, go back and review the text that you marked. If the information is still confusing, consult a classmate or a teacher.

A Mighty Impact!

What does science affect?

For centuries, people have been asking questions and seeking answers. Even before there were people known as scientists, people engaged in scientific exploration. Science has had a great impact on all of us. Most likely, you can think of ways science affects your life already. You may be surprised to discover how large the influence of science really is.

The Way We Think

How do you see yourself? People used to think that Earth was the center of the universe. They thought the objects in the sky moved around them. They thought the sky existed only for them to look at. These beliefs made people feel very special.

We now know Earth is just one planet in one solar system. Earth orbits the sun and rotates once each day. When people realized this, they had to rethink their place in the universe. They had to rethink just how special they believed themselves to be. Scientific findings affect how we see ourselves.

Active Reading

5 Apply As you read, underline examples of advances in science that have impacted you today.

Space science, 100 BCE

Space science, Today

Visualize It!

6 Explain Why might learning of the vastness of outer space affect how people see themselves?

_____

_____

_____

Modern agriculture is changing where we can grow things. These basil plants are grown using hydroponics on a floating barge!

The Way We Live Our Lives

Our daily activities have been affected by advances in science, too. In industrialized countries, many people enjoy clean water and sanitary living conditions. Scientists frequently find new ways for us to conserve and protect resources. Medicines have eliminated many health concerns. Cars, trains, and airplanes take us where we want to go. Weather forecasts tell us what to expect, and then we can dress appropriately. Satellites and cables allow us to communicate with others from all over the world. Most of these things were not even imaginable just 100 years ago.

Society became more complex with the beginning of farming. People joined together to grow crops for the benefit of all. World population has been able to grow so large today because of advances in farming. We can now grow crops in soil once thought to be infertile. Thanks to science, we can even grow plants with no soil at all! Hydroponics (HY•druh•pahn•iks), or growing plants without soil, may one day allow us to live in outer space.

7 Compare When your grandparents were growing up, they ate mostly foods grown or produced near them. Describe how the food you eat is different from the food your grandparents ate as a result of science's impact on agriculture and transportation.

_____

_____

_____

_____

© Houghton Mifflin Harcourt Publishing Company • Image Credits: (tl) ©Frances Roberts/Alamy; (tr) ©Michael Keller/Corbis; (b) ©Bob Krist/Corbis

It Takes All Kinds

Who contributes to science?

Myra Logan was the first female to perform open-heart surgery. She also played piano and contributed to the civil rights movement. Leonardo da Vinci was a great artist. He also drew designs for flying machines and studied human anatomy. Logan and da Vinci are just two of the many people who have contributed to science. People who contribute to science come from all backgrounds, fields of interest, and skill groups. So who contributes to science?

Active Reading **8 Identify** As you read, underline some characteristics of people who do scientific research.

Those Who Do Scientific Research

Scientists are curious, creative, and enjoy solving problems. Scientists do research to answer questions and to investigate and challenge prevailing ideas. Some scientists work in life science, like immunologist Cesar Milstein, who researches viruses like AIDS. Physicist Chien Shiung Wu, a physical scientist, spent time in laboratories with radioactive elements. Mary Leakey, an archaeologist and Earth scientist, unearthed ape fossils in the field.

Leonardo da Vinci and his design for a flying machine

Klaus Radermacher uses robots and computers to make custom prosthetics. Prosthetics are artificial body parts that can replace missing, damaged, or diseased parts.

Visualize It!

9 Predict What problem might Radermacher have been trying to solve when he began his research?

_____

_____

_____

_____

© Houghton Mifflin Harcourt Publishing Company • Image Credits: (bkgd) ©Stockbyte/Getty Images; (t) ©SSPL/Getty Images; (c) ©Stefano Bianchetti/Corbis; (b) ©Dung Vo Trung/Corbis

People in Many Fields

The number of men and women who get paid to do scientific research is not very high. However, the opportunities open to those who are willing to learn and think like a scientist in other fields are almost limitless.

Many occupations use science. Medical and dental technicians help doctors and dentists keep people in good health. Architects use the laws of physics to design stable homes and offices. People who dye and style hair use chemistry when mixing hair dye and relaxing solutions. In the growing field of forensics, police officers use science to help them solve crimes. Auto engineers use physics to design aerodynamic cars.

Forensic technician

Auto engineers design vehicles.

10 Infer What might motivate someone to study forensics?

_____

_____

_____

_____

11 Describe Fill in the second column with a description of how a person might use science in each of the careers. Fill in the last row of the table with a career you might like to have.

Career	Science applications
Firefighter	
Pharmacist	
Chef	

Anyone Who Asks Scientific Questions and Seeks Answers

An important point to remember is that anyone can think and act like a scientist and do science. Have you wondered why certain plants always flower at about the same time of year? Have you wondered what the center of Earth is like? Have you wondered why sugar dissolves faster in hot liquids than in cold ones? If you have asked questions and thought about finding the answers, you have acted like a scientist.

Do not be embarrassed to ask impossible questions. A lot of what we take for granted today was once thought impossible. You may even discover that you are asking the same questions many scientists still ask.

Active Reading

12 Identify As you read, underline questions that science can help you answer.

Inquiry

13 Relate Questions about the world can pop into your mind at any time. Write down something you've thought about recently as you've gone about your usual activities. Then write how you might investigate it.

_____

_____

_____

_____

_____

_____

Is time travel possible?

Can a computer be built that can sense people's feelings?

Can plants be used to "clean up" the increased levels of carbon dioxide in our atmosphere?

Think Outside the Book

14 State What is your daring dream? Write a scientific question you would like to answer, regardless of how impossible it might seem to do.

Why It Matters

Let the Games Begin

Robotics tournaments, model car races, and science fairs offer opportunities for you to explore and share your interest in science with others. You may even win a prize doing it!

Robot Challenge
This robot was built and operated by students at a San Diego robotics competition. Robots aren't just for competitions, though. Robots can be built for search and rescue missions, manufacturing, and other roles.

Fast and Friendly
This student is racing a model car he built. The car is powered by hydrogen fuel cells. Hydrogen fuel cells may be an environmentally friendly power source for cars of the future!

Extend

Inquiry

15 Select Which would you be most interested in entering: a science fair, a robotics competition, or a model car race? Why?

16 Identify Use the Internet to find a science competition in your area. Consider visiting it!

17 Plan Make a poster, draw a model, or write a paragraph explaining an idea you have for a science competition.

© Houghton Mifflin Harcourt Publishing Company • Image Credits: (t) ©Mike Blake/Reuters/Corbis; (b) ©Science Source/Photo Researchers

57

Visual Summary

To complete this summary, check the box that indicates true or false. Then use the key below to check your answers. You can use this page to review the main concepts of the lesson.

Science and Society

Impact of Science

The work of scientists has changed the way we live and think about the world.

	T	F	
18	☐	☐	As science has advanced, technology has advanced.
19	☐	☐	Agriculture and medicine are affected by science.

Who Does Science

Scientists are curious about the world and enjoy exploring it. They may work in laboratories, in the field, or in other locations.

	T	F	
20	☐	☐	Only people who work in science use scientific thinking skills.
21	☐	☐	People from all backgrounds, interests, and cultures can contribute to science.

Answers: 18. T; 19. T; 20. F; 21. T

22 Predict Identify two changes in your world that might occur if funding for scientific research were cut drastically.

© Houghton Mifflin Harcourt Publishing Company • Image Credits: (t) ©Frances Roberts/Alamy; (b) ©Dung Vo Trung/Corbis

Vocabulary

Fill in the blanks with the term or phrase that best completes the following sentences.

1 A(n) _____ may work in a lab or in the field and conducts research to discover new things.

2 The impact of science on _____ includes improvements in medicine, new technology, and more diverse food sources.

Key Concepts

3 Apply Identify two areas of science or technology that make your life easier, safer, or otherwise better than your grandparents' lives were.

_____

_____

_____

_____

_____

_____

4 List Name three characteristics of scientists that are important to their work but are also found in nonscientists.

_____

_____

_____

Critical Thinking

5 Devise Imagine that one tree outside your school looks unhealthy, although all the other trees seem healthy and strong. Describe how you could apply scientific thinking to the situation.

_____

_____

_____

_____

_____

_____

_____

Use this table to answer the following questions.

Scientists and Their Contributions		
When	**Who**	**What**
1660s	Robert Hooke	Identified and coined the word *cells* using early microscopes
Late 1700s	Antoine Lavoisier	Identified oxygen and oxygen's role in respiration and combustion
Early 1900s	Marie Curie	Experimented with radioactivity and identified new chemical elements
Early 1980s	Luis Alvarez	Used geological evidence to show that a meteor struck Earth and proposed that this led to the extinction of dinosaurs

6 Categorize The main branches of science are life science, physical science, and Earth and space science. Identify a branch of science that was affected by each of these scientists.

_____

_____

_____

7 Justify Why do you think the work of scientists cannot be pinned down to a single year?

_____

_____

_____

8 Debate Do you think the contributions of these scientists are still valuable, even though some were made hundreds of years ago? Explain your answer.

_____

_____

_____

_____

_____

My Notes

Unit 1 **Summary**

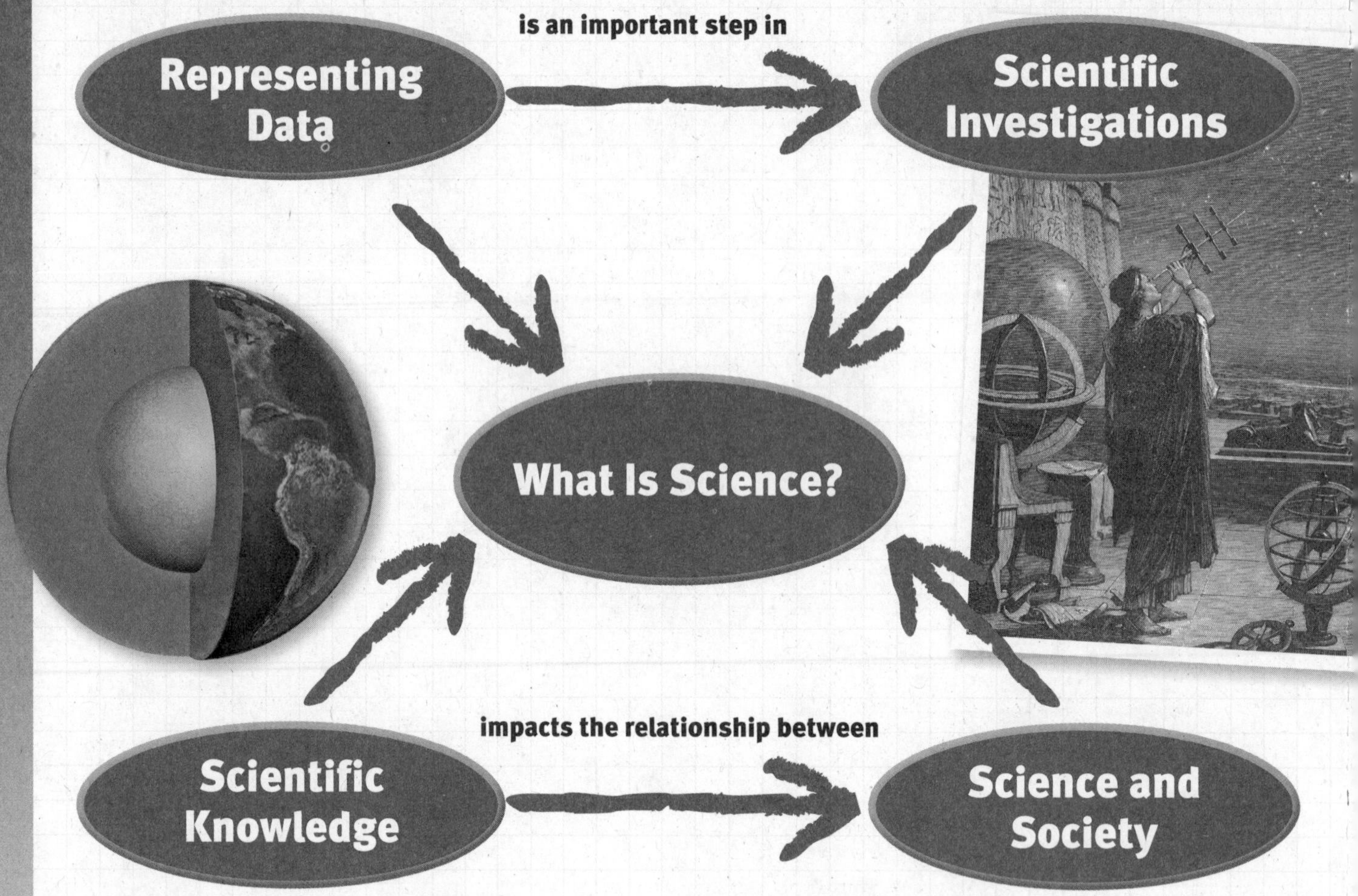

Representing Data is an important step in **Scientific Investigations**

What Is Science?

Scientific Knowledge impacts the relationship between **Science and Society**

---

1 Interpret The Graphic Organizer above shows that scientific knowledge can impact society. Explain why this is so.

_____

_____

_____

2 Distinguish Explain the difference between scientific investigations and scientific knowledge.

_____

_____

_____

3 Judge "Representing data is not an important part of scientific investigations." Describe why this statement is incorrect.

_____

_____

_____

4 Support Explain why there is not one "scientific method."

_____

_____

_____

Name _____

Multiple Choice

Identify the choice that best completes the statement or answers the question.

1   Scientists do many types of work. Their work often includes making field observations, conducting surveys, creating models, and carrying out experiments. Which description characterizes an experiment?

   A.   observation of plants or animals in their natural environment

   B.   physical or mathematical representation of an object or process

   C.   an organized procedure to study something under controlled conditions

   D.   collection of data from the unregulated world for comparative purposes

2   Raul wants to investigate how the angle of a ramp affects the speed of an object rolling down the ramp. He can conduct his investigation in a number of different ways. Which investigation should he perform?

   F.   observe different bicyclists riding down hills of varying steepness

   G.   record the time it takes one bicyclist to ride down hills of varying steepness

   H.   perform an experiment in a lab in which the angle of the ramp is controlled and the speed of a rolling cart is measured

   I.   observe video of various objects rolling down hills and estimate the angle of the hill and the speed of the object

3   Lida fills two balloons with the same amount of air. Balloon 1 remains at room temperature. Lida places balloon 2 in a freezer. The following diagram shows that the volume of the balloon in the freezer shrinks.

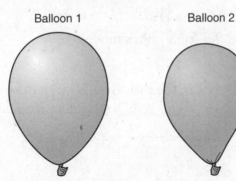

Balloon 1   Balloon 2

Which statement is a law that describes the results of Lida's balloon experiment?

   A.   Decreasing the amount of a gas decreases its temperature.

   B.   The volume of a gas increases when the temperature decreases.

   C.   The volume of a gas decreases when the temperature decreases.

   D.   Decreasing temperature decreases the volume of a gas because the molecules slow down.

4 Ryan made a list of activities that are scientific and activities that are not scientific. Which activity should Ryan classify as **not** scientific?

   F. sorting rocks by color and size

   G. measuring the height of a plant every day

   H. climbing to the top of a very tall mountain

   I. making notes about how many hours the sun shines each day

5 The diagram shows Niels Bohr's theory about how electrons are arranged in atoms. He thought electrons traveled on specific paths around a nucleus. The current theory is that electrons exist in certain cloudlike regions around a nucleus.

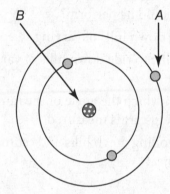

How would a model of the current theory **differ** from Bohr's model?

   A. It would be the same as Bohr's model.

   B. Object A would differ from Bohr's model.

   C. Object B would differ from Bohr's model.

   D. Both objects A and B would differ from Bohr's model.

6 Bryce observes that the sun always rises in the east. He talks with others and finds that everyone has the same observation. Which statement is a scientific law?

   F. The sun rises in the east.

   G. Why does the sun rise in the east?

   H. The sun appears in the east because of Earth's rotation pattern.

   I. If the sun appears in the east, then I am in the Western Hemisphere.

7 Scientists use different types of tools to investigate how and why things happen. Here are some examples of these tools:

• a diagram of a food chain in the Everglades

• a plastic replica of the human digestive system

• a mathematical equation for finding the speed of an object

Which word describes **all** of these examples?

A. experiment

B. hypothesis

C. model

D. observation

8 Three different lab groups perform experiments to determine the density of the samples of iron. They have all rounded the density to the nearest whole number.

Group	Mass of iron (g)	Volume of iron (cm³)	Density of iron (g/cm³)
1	32	4	8
2	48	6	8
3	?	5	8

What is the mass of iron for group 3?

F. 5 g

G. 8 g

H. 40 g

I. 64 g

9 Lee wants to make sure she understands the components of a good scientific investigation. She knows that it should be controlled and have a large sample size. Also, she thinks that the results should be communicated to other scientists. Which is another component that is necessary for a good investigation?

A. It must be conducted in a big lab.

B. It must be run by a university scientist.

C. It must be done with expensive equipment.

D. It must be able to be replicated by other scientists.

10 A friend who knows a lot about science reads in a book that a piece of black paper will get warmer in sunlight than a piece of white paper. Which of these is a scientific reaction to this information?

F. Accept the statement as true because your friend knows about science.

G. Design an experiment to show whether the statement is correct or incorrect.

H. Believe the statement because it was written in a book, so you can trust it to be true.

I. Tell your friend that the statement makes no sense because color does not affect temperature.

11 University of Florida scientists developed a new type of wound dressing that keeps bacteria out of the wound. What is a conclusion that you can make from this information?

A. Scientific discoveries always lead to new technologies.

B. Scientists often respond to the needs in our society.

C. Scientific advances are always made in the field of medicine.

D. Scientists may make discoveries that have no impact on society.

12 Joe tells Mai his theory about why sea turtles nest on the beach instead of in the ocean. He says, "The turtle eggs would sink to the bottom of the ocean, and the baby turtles would drown." Joe says his uncle, a fisherman, told Joe this information. Mai tells Joe that his theory is not scientific. Why does Joe's idea not meet the requirements to be a scientific theory?

F. Joe's idea is already a scientific law.

G. Joe's idea is not supported by scientific evidence.

H. Joe's idea is a good guess that can be tested by experiments.

I. Joe and his uncle are not scientists.

Matter

At room temperature, gold is a solid. But at very high temperatures, solid gold becomes a liquid that flows.

Big Idea 8

Properties of Matter

Big Idea 9

Changes in Matter

What do you think?

Gold is a shiny metal that can be used to make jewelry. Water is a clear liquid that makes up over half of the human body. Though gold and water have different properties, they are both made of matter. What is matter?

Unit 2
Matter

Matter Up Close

Matter is anything that has mass and takes up space. All things, large and small, on Earth are made up of matter! Atoms are the smallest parts of the matter you see. You can't see atoms with your eyes alone.

Fly, about 7×10^{-3} m
The eye of a fly has been magnified so that you can see more detail. Magnification allows us to see things we cannot see with the human eye alone.

Grain of salt, about 5×10^{-4} m

This seasoning and preservative can be harvested from sea water.

Table salt

Rhinovirus, about 3×10^{-8} m

Watch out for this virus—it causes the common cold.

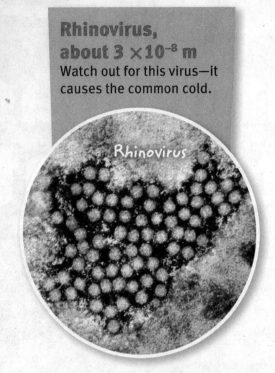

Rhinovirus

Helium atom, about 3×10^{-11} m

Atoms are so small that they cannot be viewed with traditional light microscopes. Often, they are represented by models such as this one.

Object	Width
Grain of salt	5×10^{-4} m (or 0.0005 m)
Rhinovirus	3×10^{-8} m (or 0.00000003 m)
Helium atom	3×10^{-11} m (or 0.00000000003 m)

Take It Home   Size Is Relative

By looking at ratios of sizes, you can compare the relative sizes of objects. How many times greater is the size of a grain of salt than a rhinovirus particle? You can write a ratio to find the answer:

$$\frac{\text{grain of salt}}{\text{rhinovirus}} = \frac{0.0005 \text{ m}}{0.00000003 \text{ m}} \approx 17{,}000$$

A grain of salt is about 17,000 times the size of a rhinovirus.

A Determine how many times greater a rhinovirus is than a helium atom.

B Measure the width of one of your textbooks to the nearest millimeter. How many helium atoms could you line up across the book?

Introduction to Matter

ESSENTIAL QUESTION

What properties define matter?

By the end of this lesson, you should be able to relate mass, weight, volume, and density to one another.

Hot air takes balloons aloft because hot air is less dense than the cooler air around it.

Sunshine State Standards

SC.8.P.8.2 Differentiate between weight and mass recognizing that weight is the amount of gravitational pull on an object and is distinct from, though proportional to, mass.

SC.8.P.8.3 Explore and describe the densities of various materials through measurement of their masses and volumes.

MA.6.A.3.6 Construct and analyze tables, graphs, and equations to describe linear functions and other simple relations using both common language and algebraic notation.

LA.6.2.2.3 The student will organize information to show understanding (e.g., representing main ideas within text through charting, mapping, paraphrasing, summarizing, or comparing/contrasting).

Engage Your Brain

1 Describe Fill in the blank with the word or phrase that you think correctly completes the following sentences.

A(n) _____ can hold a greater volume of water than a mug.

A hamster weighs less than a(n)

_____ .

A bowling ball is harder to lift than a basketball because _____

_____ .

2 Explain List some similarities and differences between the golf ball on the left and the table-tennis ball on the right in the photo.

_____

_____

_____

_____

_____

Active Reading

3 Apply Many scientific words, such as *matter*, also have everyday meanings. Use context clues to write your own definition for each meaning of the word *matter*.

Example sentence
What is this gooey <u>matter</u> on the table?

Matter:

_____

_____

_____

Example sentence
Please vote! Your opinions <u>matter</u>.

Matter:

_____

_____

_____

Vocabulary Terms

- matter
- mass
- weight
- volume
- density

4 Identify This list contains the vocabulary terms you'll learn in this lesson. As you read, circle the definition of each term.

What's the MATTER?

What is matter?

Suppose your class takes a field trip to a museum. During the course of the day you see mammoth bones, sparkling crystals, hot-air balloons, and an astronaut's space suit. All of these things are matter.

As you will see, **matter** is anything that has mass and takes up space. Your body is matter. The air that you breathe and the water that you drink are also matter. Matter makes up the materials around you.

However, not everything is matter. Light and sound, for example, are not matter. Light does not take up space or have mass in the same way that a table does. Although air is matter, a sound traveling through air is not.

Active Reading 5 **Explain** How can you tell if something is matter?

_____

_____

_____

Visualize It!

6 Identify Name three examples of matter found in this photo.

_____

_____

What is mass?

You cannot always tell how much matter is in an object simply by observing the object's size. But you *can* measure the object's mass. **Mass** describes the amount of matter in an object.

Compare the two balloons at the right. The digital scales show that the balloon filled with compressed air has a greater mass than the other balloon. This is because the compressed air adds mass to the balloon. Air may seem to be made of nothing, but it has mass. The readings on the scale are in grams (g). A gram is the unit of mass you will use most often in science class.

Objects that are the same size can be made up of different amounts of matter. For example, a large sponge is about the same size as a brick. But the brick contains more matter. Therefore, the brick has a greater mass than the sponge.

The readings on these digital scales show that all matter, even air, has mass.

0.010 g

0.005 g

How does mass differ from weight?

The words *weight* and *mass* are often used as though they mean the same thing, but they do not. **Weight** is a measure of the gravitational force (grav•ih•TAY•shuhn•uhl FAWRS) on an object. Gravitational force keeps objects on Earth from floating into space. The gravitational force between an object and Earth depends partly on the object's mass. The greater that the mass of an object is, the greater the gravitational force on the object will be and the greater the object's weight will be.

An object's weight can change depending on the object's location. For example, you would weigh less on the moon than you do on Earth because the moon has less mass—and therefore exerts less gravitational force—than Earth does. However, you would have the same mass in both places. An object's mass does not change unless the amount of matter in an object changes.

The weight of this dachshund on the moon is about one-sixth of its weight on Earth.

Active Reading **7 Explain** Why do astronauts weigh less on the moon than they do on Earth?

_____

_____

_____

The balance below works by moving the masses on the right along the beams until they "balance" the pan on the left. Moving the masses changes the amount of force the levers exert on the pan. The more massive the object on the pan, the more force will be needed on the levers to balance the two sides.

8 Infer Would this balance give the same value for mass if used on the moon? Explain.

_____

_____

_____

_____

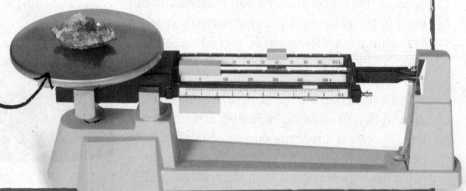

A triple-beam balance can be used to measure the mass of small objects such as this geode fragment.

The spring scale gives weight in pounds (lb).

How are mass and weight measured?

Mass is often measured by using a triple-beam balance such as the one shown above. The balance compares an object's mass to known standards of mass called *countermasses*. The countermasses slide across each of three beams. When the countermasses balance the mass of the object in the balance pan, the pointer will rest at 0. Then, the mass can be read from the position of the countermasses on the beams.

Weight is measured with devices such as the spring scale shown at the left. The spring measures the force between the mass in the pan and Earth. The more massive the object placed in the pan, the more forceful is the attraction between it and Earth, and the more the spring will stretch. Greater stretch means greater weight.

Because weight is a measure of gravitational force, it is given in units of force. You probably are most familiar with weight given in pounds (lb), like the units shown on the scale. The standard scientific unit for weight, however, is the newton (N). A 100-g mass weighs approximately 1 N on Earth. One newton is about one-fourth of a pound.

Measuring Space

How is the amount of space occupied by matter measured?

All matter takes up space. The amount of space that an object takes up, or occupies, is known as the object's **volume.**

Objects with the similar volumes do not always have the same mass. In the photos, the bowling ball and the balloon have about the same volume, but the bowling ball contains a lot more mass than the balloon. You know this because the bowling ball weighs much more than the balloon. The different masses take up about the same amount of space, so both objects have about the same volume.

Active Reading **9 Define** What does volume measure?

_____

_____

The bowling ball has a lot more mass than the balloon.

The balloon is similar in volume but has much less mass than the bowling ball.

Think Outside the Book (Inquiry)

10 Infer Big things can look very small when seen from far away. Describe how you know big things far away aren't really small.

How can volume be determined?

There are different ways to find the volume of an object. For objects that have well-defined shapes, you can take a few measurements and calculate the volume using a formula. For objects that are irregularly shaped, such as a rock, you can use water displacement to measure volume. For liquids, you can use a graduated cylinder.

Using a Formula

Some objects have well-defined shapes. For these objects, the easiest way to find their volume is to measure the dimensions of the object and use a formula. Different shapes use different volume formulas. For example, to find the volume of a rectangular box, you would use a different formula than if you were to find the volume of a spherical ball.

> To find the volume of a rectangular box, use the following formula:
>
> $$\text{Volume} = (\text{length})(\text{width})(\text{height})$$
> $$V = lwh$$

The volume of a solid is measured in units of length cubed. For example, if you measure the length, width, and height of a box in centimeters (cm), the volume of the box has units of centimeters multiplied by centimeters multiplied by centimeters, or cubic centimeters (cm^3). In order to calculate volume, make sure that all the measurements are in the same units.

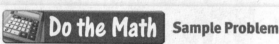 **Do the Math** **Sample Problem**

Find the volume of the lunch box.

Identify

A. What do you know?

length = 25 cm, width = 18 cm, height = 10 cm

B. What do you want to find? Volume

Plan

C. Draw and label a sketch: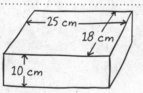

D. Write the formula: $V = lwh$

E. Substitute into the formula: $V = (25 \text{ cm})(18 \text{ cm})(10 \text{ cm})$

Solve

F. Multiply: $(25 \text{ cm})(18 \text{ cm})(10 \text{ cm}) = 4{,}500 \text{ cm}^3$

G. Check that your units agree: The given units are centimeters, and the measure found is volume. Therefore, the units should be cm^3. The units agree.

Answer: $4{,}500 \text{ cm}^3$

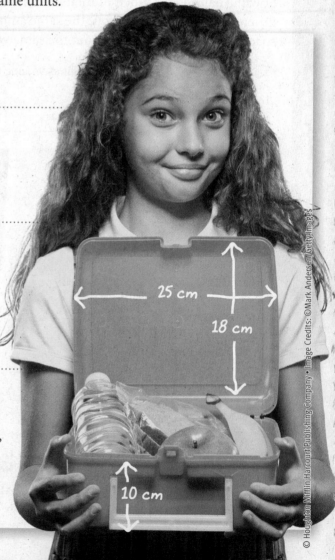

The volume of your locker will tell you how much stuff will fit inside.

30 cm

200 cm

40 cm

Do the Math   You Try It

11 Calculate Find the volume of a locker that is 30 cm long, 40 cm wide, and 200 cm high.

Identify

A. What do you know?

B. What do you want to find?

Plan

C. Draw and label a sketch:

D. Write the formula:

E. Substitute the given values into the formula:

Solve

F. Multiply:

G. Check that your units agree:

Answer:

Using Water Displacement

In the lab, you can use a beaker or graduated cylinder to measure the volume of liquids. Graduated cylinders are used to measure liquid volume when accuracy is important. The volume of liquids is often expressed in liters (L) or milliliters (mL). Milliliters and cubic centimeters are equivalent; in other words, 1 mL = 1 cm^3. The volume of any amount of liquid, from one raindrop to an entire ocean, can be expressed in these units.

Two objects cannot occupy the same space at the same time. For example, as a builder stacks bricks to build a wall, she adds each brick on top of the other. No brick can occupy the same place that another brick occupies. Similarly, when an object is placed in water, the object pushes some of the water out of the way. This process, called *displacement*, can be used to measure the volume of an irregularly shaped solid object.

In the photos at the right, you can see that the level of the water in the graduated cylinder has risen after the chess piece is placed inside. The volume of water displaced is found by subtracting the original volume in the graduated cylinder from the new volume. This is equal to the volume of the chess piece.

When deciding the units of the volume found using water displacement, it is helpful to remember that 1 mL of water is equal to 1 cm^3. Therefore, you can report the volume of the object in cubic centimeters.

Do the Math

You Try It

12 Calculate The two images below show a graduated cylinder filled with water before and after a chess piece is placed inside. Use the images to calculate the volume of the chess piece.

Volume without chess piece = _____

Volume with chess piece = _____

Volume of chess piece = _____

Don't forget to check the units of volume of the chess piece!

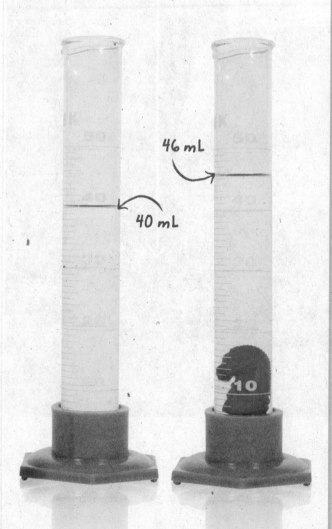

46 mL

40 mL

Packing It In!

What is density?

Mass and volume are properties of all substances. These two properties are related to another property called density (DEN•sih•tee). **Density** is a measure of the amount of mass in a given volume. Objects containing the same amount of mass can take up different amounts of space. For example, the pile of feathers above takes up more space than the tomato. But they have the same mass. This is because the tomato is more dense. The tomato has more mass in a smaller space.

The density of a given substance remains the same no matter how much of the substance you have. For example, if you divide a piece of clay in half, both halves will have the same density as the original piece.

The tomato and the pile of feathers have similar masses, but the tomato has less volume. This means that the tomato is more dense.

Active Reading

13 Explain What is density?

_____

_____

_____

14 Predict Circle the item in each pair that is more dense.

Golf ball	Empty milk carton	Foam ball
Table-tennis ball	Milk carton full of milk	Baseball

How is density determined?

Units for density consist of a mass unit divided by a volume unit. Units that are often used for density are grams per cubic centimeter (g/cm³) for solids, and grams per milliliter (g/mL) for liquids. In other words, density is the mass in grams divided by the volume in cubic centimeters or milliliters.

To find an object's density (D), find its mass (m) and its volume (V). Then, use the given formula to calculate the density of the object.

$$D = \frac{m}{V}$$

The density of water is 1 g/mL (g/cm³). Any object with a density greater than 1 g/mL will sink in water and with a density less than 1 g/mL will float. Density, therefore, can be a useful thing to know. The sample problem below shows how to calculate the density of a volcanic rock called pumice.

Pumice and obsidian are two igneous volcanic rocks with very different densities.

Do the Math

Sample Problem

Pumice is an igneous volcanic rock, formed by the rapid cooling of lava. What is the density of a 49.8 g piece of pumice that has a volume of 83 cm³?

Identify

A. What do you know?

mass = 49.8 g, volume = 83 cm³

B. What do you want to find? Density

Plan

C. Write the formula: $D = \frac{m}{V}$

D. Substitute the given values into the formula:

$D = \frac{49.8\ g}{83\ cm^3}$

Solve

E. Divide: $\frac{49.8\ g}{83\ cm^3} = 0.6\ g/cm^3$

F. Check that your units agree: The given units are grams and cubic centimeters, and the measure found is density. Therefore, the units should be g/cm³. The units agree.

Answer: 0.6 g/cm³

You Try It

15 Calculate Obsidian is another type of igneous rock. What is the density of a piece of obsidian that has a mass of 239.2 g and a volume of 92 cm³?

Identify

A. What do you know?

B. What do you want to find?

Plan

C. Write the formula:

D. Substitute the given values into the formula:

Solve

E. Divide:

F. Check that your units agree:

Answer:

Do the Math

Sample Problem

A basalt rock displaces 16 mL of water. The density of the rock is 3.0 g/cm³. What is the mass of the rock?

Identify

A. What do you know?

volume = 16 mL, density = 3.0 g/cm³

B. What do you want to find? Mass

Plan

C. Rearrange the formula $D = \dfrac{m}{V}$ to solve for mass. You can do this by multiplying each side by V.

$$D = \frac{m}{V}$$
$$m = D \cdot V$$

D. Substitute the given values into the formula. Recall that 1 mL = 1 cm³, so 16 mL = 16 cm³.

$$m = \frac{3.0 \text{ g}}{\text{cm}^3} \cdot 16 \text{ cm}^3$$

Solve

E. Multiply: $\dfrac{3.0 \text{ g}}{\text{cm}^3} \cdot 16 \text{ cm}^3 = 48 \text{ g}$

F. Check that your units agree: The given units are g/cm³ and mL, and the measure found is mass. Therefore, the units should be g. The units agree.

Answer: 48 g

You Try It

16 Calculate A rhyolite rock has a volume of 9.5 mL. The density of the rock is 2.6 g/cm³. What is the mass of the rock?

Identify

A. What do you know?

B. What do you want to find?

Plan

C. Write the formula:

D. Substitute the given values into the formula:

Solve

E. Multiply:

F. Check that your units agree:

Answer:

Kilauea is the youngest volcano on the Big Island of Hawaii. "Kilauea" means "spewing" or "much spreading," apparently in reference to the lava flows that it erupts.

Visual Summary

To complete this summary, check the box that indicates true or false. Then, use the key below to check your answers. You can use this page to review the main concepts of the lesson.

Relating Mass, Weight, Volume, and Density

Mass is the amount of matter in an object. Weight is a measure of the gravitational force on an object.

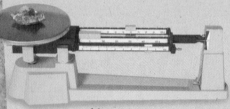

Mass

Weight

	T	F	
17	☐	☐	An object's weight is the amount of space it occupies.
18	☐	☐	The mass of an object is equal to its weight.

Volume is the amount of space that matter in an object occupies.
To find the volume of a rectangular box, use the formula:

$$V = lwh$$

	T	F	
19	☐	☐	The volume of a solid can be expressed in units of cm^3.

Density describes the mass of a substance in a given volume.
To find the density of a substance, use the formula:

$$D = \frac{m}{V}$$

	T	F	
20	☐	☐	An object that floats in water is less dense than water.

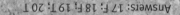

Answers: 17 F; 18 F; 19 T; 20 T

21 Describe Write a set of instructions that describe how to find the density of an object. Write the instructions so that they work for a regularly shaped object and for an irregularly shaped object.

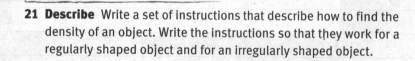

Lesson Review

Vocabulary

Fill in the blank with the term that best completes the following sentence.

1 _____ is the amount of space that matter in an object occupies.

2 _____ is anything that has mass and takes up space.

3 _____ is the amount of matter in an object.

4 _____ is a measure of the amount of matter in a given amount of space.

5 _____ is a measure of the gravitational force on an object.

Key Concepts

6 Classify Is air matter? How can you tell?

_____

_____

_____

7 Describe Is it possible for an object's weight to change while its mass remains constant? Explain.

_____

_____

_____

8 Compare Explain why a golf ball is heavier than a table-tennis ball, even though the balls are the same size.

_____

_____

9 Calculate A block of wood has a mass of 120 g and a volume of 200 cm³. What is the density of the wood?

Critical Thinking

Use this table to answer the following questions.

Substance	Density (g/cm³)
Zinc (solid)	7.13
Silver (solid)	10.50
Lead (solid)	11.35

10 Identify Suppose that 273 g of one of the substances listed above displaces 26 mL of water. What is the substance?

_____

_____

_____

11 Evaluate How many mL of water would be displaced by 408 g of lead?

_____

_____

_____

12 Predict How can you determine that a coin is not pure silver if you know the mass and volume of the coin?

_____

_____

_____

_____

13 Calculate A truck whose bed is 2.5 m long, 1.5 m wide, and 1.0 m high is delivering sand for a sand-sculpture competition. About how many trips must the truck make to deliver 7 m³ of sand?

Determining Relevant Information

Sunshine State Standards

SC.8.N.1.6 Understand that scientific investigations involve the collection of relevant empirical evidence, the use of logical reasoning, and the application of imagination in devising hypotheses, predictions, explanations and models to make sense of the collected evidence.

SC.8.N.2.1 Distinguish between scientific and pseudoscientific ideas.

Many people and companies claim to use scientific evidence to support their ideas, arguments, or products. Some of this evidence may be strong and well-supported by scientific investigation. But some evidence may be weak and not supported by scientific investigation. Some information may seem impressive, but may not actually support the claims being made. How can you recognize the difference? How can you tell if the information is relevant?

Tutorial

The advertisement below highlights some things that you should consider as you try to identify whether information is relevant.

Grow your best Indian blanket wildflowers using new Fertilizer Formulation!

Fertilizer Formulation

We tested 20 patches of Indian blanket wildflowers in the Valdosta, Georgia, area. Plants that received the recommended amount of fertilizer grew an average of 30% taller. This fertilizer is made of all-natural ingredients and provides the best mixture of nutrients for any garden.

Everyone should use this fertilizer!

Limited Samples Be alert to any mention of specific times, places, or objects. Information that is relevant in one instance might not be relevant for your purpose. In this case, one type of wildflower in one place is mentioned. If you grow a different plant in a different area, this information is not relevant.

Comparisons Strong, relevant information would compare the results of two similar products or events. When a comparison is made, ask yourself what things are being compared. Relevant information might include comparisons of the results of a controlled experiment. In this advertisement, there is no mention of whether the comparison is for plants that had no fertilizer or plants that were given a similar competing fertilizer.

Unclear Connections While the all-natural ingredients may be good for plants, there is no connection made between these ingredients and how the fertilizer works or that they work better than artificial ingredients. An explanation of which ingredients the fertilizer uses and why they work better than artificial ingredients would make the connection more clear.

You Try It!

Read the following advertisement, and answer the questions below to determine which information is relevant to the claims being made.

GroBig Soil Additive

GroBig will work on all types of wildflowers!

Buy GroBig today, and watch your flowers grow!
$19.95 per liter

"I've found the secret to the best wildflower garden—using GroBig Soil Additive. Now, you can have your best garden, too."
— A. Gardener

Botanists at a private nursery near Tampa, Florida, selected two tall samples of a common wildflower, the narrow-leaved sunflower. One plant received the recommended amount of GroBig Soil Additive. The other did not. After 2 weeks, the plant given GroBig Soil Additive had grown 4 cm. The other plant had grown just 2 cm. What a difference!

1 Identifying Conclusions Identify the claim that the advertisers are making.

_____

_____

_____

2 Identifying Evidence What evidence or information does the writer use to support the claims? Underline two examples to support your answer. Then, identify whether the information is relevant or irrelevant.

Relevant	Irrelevant

3 Applying Concepts List three questions you would need to answer in order to support the claims being made about GroBig.

_____

_____

_____

_____

_____

_____

Take It Home

Find an article or advertisement in a newspaper or magazine that contains a scientific claim and supporting information. Identify relevant or irrelevant information in the article or advertisement. Write a paragraph that summarizes the article or advertisement and its scientific evidence.

Properties of Matter

ESSENTIAL QUESTION

What are physical and chemical properties of matter?

By the end of this lesson, you should be able to classify and compare substances based on their physical and chemical properties.

🌀 Sunshine State Standards

SC.8.P.8.4 Classify and compare substances on the basis of characteristic physical properties that can be demonstrated or measured; for example, density, thermal or electrical conductivity, solubility, magnetic properties, melting and boiling points, and know that these properties are independent of the amount of the sample.

MA.6.A.3.6 Construct and analyze tables, graphs, and equations to describe linear functions and other simple relations using both common language and algebraic notation.

LA.6.2.2.3 The student will organize information to show understanding (e.g., representing main ideas within text through charting, mapping, paraphrasing, summarizing, or comparing/contrasting).

To harvest cranberries, the dry beds are flooded with water. Next, water reels loosen the berries from the vines. Since cranberries are less dense than water, they float. Harvesters take advantage of this property to gather and easily float them towards collection sites.

Engage Your Brain

1 Predict Check T or F to show whether you think each statement is true or false.

T	F	
☐	☐	Liquid water freezes at the same temperature at which ice melts: 0 °C.
☐	☐	A bowling ball weighs less than a Styrofoam ball of the same size.
☐	☐	An object with a density greater than the density of water will float in water.
☐	☐	Solubility is the ability of one substance to dissolve in another.

2 Describe If you were asked to describe an orange to someone who had never seen an orange, what would you tell the person?

_____

_____

_____

_____

_____

Active Reading

3 Synthesize Many English words have their roots in other languages. The root of the word *solubility* is the Latin word *solvere*, which means "to loosen." Make an educated guess about the meaning of the word *solubility*.

_____

_____

_____

Vocabulary Terms

- **physical property**
- **chemical property**

4 Apply As you learn the definition of each vocabulary term in this lesson, create your own definition or sketch to help you remember the meaning of the term.

Physical Education

What are physical properties of matter?

What words would you use to describe a table? A chair? A piece of cloth? You would probably say something about the shape, color, and size of each object. Next, you might consider whether the object is hard or soft, smooth or rough. Normally, when describing an object, you identify what it is about that object that you can observe without changing its identity.

They Are Used to Describe a Substance

A characteristic of a substance that can be observed and measured without changing the identity of the substance is called a **physical property**. Gold is one metal prized for its physical properties. Gold can be bent and shaped easily and has a lasting shine. Both properties make it an excellent metal for making coins and jewelry.

All of your senses can be used to detect physical properties. Color, shape, size, and texture are a few of the physical properties you encounter. Think of how you would describe an object to a friend. Most likely, your description would be a list of the object's physical properties.

Active Reading **5 Describe** Does observing a physical property of a substance change the identity of the substance? Explain.

_____

_____

_____

_____

_____

Gold is a highly sought-after metal for making jewelry. Gold is dense, soft, and shiny, and it is resistant to tarnishing. Gold is often mixed with other metals to make it stronger.

In this factory, gold is being purified by the process of smelting. This process uses pressure, high heat, and chemicals to remove impurities from the gold.

They Can Be Observed without Changing the Identity of a Substance

The physical properties of an object can be observed with the senses. Some properties can be measured, too. For example, you can look at a table to observe its relative size. Or, you can measure its length, width, and height by using a tool like a measuring tape. When you observe a physical property, you do not change the substance's identity. The material that makes up the table keeps its identity.

Imagine that you conducted an experiment to measure the temperature at which water boils. This temperature, called the boiling point, is a physical property. You placed a beaker of water over a heating source and measured the increase in water temperature using a thermometer. Once the water reached its boiling point, some of the water had become a gas. In this experiment, the water had to change to a gas before you could record the boiling point of water. However, the water did not change in identity. It is water whether it is a solid, liquid, or gas.

Visualize It!

6 Observe Describe the physical properties of objects you see in this photo.

_____

_____

_____

_____

_____

Think Outside the Book

7 Apply Describe a common object by naming its properties. Trade your mystery-object description with a classmate's and try to guess what object he or she has described.

Common Physical Properties

On these two pages, you can read about some common physical properties. The physical properties of a substance often describe how the substance can be useful.

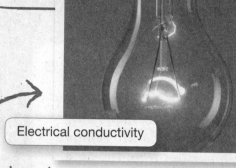

Visualize It!

Electrical conductivity

Electrical conductivity is a measure of how well an electric current can move through a substance.

Density

Density is a measure of the amount of mass in a given amount of volume.

8 Explain The photo above shows oil and vinegar in a pitcher. The top layer is the oil. Describe the density of the vinegar compared to the density of the oil.

_____

_____

_____

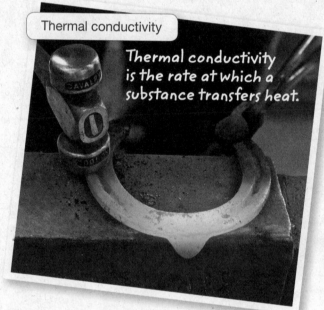

Thermal conductivity

Thermal conductivity is the rate at which a substance transfers heat.

Solubility

Solubility is the ability of a substance to dissolve in another substance. This powdered drink mix is dissolving in water. When fully dissolved, the particles of the drink mix will be spread throughout the water.

9 Predict If you let all of the liquid evaporate out of the pitcher, would you be able to see the solid particles of the drink mix? Explain.

_____

_____

_____

_____

Unit 2 Matter

© Houghton Mifflin Harcourt Publishing Company • Image Credits: (tr) ©Photos India/Photolibrary; (br) ©Phil Degginger/Alamy

Malleability

Malleability (MAL·ee·uh·bil·i·tee) is the ability of a substance to be rolled or pounded into various shapes. Aluminum has the property of malleability.

10 Identify Name something made of aluminum and explain why malleability is a useful property.

_____

_____

_____

Luster

Many metals often have a shine, or luster, that make them prized by decorators.

Some metals exert a magnetic attraction. Magnetic attraction can act at a distance.

Magnetic attraction

Melting point

The melting point of a substance is the temperature at which it changes from a solid to a liquid.

Boiling water beneath the surface of Earth powers this geyser.

Boiling point

Inquiry

11 Infer Compare what happens when a geyser erupts to what happens when a tea kettle whistles.

_____

_____

_____

_____

_____

Identity Theft

What are chemical properties of matter?

Active Reading 12 **Identify** As you read, underline the definition of a chemical property.

Physical properties are not the only properties that describe matter. A **chemical property** describes a substance's ability to change into a new substance with different properties. Common chemical properties include flammability and reactivity with substances such as oxygen, water, and acids.

They Describe How a Substance Changes

Can you think of a chemical property for the metal iron? When left outdoors in wet weather, iron rusts. The ability to rust is a chemical property of iron. The metal silver does not rust, but eventually a darker substance, called tarnish, forms on its surface. You may have noticed a layer of tarnish on some silver spoons or jewelry. Rusting and tarnishing are chemical properties because the metal changes. After rusting or tarnishing, a portion of the metal is no longer the metal but a different substance.

13 **Predict** Why do automobiles rust more easily in wet climates than drier climates?

_____

_____

_____

_____

Iron can form rust, turning a once shiny car into a crumbling relic.

They Can Be Observed by Attempting to Change the Identity of a Substance

One way to identify a chemical property is to observe the changes that a substance undergoes. Wood for a campfire has the chemical property of flammability—the ability to burn. When wood burns, new substances are formed: water, carbon dioxide, and ash. These new substances have different properties than the wood had. Reactivity is another chemical property that can be identified by observing changes. Reactivity is the ability of a substance to interact with another substance and form one or more new substances.

You can also observe a chemical property of a substance by attempting to change the substance, even if no change occurs. For example, you can observe that gold is nonflammable by attempting to burn it. A chemical property of gold is that it is nonflammable.

Reactivity is a chemical property. Vinegar and baking soda react to make a salt, water, and carbon dioxide gas.

Flammability, or the ability of a substance to burn, is a chemical property. For example, the wood building in the photo is flammable, and the suits that help keep the firefighters safe are flame resistant.

Property Boundaries

What is the difference between physical and chemical properties?

A physical property can always be observed without changing the identity of a substance. The mass of a log can be observed without changing the log. A chemical property, however, is observed by attempting to change the identity of a substance. To witness a log's flammability, you must try to set the log on fire.

A substance always has physical and chemical properties. For example, a log is flammable even when it's not burning.

Active Reading 14 **Compare** Describe the difference between a physical property and a chemical property.

_____

_____

_____

_____

Visualize It!

Bending an iron nail will change its shape but not its identity.

An iron nail can react with oxygen in the air to form iron oxide, or rust.

15 **Distinguish** What type of property is being shown by each nail?

_____

_____

16 **Predict** Check the correct box to show whether each property of an iron nail is a physical or a chemical property.

Malleable	☐ Physical ☐ Chemical
Reacts with oxygen	☐ Physical ☐ Chemical
Magnetic	☐ Physical ☐ Chemical
Nonflammable	☐ Physical ☐ Chemical

At the Scene

The collection and study of physical evidence in a criminal investigation is known as *forensic science*. Forensic scientists are experts in observing the physical and chemical properties of evidence at crime scenes.

Arson Investigation

A forensic scientist can gently heat ashes from an arson scene to help determine what chemicals were used to start the fire. If detectives know how the fire began, then they might be able to determine who is responsible for the crime.

Studying Paint

Flecks of paint left on a tree where a car hit it can be examined with a special microscope. How the paint absorbs light can reveal what chemicals were used in the paint. This information could help authorities determine what kind of vehicle a criminal suspect drove.

Fiber Analysis

Magnified fibers, like those shown above, can provide clues, too. An acrylic fiber might be material from a boat cover or a rug. Or, polyester could have come from a suspect's shirt.

Extend

Inquiry

17 Identify List physical and chemical properties used to identify evidence at a crime scene.

18 Predict When examining evidence, why might investigators want to be more careful examining chemical properties than physical properties?

19 Evaluate By examining the physical and chemical properties of evidence at a crime scene, investigators can often be more certain about what a suspicious substance is *not* than about what it *is*. Why do you think this is the case?

Identify Yourself

How can physical and chemical properties identify a substance?

Properties unique to a substance are its *characteristic properties*. Characteristic properties can be physical properties, such as density, or chemical properties, such as flammability. Characteristic properties stay the same regardless of the amount of a sample. They can help identify a substance.

Iron pyrite is one of several minerals having a color similar to that of gold. Miners can find iron pyrite near deposits of gold, and sometimes mistake it for gold. Color and location, however, are about the only properties iron pyrite shares with gold. The two substances have quite different characteristic properties.

For example, gold flattens when hit with a hammer, but iron pyrite shatters. When rubbed on a ceramic plate, gold leaves a yellow streak, but iron pyrite leaves a greenish black one. Gold keeps its shine even if beneath the sea for years, but iron pyrite turns green if exposed to water.

An easy way for miners to tell iron pyrite and gold apart is by using the property of density. Miners collect gold by sifting through dirt in pans. Because of its high density, gold stays in the pan while dirt and most other substances wash over the side as the miner swirls the contents in the pan. Since gold has a density almost four times that of iron pyrite, distinguishing gold from iron pyrite should be an easy task for the experienced miner.

> To find the density of a substance, use the following formula, where D is density, m is mass, and V is volume:
>
> $$D = \frac{m}{V}$$

20 Infer Check the box to show which would tell you for sure if you had a sample of real gold.

	Yes	No
Color of your sample.	☐	☐
What happens when you strike your sample with a hammer.	☐	☐
The location where your sample was found.	☐	☐

In pan mining, as the contents in the pan are swirled, less dense substances are washed away.

 **Do the Math**

Sample Problem

A sample of gold has a mass of 579 g. The volume of the sample is 30 cm³. What is the density of the gold sample?

Identify

A. What do you know?

mass = 579 g, volume = 30 cm³

B. What do you want to find? Density

Plan

C. Write the formula: $D = \dfrac{m}{V}$

D. Substitute the given values into the formula:

$D = \dfrac{579 \text{ g}}{30 \text{ cm}^3}$

Solve

E. Divide: $\dfrac{579 \text{ g}}{30 \text{ cm}^3} = 19.3 \text{ g/cm}^3$

F. Check that your units agree:

The given units are grams and cubic centimeters, and the measure found is density. Therefore, the units should be g/cm³. The units agree.

Answer: 19.3 g/cm³

You Try It

21 Calculate A student finds an object with a mass of 64.54 g and a volume of 14 cm³. Find the density of the object. Is the object gold?

Identify

A. What do you know?

B. What do you want to find?

Plan

C. Write the formula:

D. Substitute the given values into the formula:

Solve

E. Divide:

F. Check that your units agree:

Answer:

	Yes	No
Is the object gold?	☐	☐

Gold

Iron pyrite

Visual Summary

To complete this summary, circle the correct word. Then use the key below to check your answers. You can use this page to review the main concepts of the lesson.

Physical and Chemical Properties

A physical property is a property that can be observed or measured without changing the identity of the substance.

22 Solubility / Flammability is a physical property.

23 The melting point of a substance is the temperature at which the substance changes from a solid to a gas / liquid.

A chemical property is a property that describes a substance's ability to form new substances.

24 Reactivity with water / Magnetism is a chemical property.

25 Flammability is the ability of a substance to transfer heat / burn.

The properties that are most useful in identifying a substance are its characteristic properties. Characteristic properties can be physical properties or chemical properties.

26 The characteristic properties of a substance do / do not depend on the size of the sample.

Answers: 22 Solubility; 23 liquid; 24 Reactivity with water; 25 burn; 26 do not

27 Synthesize You have two solid substances that look the same. What measurements would you take and which tests would you perform to determine whether they actually are the same?

Lesson Review

Vocabulary

Fill in the blanks with the term that best completes the following sentences.

1 Flammability is an example of a _____ property.

2 Electrical conductivity is an example of a _____ property.

Key Concepts

3 Identify What are three physical properties of aluminum foil?

_____

_____

_____

4 Describe What effect does observing a substance's physical properties have on the substance?

_____

_____

_____

_____

5 Explain Describe how a physical property, such as mass or texture, can change without causing a change in the substance.

_____

_____

_____

_____

6 Justify Must new substances be formed when you observe a chemical property? Explain.

_____

_____

_____

_____

_____

_____

Critical Thinking

Use this table to answer the following question.

Element	Melting Point (°C)	Boiling Point (°C)
Bromine	−7.2	59
Chlorine	−100	−35
Iodine	110	180

7 Infer You are given samples of the substances shown in the table. The samples are labeled A, B, and C. At room temperature, sample A is a solid, sample B is a liquid, and sample C is a gas. What are the identities of samples A, B, and C? (Hint: Room temperature is about 20 °C.)

_____

_____

_____

8 Conclude The density of gold is 19.3 g/cm³. The density of iron pyrite is 5.0 g/cm³. If a nugget of iron pyrite and a nugget of gold each have a mass of 50 g, what can you conclude about the volume of each nugget?

_____

_____

_____

9 Predict Suppose you need to build a raft to cross a fast-moving river. Describe the physical and chemical properties of the raft that would be important to ensure your safety.

_____

_____

_____

_____

_____

_____

Shirley Ann Jackson

PHYSICIST AND EDUCATOR

How can you make contributions to many areas of science all at once? One way is to promote the study of science by others. This is precisely what physicist Dr. Shirley Ann Jackson does as the president of Rensselaer Polytechnic Institute in Troy, New York.

Earlier in her career, she was a research scientist, investigating the electrical and optical properties of matter. Engineers used her research to help develop products for the telecommunications industry. She later became a professor of physics at Rutgers University in New Jersey.

In 1995, President Bill Clinton appointed Dr. Jackson to chair the U.S. Nuclear Regulatory Commission (NRC). The NRC is responsible for promoting the safe use of nuclear energy. At the NRC, Dr. Jackson used her knowledge of how the particles that make up matter interact and can generate energy. She also used her leadership skills. She helped to start the International Nuclear Regulators Association. This group made it easier for officials from many nations to discuss issues of nuclear safety.

Dr. Jackson's interest in science started when she observed bees in her backyard. She is still studying the world around her, making careful observations, and taking actions based on what she learns. These steps for learning were the foundation for all her later contributions to science. As a student, Dr. Jackson learned the same things about matter and energy that you are learning.

Nuclear power plant

Language Arts Connection

Research how nuclear energy is generated, what it can be used for, and what concerns surround it. Write a summary report to the government outlining the risks and benefits of using nuclear energy.

JOB BOARD

Chemical Technician

What You'll Do: Help chemists and chemical engineers in laboratory tests, observe solids, liquids, and gases for research or development of new products. You might handle hazardous chemicals or toxic materials.

Where You Might Work: Mostly indoors in laboratories or manufacturing plants, but may do some research outdoors.

Education: An associate's degree in applied science or science-related technology, specialized technical training, or a bachelor's degree in chemistry, biology, or forensic science is needed.

Other Job Requirements: You need to follow written steps of procedures and to accurately record measurements and observations. You need to understand the proper handling of hazardous materials.

Chef

What You'll Do: Prepare, season, and cook food, keep a clean kitchen, supervise kitchen staff, and buy supplies and equipment.

Where You Might Work: Restaurants, hotels, the military, schools, and in your own kitchen as a private caterer.

Education: Many chefs gain on-the-job training without formal culinary school training. However, you can also learn cooking skills at culinary institutes and earn a two-year or four-year degree.

Other Job Requirements: Your job will require you to be on your feet for many hours and lift heavy equipment and boxes of food.

PEOPLE IN SCIENCE NEWS

Andy Goldsworthy

Changing Matter Is Art

Andy Goldsworthy is interested in how matter changes over time. He is inspired by the changes that occur in nature. As a sculptor, he uses materials found in nature, like snow, ice, twigs, and leaves. Many of his sculptures do not last for very long, but these materials show the changing state of matter. For example, for one of his art projects, he made 13 large snowballs in the winter and placed them in cold storage. In the middle of summer, he placed the snowballs around London. It took five days for the snowballs to melt. During that time they were reminders of a wider world of nature. Movement, change, light, growth, and decay are factors that affect his pieces. Because his work is constantly changing, Goldsworthy takes photographs of his sculptures.

© Houghton Mifflin Harcourt Publishing Company • Image Credits: (bkgd) ©Dale O'Dell/Alamy; (br) ©Julian Calder/Corbis

Physical and Chemical Changes

ESSENTIAL QUESTION

What are physical and chemical changes of matter?

By the end of this lesson, you should be able to distinguish between physical and chemical changes of matter.

Sunshine State Standards

SC.8.N.1.6 Understand that scientific investigations involve the collection of relevant empirical evidence, the use of logical reasoning, and the application of imagination in devising hypotheses, predictions, explanations and models to make sense of the collected evidence.

SC.8.P.9.1 Explore the Law of Conservation of Mass by demonstrating and concluding that mass is conserved when substances undergo physical and chemical changes.

SC.8.P.9.2 Differentiate between physical changes and chemical changes.

SC.8.P.9.3 Investigate and describe how temperature influences chemical changes.

LA.6.4.2.2 The student will record information (e.g., observations, notes, lists, charts, legends) related to a topic, including visual aids to organize and record information and include a list of sources used.

Rusty beams are all that remain of these large boats. The rust is the result of an interaction of the iron beams with water and air.

Engage Your Brain

1 Predict Check T or F to show whether you think each statement is true or false.

T   F

☐ ☐ When an ice cube melts, it is still water.

☐ ☐ Matter is lost when a candle is burned.

☐ ☐ When your body digests food, the food is changed into new substances.

2 Describe Write a word or phrase beginning with each letter of the word CHANGE that describes changes you have observed in everyday objects.

C _____

H _____

A _____

N _____

G _____

E _____

Active Reading

3 Apply Use context clues to write your own definitions for the words *interact* and *indicate*.

Example sentence
As the two substances <u>interact</u>, gas bubbles are given off.

interact:

_____

_____

_____

Example sentence
A color change may <u>indicate</u> that a chemical change has taken place.

indicate:

_____

_____

_____

Vocabulary Terms

- physical change
- chemical change
- law of conservation of mass

4 Apply As you learn the definition of each vocabulary term in this lesson, create your own definition or sketch to help you remember the meaning of the term.

Change of Appearance

What are physical changes of matter?

A physical property of matter is any property that can be observed or measured without changing the chemical identity of the substance. A **physical change** is a change that affects one or more physical properties of a substance. Physical changes occur when a substance changes from one form to another. However, the chemical identity of the substance remains the same.

Changes in Observable Properties

The appearance, shape, or size of a substance may be altered during a physical change. For example, the process of turning wool into a sweater requires that the wool undergo physical changes. Wool is sheared from the sheep. The wool is then cleaned, and the wool fibers are separated from one another. Shearing and separating the fibers are physical changes that change the shape, volume, and texture of the wool.

Physical Changes Turn Wool into a Sweater

Ⓐ Wool is sheared from the sheep. The raw wool is then cleaned and placed into a machine that separates the wool fibers from one another.

Ⓑ The wool fibers are spun into yarn. Again, the shape and volume of the wool change. The fibers are twisted so that they are packed more closely together and are intertwined with one another.

Ⓒ The yarn is dyed. The dye changes the color of the wool, but it does not change the wool into another substance. This type of color change is a physical change.

Changes That Do Not Alter the Chemical Identity of the Substance

During the process of turning wool into a sweater, many physical changes occur in the wool. However, the wool does not change into some other substance as a result of these changes. Therefore, physical changes do not change the chemical identity of a substance.

Another example of a physical change happens when you fill an ice cube tray with water and place it inside a freezer. If the water gets cold enough, it will freeze to form ice cubes. Freezing water does not change its chemical makeup. In fact, you could melt the ice cube and have liquid water again! Changes of state, and all physical changes, do not change the chemical makeup of the substance.

6 Identify The list below gives several examples of physical changes. Write your own examples of physical changes on the blank lines.

Examples of Physical Changes
Stretching a rubber band
Dissolving sugar in water
Cutting your hair
Melting butter
Bending a paper clip
Crushing an aluminum can

_____

_____

_____

_____

D Knitting the yarn into a sweater also does not change the wool into another substance. A wool sweater is still wool, even though it no longer resembles the wool on the sheep.

Visualize It!

7 Analyze How does the yarn in the sweater differ from the wool on the sheep?

_____

_____

_____

What are chemical changes of matter?

Think about what happens to the burning logs in a campfire. They start out dry, rough, and dense. After flames surround them, the logs emerge as black and powdery ashes. The campfire releases a lot of heat and smoke in the process. Something has obviously happened, something more than simply a change of appearance. The wood has stopped being wood. It has undergone a chemical change.

Changes in Substance Identity

A **chemical change** occurs when one or more substances change into entirely new substances with different properties. For example, in the campfire, the dry, dense wood became the powdery ashes—new substances with different properties. When a cake is baked, the liquid cake batter becomes the solid, spongy treat. Whenever a new substance is formed, a chemical change has occurred.

Be aware that chemical *changes* are not exactly the same as chemical *properties*. Burning is a chemical change; flammability is a chemical property. The chemical properties of a substance describe which chemical changes can or cannot happen to that substance. Chemical changes are the *processes* by which substances actually change into new substances. You can learn about a substance's chemical properties by watching the chemical changes that substance undergoes.

Visualize It!

8 Identify Use the boxes provided to identify the wood, ashes, and flames involved in the chemical change. Then write a caption describing the chemical changes you see in the photo.

_____

_____

_____

_____

the inside

Changes to the Chemical Makeup of a Substance

In a chemical change, a substance's identity changes because its chemical makeup changes. This happens as the particles and chemical bonds that make up the substance get rearranged. For example, when iron rusts, molecules of oxygen from the air combine with iron atoms to form a new compound. Rust is not iron or oxygen. It is a new substance made up of oxygen and iron joined together.

Because chemical changes involve changes in the arrangements of particles, they are often influenced by temperature. At higher temperatures, the particles in a substance have more average kinetic energy. They move around a lot more freely and so rearrange more easily. Therefore, at higher temperatures, chemical reactions often happen more quickly. Think of baking a cake. The higher the temperature of the oven, the less time the cake will need to bake because the faster the chemical reactions occur.

Active Reading **9 Explain** How do higher temperatures influence a chemical change?

_____

_____

_____

Think Outside the Book (Inquiry)

10 Infer Think of ways you control temperature to influence chemical changes during a typical day. (Hint: Cooking, Art class)

Look for the signs

How can you tell a chemical change has happened?

Physical changes and chemical changes are different. Chemical changes result in new substances, while physical changes do not. However, it may not be obvious that any new substances have formed during a chemical change. Here are some signs that a chemical change may have occurred. If you observe two or more of these signs during a change, you likely are observing a chemical change.

Active Reading **11 Compare** How are physical and chemical changes different?

_____

_____

_____

_____

Production of an Odor

Some chemical changes produce odors. The chemical change that occurs when an egg is rotting, for example, produces the smell of sulfur. Milk that has soured also has an unpleasant smell—because bacteria have formed new substances in the milk. And if you've gone outdoors after a thunderstorm, you've probably noticed a distinct smell. This odor is an indication that lightning has caused a chemical change in the air.

Production of a Gas

Chemical changes often cause fizzing or foaming. For example, a chemical change is involved when an antacid tablet is dropped into a glass of water. As the tablet makes contact with the water and begins to react with it, bubbles of gas appear. One of the new substances that is formed is carbon dioxide gas, which forms the bubbles that you see.

It is important to note that some physical changes, such as boiling, can also produce gas bubbles. Therefore, the only way to know for sure whether a chemical change has taken place is to identify new substances.

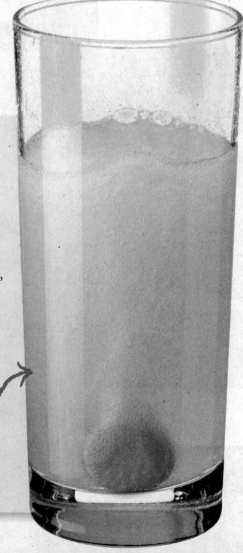

Bubbles form when an antacid tablet reacts with water. The bubbles contain a new, gaseous substance, which signals that a chemical change has happened.

Formation of a Precipitate

Chemical changes may result in products in different physical states. Liquids sometimes combine to form a solid called a *precipitate*. For example, colorless potassium iodide and lead nitrate combine to form the bright yellow precipitate lead iodide, as shown below.

Bright yellow lead iodide precipitates from the clear solution.

Change in Color

A change in color is often an indication of a chemical change. For example, when gray iron rusts, the product that forms is brown.

Change in Energy

Chemical changes can cause energy to change from one form into another. For example, in a burning candle, the chemical energy stored in the candle converts to heat and light energy.

A change in temperature is often a sign of a chemical change. The change need not always be as dramatic as the one in the photo, however.

The reaction of powdered aluminum with a metal oxide releases so much heat that it is often used to weld metals together. Here it is being used to test the heat-resistant properties of steel.

12 Infer List the observations you might make as you witness each of the changes below. Then classify each change as a physical change or a chemical change.

Change	Signs/observations	Type of change
Boiling water		
Baking a cake		
Burning wood		
Painting a door		

Conservation is the Law

What is the law of conservation of mass?

If you freeze 5 mL of water and then let the ice melt, you have 5 mL of water again. You can freeze and melt the water as much as you like. The mass of water will not change.

This does not always seem true for chemical changes. The ashes remaining after a fire contain much less mass than the logs that produced them. Mass seems to vanish. In other chemical changes, such as those that cause the growth of plants, mass seems to appear out of nowhere. This puzzled scientists for years. Where did the mass go? Where did it come from?

In the 1770s, the French chemist Antoine Lavoisier (an•TWAHN luh•VWAH•zee•ay) studied chemical changes in which substances seemed to lose or gain mass. He showed that the mass was most often lost to or gained from gases in the air. Lavoisier demonstrated this transformation of mass by observing chemical changes in sealed glass bulbs. This was the first demonstration of the *law of conservation of mass*. The **law of conservation of mass** states that in ordinary chemical and physical changes, mass is not created or destroyed but is only transformed into different substances.

The examples at the right will help you understand how the law works in both physical and chemical changes. In the top example, the second robot may have a different shape than the first, but it clearly has the same parts. In the second example, vinegar and baking soda undergo a chemical change. Mix the baking soda with the vinegar in the flask, and mass seems to vanish. Yet the balloon shows that what really happens is the production of a gas—carbon dioxide gas.

Active Reading **13 Identify** What is the law of conservation of mass?

_____

_____

_____

The water may freeze or the ice may melt, but the amount of matter in this glass will stay the same.

Conservation of Mass in Physical Changes

When the long gray piece is moved from its arms to its waist, the toy robot gets a new look. It's still a toy robot—its parts are just rearranged. Most physical changes are reversible. All physical changes follow the law of conservation of mass.

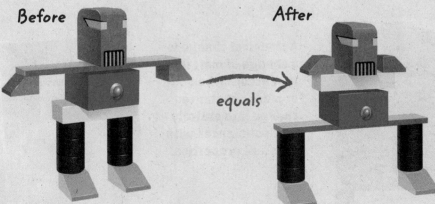

Before   equals   After

Visualize It!

14 Describe How is the physical change in the robot reversible, and how can you tell that the change follows the law of conservation of mass?

_____

_____

_____

_____

_____

Conservation of Mass in Chemical Changes

When vinegar and baking soda are combined, they undergo a chemical change. The balloon at the right is inflated with carbon dioxide gas that was produced as a result of the change. The mass of the starting materials is the same as the mass of the products. Without the balloon to catch it, however, the gas would seem to disappear.

Before

vinegar

baking soda

After

equals

When vinegar and baking soda combine, carbon dioxide gas is produced.

Visualize It!

15 Infer What would you observe about the mass in the flask if you did not put the balloon on top? Why?

_____

_____

111

Visual Summary

To complete this summary, circle the correct word or phrase. Then use the key below to check your answers. You can use this page to review the main concepts of the lesson.

How Matter Changes

A physical change is a change of matter from one form to another without a change in the identity of the substance.

16 Burning / Dying wool is an example of a physical change.

A chemical change is a change of matter that occurs when one or more substances change into entirely new substances with different properties.

17 The formation of a precipitate signals a physical / chemical change.

Chemical changes often cause the production of an odor, fizzing or foaming, the formation of a precipitate, or changes in color or temperature.

18 This physical / chemical change results in the formation of new substances.

The law of conservation of mass states that mass cannot be created or destroyed in ordinary chemical and physical changes.

19 The mass of the toy on the right is the same as / different from the mass of the toy on the left.

Answers: 16 Dying; 17 chemical; 18 chemical; 19 the same as

20 Explain Do changes that cannot be easily reversed, such as burning, observe the law of conservation of mass? Explain.

Lesson Review

Vocabulary

In your own words, define the following terms.

1 physical change

_____

_____

_____

2 chemical change

_____

_____

_____

3 law of conservation of mass

_____

_____

_____

Key Concepts

4 Identify Give an example of a physical change and an example of a chemical change.

_____

_____

_____

_____

5 Compare How is a chemical change different from a physical change?

_____

_____

_____

_____

6 Apply Suppose a log's mass is 5 kg. After burning, the mass of the ash is 1 kg. Explain what may have happened to the other 4 kg.

_____

_____

_____

Critical Thinking

Use this photo to answer the following question.

7 Analyze As the bright sun shines upon the water, the water slowly disappears. The same sunlight gives energy to the surrounding plants to convert water and carbon dioxide into sugar and oxygen gas. Which change is physical and which is chemical?

_____

_____

_____

8 Compare Relate the statement "You can't get something for nothing" to the law of the conservation of mass.

_____

_____

_____

_____

_____

9 Infer Sharpening a pencil leaves behind pencil shavings. Is sharpening a pencil a physical change or a chemical change? Explain.

_____

_____

_____

_____

States of Matter

ESSENTIAL QUESTION

How do particles in solids, liquids, and gases move?

By the end of this lesson, you should be able to model the motion of particles in solids, liquids, and gases.

Sunshine State Standards

SC.8.N.1.1 Define a problem from the eighth grade curriculum using appropriate reference materials to support scientific understanding, plan and carry out scientific investigations of various types, such as systematic observations or experiments, identify variables, collect and organize data, interpret data in charts, tables, and graphics, analyze information, make predictions, and defend conclusions.

SC.8.N.3.1 Select models useful in relating the results of their own investigations.

SC.8.P.8.1 Explore the scientific theory of atoms (also known as atomic theory) by using models to explain the motion of particles in solids, liquids, and gases.

LA.6.4.2.2 The student will record information (e.g., observations, notes, lists, charts, legends) related to a topic, including visual aids to organize and record information and include a list of sources used.

At these hot springs in Japan, you can find water in the form of a solid, a liquid, and a gas.

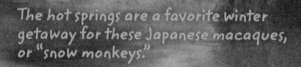

The hot springs are a favorite winter getaway for these Japanese macaques, or "snow monkeys."

Engage Your Brain

1 Predict Check T or F to show whether you think each statement is true or false.

T   F

☐   ☐   Atoms combine in different ways to make up all the substances you encounter every day.

☐   ☐   Saltwater can be separated into salt and water.

☐   ☐   A mixture of soil has the same chemical composition throughout.

2 Apply Think of a substance that does not dissolve in water. Draw a sketch below that shows what happens when this substance is added to water.

 Active Reading

3 Synthesize Many English words have their roots in other languages. Use the Greek words below to make an educated guess about the meanings of the words *homogeneous* and *heterogeneous*.

Greek word	Meaning
genus	type
homos	same
heteros	different

Example sentence
Saltwater is <u>homogeneous</u> throughout.

homogeneous:

_____

_____

Example sentence
A <u>heterogeneous</u> mixture of rocks varies from handful to handful.

heterogeneous:

_____

_____

Vocabulary Terms

- atom
- element
- compound
- mixture
- pure substance
- heterogeneous
- homogeneous

4 Identify This list contains the key terms you'll learn in this lesson. As you read, circle the defnition of each term.

A Great Combination

How can matter be classified?

What kinds of food could you make with the ingredients shown below? You could eat slices of tomato as a snack. Or, you could combine tomato slices with lettuce to make a salad. Combine more ingredients, such as bread and cheese, and you have a sandwich. Just as these meals are made up of simpler foods, matter is made up of basic "ingredients" known as *atoms*. **Atoms** are the smallest unit of an element that maintains the properties of that element. Atoms, like the foods shown here, can be combined in different ways to produce different substances.

The substances you encounter every day can be classified into one of the three major classes of matter: *elements, compounds,* and *mixtures*. Atoms are the basic building blocks for all three types of matter. Elements, compounds, and mixtures differ in the way that atoms are combined.

Active Reading **5 Compare** What do elements, compounds, and mixtures have in common?

_____

_____

Think Outside the Book **Inquiry**

6 Predict If you have ever baked a cake or bread, you know that the ingredients that combine to make it taste different from the baked food. Why do you think that is?

Just as these ingredients combine to make a tasty sandwich, atoms are the basic "ingredients" that make up matter.

© Houghton Mifflin Harcourt Publishing Company

Matter Can Be Classified into Elements, Compounds, and Mixtures

You can think of atoms as the building blocks of matter. Like these toy blocks, atoms can be connected in different ways. The models below show how atoms make up elements and compounds. Elements and compounds, in turn, make up mixtures.

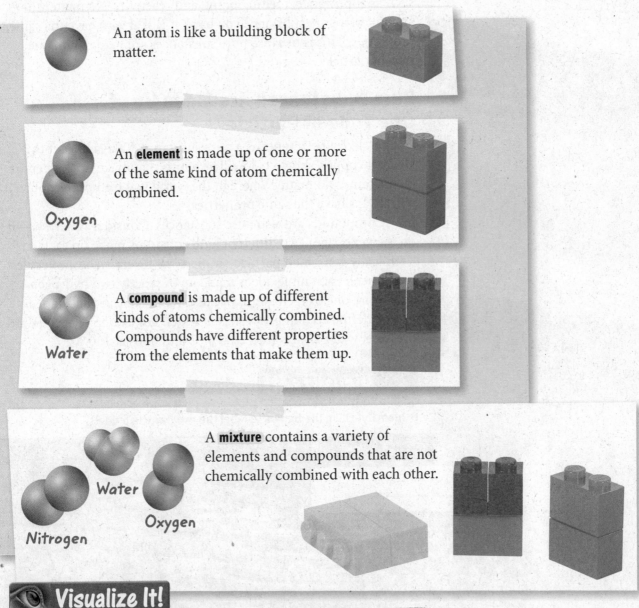

An atom is like a building block of matter.

An **element** is made up of one or more of the same kind of atom chemically combined.

Oxygen

A **compound** is made up of different kinds of atoms chemically combined. Compounds have different properties from the elements that make them up.

Water

A **mixture** contains a variety of elements and compounds that are not chemically combined with each other.

Nitrogen   Water   Oxygen

Visualize It!

7 Analyze Why are the spheres representing nitrogen and oxygen different colors?

_____

_____

_____

_____

Pure Genius

What are pure substances?

Elements and compounds are **pure substances**. A pure substance is a substance that has definite physical and chemical properties such as appearance, melting point, and reactivity. No matter the amount of a pure substance you have, it will always have the same properties. This is because pure substances are made up of one type of particle.

Pure Substances Are Made Up of One Type of Particle

Copper, like all elements, is a pure substance. Take a look at the element copper, shown below. The atoms that make up copper are all the same. No matter where in the world you find pure copper, it will always have the same properties.

Compounds are also pure substances. Consider water, shown on the next page. Two different kinds of atoms make up each chemically combined particle, or *molecule*. Every water molecule is identical. Each molecule is made up of exactly two hydrogen atoms and one oxygen atom. Because water is a pure substance, we can define certain properties of water. For example, at standard pressure, water always freezes at 0 °C and boils at 100 °C.

Visualize It!

8 Identify Fill in the blanks to label the two particle models.

A Copper _____

9 Explain Copper is an element. How do these images of copper illustrate this?

_____

_____

_____

_____

© Houghton Mifflin Harcourt Publishing Company • Image Credits: (bkgd) ©Imagewerks//Getty Images; (b) ©Allan Shoemake/Photographer's Choice/Getty Images

Pure Substances Cannot Be Formed or Broken Down by Physical Changes

Physical changes such as melting, freezing, cutting, or smashing do not change the identity of pure substances. For example, if you cut copper pipe into short pieces, the material is still copper. And if you freeze liquid water, the particles that make up the ice remain the same: two hydrogen atoms combined with one oxygen atom.

The chemical bonds that hold atoms together cannot be broken easily. To break or form chemical bonds, a chemical change is required. For example, when an electric current is passed through water, a chemical change takes place. The atoms that make up the compound break apart into two elements: hydrogen and oxygen. When a pure substance undergoes a chemical change, it is no longer that same substance. A chemical change changes the identity of the substance. Individual atoms cannot be broken down into smaller parts by normal physical or chemical changes.

Active Reading **11 Identify** What happens when a pure substance undergoes a chemical change?

_____

_____

_____

_____

B Water _____

10 Explain Water is a compound. How do these images of water illustrate this?

_____

_____

_____

Classified Information

How can elements be classified?

📖 Active Reading

12 Identify As you read, underline the ways in which elements are organized on the periodic table.

Differences in physical and chemical properties allow us to classify elements. By knowing the category to which an element belongs, you can predict some of its properties. Elements are broadly classified as metals, nonmetals, or metalloids. Most metals are shiny, conduct heat and electricity well, and can be shaped into thin sheets and wires. Nonmetals are not shiny and do not conduct heat or electricity well. Metalloids have some properties of both metals and nonmetals.

There are over 100 elements known to exist. Each element has a place in an arrangement called the periodic table of the elements. The periodic table is a useful tool that can help you to identify elements that have similar properties. Metals, nonmetals, and metalloids occupy different regions in the periodic table. Metals start at the left and make up most of the elements in the periodic table. Nonmetals are at the right and are often shaded with a color different from that of the metals. Not surprisingly, the metalloids lie between the metals and nonmetals. In many instances, you can even predict which elements combine with others to form compounds based on their positions in the periodic table.

Aluminum, like many metals, can be formed into a thin foil.

Charcoal, made mostly of carbon atoms, is brittle and dull like many other nonmetals.

How can compounds be classified?

You are surrounded by compounds. Compounds make up the food you eat, the school supplies you use, and the clothes you wear— even you! There are so many compounds that it would be very difficult to list or describe them all. Fortunately, these compounds can be grouped into a few basic categories by their properties.

13 Classify Read about some of the ways in which compounds can be classified. Then fill in the blanks to complete the photo captions.

By Their pH

Compounds can be classified as acidic, basic, or neutral by measuring a special value known as *pH*. Acids have a pH value below 7. Vinegar contains acetic acid, which gives a sharp, sour taste to salad dressings. Bases, on the other hand, have pH values greater than 7. Baking soda is an example of a basic compound. Bases have a slippery feel and a bitter taste. Neutral compounds, such as pure water and table salt, have a pH value of 7. Water and salt are formed when an acid and a base react. A type of paper called litmus paper can be used to test whether a compound is an acid or a base. Blue litmus paper turns red in the presence of an acid. Red litmus paper turns blue in the presence of a base. Although some foods are acidic or basic, you should NEVER taste, smell, or touch a chemical to classify them. Many acids and bases can damage your body or clothing.

Baking soda is an example of a(n) _____

As Organic or Inorganic

You may have heard of organically-grown foods. But in chemistry, the word *organic* refers to compounds that contain carbon and hydrogen. Organic compounds are found in most foods. They can also be found in synthetic goods. For example, gasoline contains a number of organic compounds, such as octane and heptane.

The compounds that make up plastic are _____ because they contain carbon.

By Their Role in the Body

Organic compounds that are made by living things are called biochemicals. Biochemicals are divided into four categories: carbohydrates, lipids, proteins, and nucleic acids. *Carbohydrates* are used as a source of energy and include sugars, starches, and fiber. *Lipids* are biochemicals that store excess energy in the body and make up cell membranes. Lipids include fats, oils, and waxes. *Proteins* are one of the most abundant types of compounds in your body. They regulate chemical activities of the body and build and repair body structures. *Nucleic acids* such as DNA and RNA contain genetic information and help the body build proteins.

Your body gets _____ such as sugars, starches, and fiber, from many of the foods you eat.

Mix and Match

What are mixtures?

Imagine that you roll out some dough, add tomato sauce, and sprinkle some cheese on top. Then you add green peppers, mushrooms, and pepperoni. What have you just made? A pizza, of course! But that's not all. You have also created a mixture.

A mixture is a combination of two or more substances that are combined physically but not chemically. When two or more materials are put together, they form a mixture if they do not change chemically to form a new substance. For example, cheese and tomato sauce do not react when they are combined to make a pizza. They keep their original identities and properties. So, a pizza is a mixture.

Mixtures Are Made Up of More Than One Type of Particle

Unlike elements and compounds, mixtures are not pure substances. Mixtures contain more than one type of substance. Each substance in a mixture has the same chemical makeup it had before the mixture formed.

Unlike pure substances, mixtures do not have definite properties. Granite from different parts of the world could contain different minerals in different ratios. Pizzas made by different people could have different toppings. Mixtures do not have defined properties because they do not have a defined chemical makeup.

👁 Visualize It!

14 Describe This student is going to make and separate a mixture of sand and salt. Complete these captions to describe what is taking place in each photo.

A Sand and salt are poured into a single beaker. The result is a mixture because

_____

_____

_____

_____

Mixtures Can Be Separated by Physical Changes

You don't like mushrooms on your pizza? Just pick them off. This change is a physical change of the mixture because the identities of the substances do not change. But not all mixtures are as easy to separate as a pizza. You cannot just pick salt out of a salt water mixture. One way to separate the salt from the water is to heat the mixture until the water evaporates. The salt is left behind. Other ways to separate mixtures are shown at the right and below.

A magnet can separate a mixture of aluminum nails and iron nails.

Active Reading **15 Devise** How could you separate a mixture of rocks and sand?

_____

_____

_____

A machine called a centrifuge separates mixtures by the densities of the components. It can be used to separate the different parts of blood.

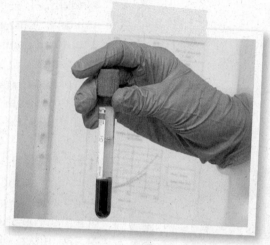

B When water is added to the sand-salt mixture,

_____

_____

_____

_____

C When the liquid is poured through a filter,

_____

_____

_____

_____

D The remaining salt water is heated until

_____

_____

_____

_____

A Simple Solution

A snow globe contains a suspension.

Active Reading

16 Identify As you read, underline the everyday examples of mixtures on this page.

How can mixtures be classified?

It is clear that something is a mixture when you can see the different substances in it. For example, if you scoop up a handful of soil, it might contain dirt, rocks, leaves, and even insects. Exactly what you see depends on what part of the soil is scooped. Such a mixture is called a heterogeneous (het•uhr•uh•JEE•nee•uhs) mixture. A **heterogeneous** mixture is one that does not have a uniform composition. In other types of mixtures, the substances are evenly spread throughout. If you add sugar to a cup of water, the sugar dissolves. Each part of the sugar-water mixture has the same sweet taste. This is called a **homogeneous** (hoh•muh•JEE•nee•uhs) mixture.

As Suspensions

The snow globe (above) contains a type of heterogeneous mixture called a *suspension*. Suspensions are mixtures in which the particles of a material are spread throughout a liquid or gas but are too large to stay mixed without being stirred or shaken. If a suspension is allowed to sit, the particles will settle out.

As Solutions

Tea is an example of a type of homogeneous mixture known as a *solution*. In a solution, one substance is dissolved in another substance. When you make tea, some of the compounds inside the tea leaves dissolve in the hot water. These compounds give your tea its unique color and taste. Many familiar solutions are liquids. However, solutions may also be gases or solids. Air is an example of a gaseous solution. Alloys, such as brass and steel, are solid solutions in which substances are dissolved in metals.

Tea is a solution.

As Colloids

Colloids are a third type of mixture that falls somewhere between suspensions and solutions. As in a suspension, the particles in a colloid are spread throughout a liquid or gas. Unlike the particles in a suspension, colloid particles are small and do not settle out quickly. Milk and gelatin are colloids. Colloids look homogeneous, but we consider them to be heterogeneous.

Gelatin is a colloid.

17 Summarize Complete the graphic organizer below by filling in
the blanks with terms from this lesson. Then add definitions or
sketches of each term inside the appropriate box.

Classifying Matter

Matter
Definition:

Matter is anything that has mass and
takes up space. Matter is made up of
building blocks called atoms.

Pure Substances
Definition:

_____
_____
_____
_____

Sketch:

Elements
Sketch:

Definition:
_____
_____
_____
_____
_____

Sketch:

Homogeneous
Definition:
_____
_____
_____
_____
_____

Suspensions
Sketch:

Colloids
Definition:
_____
_____
_____
_____
_____

Definition:
_____
_____
_____
_____
_____

Visual Summary

To complete this summary, circle the correct word or phrase. Then use the key below to check your answers. You can use this page to review the main concepts of the lesson.

Pure substances are made up of a single type of particle and cannot be formed or broken down by physical changes.

Water molecules

18 Water is a pure substance / mixture.

19 Water is a(n) element / compound.

Pure Substances and Mixtures

Mixtures are made up of more than one type of particle and can be separated into their component parts by physical changes.

20 Saltwater and sand can be separated with a magnet / filter.

21 Saltwater is a homogeneous / heterogeneous mixture.

Answers: 18 pure substance; 19 compound; 20 filter; 21 homogeneous

22 **Predict** Why do you think that the particles of a suspension settle out but the particles of a colloid do not?

Lesson Review

Vocabulary

Fill in the blanks with the term that best completes the following sentences.

1 The basic building blocks of matter are called

_____

2 A(n) _____ is a substance that is made up of a single kind of atom.

3 Elements and compounds are two types of

_____

4 A(n) _____ is a combination of substances that are combined physically but not chemically.

Key Concepts

5 Identify What kind of mixture is a solution? A suspension? A colloid?

_____

_____

_____

6 Apply Fish give off the compound ammonia, which has a pH above 7. To which class of compounds does ammonia belong?

_____

7 Compare Fill in the following table with properties of elements and compounds.

How are elements and compounds similar?	How are elements and compounds different?

Use this drawing to answer the following question.

8 Identify What type of mixture is this salad dressing?

_____

Critical Thinking

9 Explain Could a mixture be made up of only elements and no compounds? Explain.

_____

_____

_____

_____

_____

10 Synthesize Describe a procedure to separate a mixture of sugar, black pepper, and pebbles.

_____

_____

_____

_____

_____

_____

_____

_____

_____

_____

The Atom

ESSENTIAL QUESTION

What makes up an atom?

By the end of this lesson, you should be able to describe the atomic theory by identifying atoms and the parts that make them up.

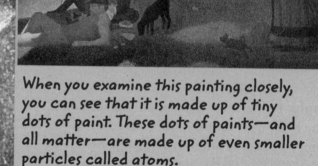

When you examine this painting closely, you can see that it is made up of tiny dots of paint. These dots of paints—and all matter—are made up of even smaller particles called atoms.

🌀 **Sunshine State Standards**

SC.8.P.8.7 Explore the scientific theory of atoms (also known as atomic theory) by recognizing that atoms are the smallest unit of an element and are composed of sub-atomic particles (electrons surrounding a nucleus containing protons and neutrons).

LA.6.2.2.3 The student will organize information to show understanding (e.g., representing main ideas within text through charting, mapping, paraphrasing, summarizing, or comparing/contrasting).

Engage Your Brain

1 Predict Check T or F to show whether you think each statement is true or false.

T F

☐ ☐ Atoms can be seen with an ordinary light microscope.

☐ ☐ Atoms have mass.

☐ ☐ Different substances are made up of different types of atoms.

2 Predict Imagine that you could shrink down to the size of an atom. Draw what you think an atom would look like if you could see it.

Active Reading

3 Synthesize Many English words have their roots in other languages. Use the Greek word below to make an educated guess about the meaning of the word *atom*.

Greek word	Meaning
atomos	unable to be divided

Example sentence
A single grain of salt contains billions of <u>atoms</u>.

atom: _____

_____

_____

Vocabulary Terms

- atom
- proton
- neutron
- nucleus
- electron
- electron cloud
- atomic number
- mass number

4 Apply As you learn the definition of each vocabulary term in this lesson, create your own definition or sketch to help you remember the meaning of the term.

As a Matter of Fact...

What is matter made of?

Imagine that you cut a piece of paper in half. Then, you cut each half in half again. Could you keep cutting the pieces in half forever? Around 440 BCE, a Greek philosopher named Democritus (di•MAHK•ri•tuhz) thought that you would eventually end up with a particle that could not be cut. He called this particle *atomos*, a Greek word meaning "not able to be divided." Aristotle (AR•ih•staht•uhl), another Greek philosopher, disagreed with Democritus's ideas. Aristotle did not believe that such a particle could make up the variety of substances found in nature. Instead, he thought that all matter was infinitely divisible. To him and many others, the idea of atoms did not make much sense. How could something exist that you couldn't see?

Within the past 200 years, scientists have come to agree that matter is made up of small particles. We use Democritus's term, *atom*, to describe these particles. The illustrations below show how ideas about the atom have changed over time.

Active Reading **5 Describe** Who was Democritus?

_____

_____

_____

Development of the Atomic Theory

Observe how models of the atom have changed over time.

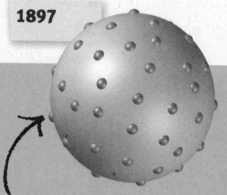

1803

John Dalton proposed that all substances are made of small particles, called atoms, that cannot be divided.

1897

J. J. Thomson performed experiments that detected smaller particles within the atom. He believed that these particles were mixed throughout the atom.

What are atoms?

An **atom** is the smallest particle into which an element can be divided and still be the same substance. In 1808, a British chemist named John Dalton published an atomic theory. Dalton's theory stated that all atoms of a particular element are identical, but are different from atoms of all other elements. Every atom of silver, for example, is the same as every other atom of silver, but different from an atom of iron. Dalton's atomic theory also assumed that atoms could not be divided into anything simpler. Scientists later discovered that this was not exactly true. They found that atoms are made of even smaller particles, called subatomic particles. As new information was discovered about atoms, scientists revised Dalton's atomic theory.

Like the tiny grains of sand that form huge beaches, tiny atoms combine to form all of the matter around us. Atoms are so small that they cannot be seen with an ordinary microscope. Only powerful instruments can produce images of atoms. How small are atoms? Think about a penny. A penny contains about 2×10^{22}, or 20,000,000,000,000,000,000,000 atoms of copper and zinc. That's over 3,000 billion times more atoms than there are people on Earth!

A big, sandy beach is made up of very small grains of sand.

These grains of sand are made up of billions of atoms.

1932

In the early 1900s, experiments by scientists such as Ernest Rutherford and James Chadwick revealed the nature of the dense center of the atom.

Today

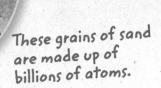

Visualize It! Inquiry

6 Analyze Today's model of the atom looks different from the models that came before it. Why do you think ideas about the structure of the atom have changed over time?

_____

_____

_____

_____

Up and Atom!

What are the parts of an atom?

As tiny as an atom is, it is made up of even smaller particles. These particles are *protons, neutrons,* and *electrons.* This model of an atom shows where these particles are found within the atom. The particles in this model are not shown in their correct proportions. If they were, the protons and neutrons would be too small to see.

Active Reading

7 Identify As you read, underline the sentences that define the three types of particles found within an atom.

The Nucleus: Protons and Neutrons

Positively-charged particles within the atom are called **protons**. The mass of a proton is about 1.7×10^{-24} g. This number can also be written as 0.0000000000000000000000017 g. Because the masses of particles in the atom are so small, scientists made a new unit for them: the unified atomic mass unit (u). Each proton has a mass of about 1 u. The relative charge of a single proton is often denoted as 1+.

Neutrons are particles having no electric charge and about the same mass as a proton, 1 u. Atoms usually have as many or more neutrons as they do protons.

Together, protons and neutrons form the **nucleus** of the atom, located at the atom's center. As you can see in this model of a beryllium atom, this nucleus contains four protons and five neutrons. Because each proton has a 1+ charge, the overall charge of this nucleus is 4+. (Remember, neutrons have no electrical charge.) The volume of the nucleus is very small compared to the rest of the atom. But protons and neutrons are the most massive particles in an atom, so the nucleus is very dense. If it were possible to have a nucleus the volume of a grape, that nucleus would have a mass greater than 9 million metric tons!

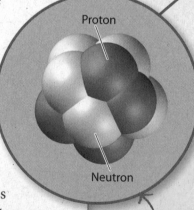

Proton

Neutron

Nucleus

The Electron Cloud

The negatively-charged particles in the atom are called **electrons**. Electrons move around the nucleus very quickly. Scientists have found that it is not possible to determine their exact positions with certainty. This is why we picture the electrons as being in an **electron cloud** around the nucleus.

Compared with protons and neutrons, electrons are very small in mass. It takes more than 1,800 electrons to equal the mass of 1 proton. The mass of an electron is so small that it is usually thought of as almost 0 u.

The charge of a single electron is represented as 1–. The charges of protons and electrons are opposite but equal. The number of protons in an atom equals the number of electrons. So the atom has a net, or overall, charge of 0. For example, this beryllium atom contains four electrons. The combined charge of the electrons is 4–. But, remember that the charge of the nucleus is 4+.

$$(4+) + (4-) = 0$$

The net charge of the atom is 0.

An atom can lose or gain electrons. When this happens, we refer to the atom as an *ion*. Ions do not have a net charge of 0.

8 Summarize Complete the following table with information about the parts of the atom.

Part of the atom	Location in the atom	Electrical charge	Relative mass
Proton			Slightly less massive than a neutron
	Nucleus		
		1–	

Take a Number!

How can we describe atoms?

Think of all the substances you see and touch every day. Are all of these substances the same? No. The substances that make up this book are quite different from the substances in the air you're breathing. If all atoms are composed of the same particles, how can there be so many different types of substances? Different combinations of protons, neutrons, and electrons produce atoms with different properties. The number of each kind of particle within an atom determines its unique properties. In turn, these different atoms combine to form the different substances all around us.

By Atomic Number

The number of protons distinguishes the atoms of one element from the atoms of another. For example, every hydrogen atom contains one proton. And every carbon atom has exactly six protons in its nucleus.

The number of protons in the nucleus of an atom is the **atomic number** of that atom. Hydrogen has an atomic number of 1 because its atoms contain just one proton. Carbon has an atomic number of 6.

Active Reading **9 Compare** How are two atoms of the same element alike?

_____

_____

_____

_____

By Mass Number

While the atoms of a certain element always have the same number of protons, they may not always have the same number of neutrons. For example, all chlorine atoms have 17 protons. But some chlorine atoms have 18 neutrons, while other chlorine atoms have 20 neutrons. These two types of chlorine atoms are called isotopes. *Isotopes* are atoms of the same element that have a different number of neutrons. Some elements have many isotopes, while other elements have just a few.

The total number of protons and neutrons in an atom's nucleus is its **mass number.** Different isotopes of chlorine have different mass numbers. What is the mass number of a chlorine atom that contains 18 neutrons?

$$17 + 18 = 35$$

The mass number of this atom is 35.

---

11 Calculate Use this model of a helium atom to find its atomic number and mass number.

Helium

Atomic number:

Mass number:

The helium in these balloons is less massive than the nitrogen in the air so the balloons float.

Think Outside the Book Inquiry

10 Apply Conduct research about how scientists can use certain isotopes in fields such as medicine or Earth science. Choose one useful isotope and create a brochure that describes its properties and uses.

Visual Summary

To complete this summary, check the box that indicates true or false. Then use the key below to check your answers. You can use this page to review the main concepts of the lesson.

Atomic theory states that matter is made up of very small particles known as atoms.

	T	F	
12	☐	☐	Each grain of sand on this beach is made up of many atoms.
13	☐	☐	Atoms can be seen with a hand lens.

The Atom

Atoms contain a positively-charged nucleus surrounded by a negatively-charged electron cloud.

	T	F	
14	☐	☐	The nucleus of an atom contains protons and electrons.

Model of a helium atom

Atoms can be characterized by their atomic number and their mass number.

	T	F	
15	☐	☐	The atomic number of helium is 2.
16	☐	☐	The mass number of this helium atom is 2.

Answers: 12 T; 13 F; 14 F; 15 T; 16 F

17 **Explain** Is there any particle of matter that is smaller than an atom? Explain.

Lesson Review

Vocabulary

Circle the term that best completes the following sentences.

1 An *atom / electron* is the smallest particle of an element that has the properties of that element.

2 Electrons are found in the *electron cloud / nucleus* of the atom.

3 *Neutrons / Protons* have a positive charge.

4 The number of protons in an atom is the same as its *atomic number / mass number.*

Key Concepts

Complete the table below with the properties of a neutral sodium atom.

Properties of a Sodium Atom	
Number of protons	11
Number of neutrons	12
5 Apply Number of electrons	
6 Apply Atomic number	
7 Apply Mass number	
8 Apply Net charge	

9 Compare Compare the charges and masses of protons, neutrons, and electrons.

_____

_____

_____

_____

_____

_____

Use this image to answer the following questions.

10 Analyze How many protons are in the nucleus of this atom?

_____

11 Analyze What is the mass number of this atom?

_____

Critical Thinking

12 Apply You can see the cells that make up your body with a light microscope. Do cells contain atoms? Explain.

_____

_____

_____

_____

_____

13 Explain If atoms are made up of smaller parts such as electrons, why are atoms considered the smallest particles of an element?

_____

_____

_____

_____

_____

_____

Mixtures in Florida

The Vinegaroon

Despite its name, the whipscorpion is not a scorpion at all. It is an arachnid, like scorpions and spiders, but it doesn't have the scorpion's poisonous stinger. Instead, it defends itself by spraying a mixture of acids. If you ever get a giant whipscorpion angry, you'll know why it's called a "vinegaroon." The mixture that it sprays is mostly acetic acid—the same acid used to make ordinary white vinegar. But the vinegar-smelling spray is about 17 times more concentrated. It also contains a small amount of caprylic acid, which boosts the power of the acid spray. This acid is used in some disinfectants and sanitizers. The acids are effective against hard exoskeletons. Although the acids can also cause mild burns to your skin and eyes, the amount of acid used is small. You might even see stores selling vinegaroons as pets.

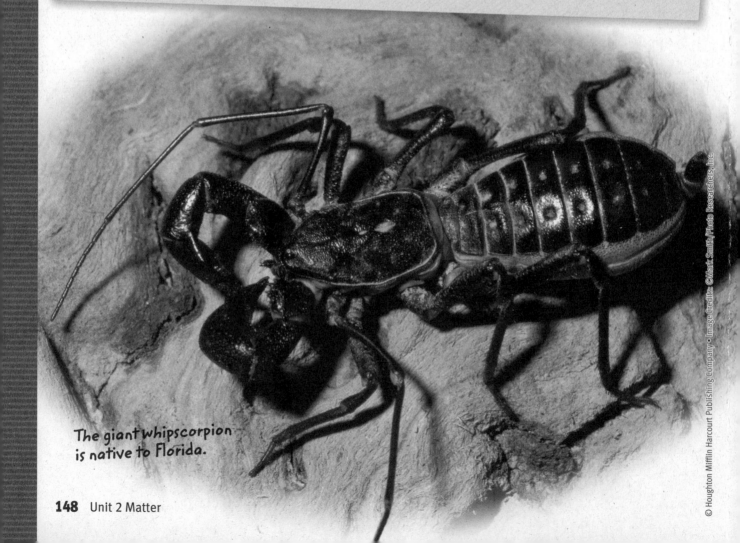

The giant whipscorpion is native to Florida.

Tabby buildings on the Kingsley Plantation

Tabby: Oyster Shell Concrete

When early settlers came to what is now the United States, they built with the materials they found. In Florida, that included shells. Tabby is a mixture of lime, water, sand, ash, and shells, which are abundant along the coastline. It is commonly called America's first concrete, and was first used by the Spanish in St. Augustine in the late 1500s. The British later carried the idea up the coast to North Carolina and Georgia. Tabby isn't as durable as modern concrete and fell out of use in the 19th century. But many tabby buildings and ruins can still be found, including those at the historic Kingsley Plantation near Jacksonville.

Florida's Sands

Florida is famous around the world for its beaches. The state has 1,900 kilometers of coastline, much of which is beautiful, sandy beach. But the sand differs from beach to beach because sand is a mixture. The material that makes up the sand depends on what washes up on shore and what gets eroded from the shoreline.

Beach sand is made up mostly of quartz, calcite, and other minerals eroded from rocks. In northwest Florida, for example, the beaches are dazzlingly white because the sand is mostly quartz. Further south, beaches are more brown because their sand contains more shell fragments. Around Daytona Beach, the sand can even be orange because of iron oxide absorbed by the shell fragments. But sand doesn't just make pretty beaches. It also contains minerals that can be important natural resources. Florida's beach sand is an important source of hafnium, which is used in nuclear control rods and in alloys that have high melting points. In northeastern Florida, the sands have a lot of titanium, which is used in making paint. In southeastern Florida, the sands are an important source of phosphate, which is used in fertilizer.

St. Joseph Peninsula State Park in Port St. Joe, Florida

The Periodic Table

ESSENTIAL QUESTION

How are elements arranged on the periodic table?

By the end of this lesson, you should be able to describe the relationship between the arrangement of elements on the periodic table and the properties of those elements.

In this market, similar foods are arranged in groups. Can you identify some of the properties each group shares?

 Sunshine State Standards

SC.8.N.1.5 Analyze the methods used to develop a scientific explanation as seen in different fields of science.

SC.8.P.8.6 Recognize that elements are grouped in the periodic table according to similarities of their properties.

Engage Your Brain

1 Describe Write a word or phrase beginning with each letter of the word GOLD that describes the properties of these gold coins.

G _____

O _____

L _____

D _____

2 Describe As you will learn in this lesson, elements are arranged by their properties on the periodic table. What other objects are often arranged by their properties?

_____

_____

_____

_____

_____

_____

Active Reading

3 Apply Many scientific words, such as *table*, also have everyday meanings. Use context clues to write your own definition for each meaning of the word *table*.

Example sentence
The books are on the <u>table</u>.

table:

_____

_____

Example sentence
A data <u>table</u> is a useful way to organize information.

table:

_____

_____

Vocabulary Terms

- periodic table
- chemical symbol
- average atomic mass
- metal
- nonmetal
- metalloid
- group
- period

4 Apply As you learn the definition of each vocabulary term in this lesson, create your own definition or sketch to help you remember the meaning of the term.

Get Organized!

What are elements?

People have long sought to find the basic substances of matter. It was once believed that fire, wind, earth, and water, in various combinations, made up all objects. By the 1860s, however, scientists considered there to be at least 60 different basic substances, or elements. They saw that many of these elements shared certain physical and chemical properties and began classifying them. Knowing what you know about the properties of matter, try classifying the elements below.

Bismuth

Sulfur

Chlorine

Visualize It!

5 Identify Observe the appearance of these six elements. Create two or three categories that group the elements by similar properties. Below each element, write the name of the category in which the element belongs.

Mercury

Copper

Bromine

© Houghton Mifflin Harcourt Publishing Company • Image Credits: (tl) ©Russell Lappa/Photo Researchers, Inc.; (tr) ©Charles D. Winters/Photo Researchers, Inc.; (bl) ©Harry Taylor/Dorling Kindersley/Getty Images; (bc) ©Charles D. Winters/Photo Researchers, Inc.

How are the elements organized?

Around this time, a Russian chemist named Dmitri Mendeleev (dih•MEE•tree men•duh•LAY•uhf) began thinking about how he could organize the elements based on their properties. To help him decide how to arrange the elements, Mendeleev made a set of element cards. Each card listed the mass of an atom of each element as well as some of the element's properties. Mendeleev arranged the cards in various ways, looking for a pattern to emerge. When he arranged the element cards in order of increasing atomic mass, the properties of those elements occurred in a *periodic,* or regularly repeating, pattern. For this reason, Mendeleev's arrangement of the elements became known as the **periodic table.** Mendeleev used the periodic pattern in his table to predict elements that had not yet been discovered.

In the early 1900s, British scientist Henry Moseley showed how Mendeleev's periodic table could be rearranged. After determining the numbers of protons in the atoms of the elements, he arranged the elements on the table in order of increasing number of protons, or *atomic number.* Moseley's new arrangement of the elements corrected some of the flaws in Mendeleev's table.

The periodic table is a useful tool to scientists because it makes clear many patterns among the elements' properties. The periodic table is like a map or a calendar of the elements.

Active Reading

6 Explain How did Henry Moseley revise Mendeleev's periodic table?

_____

_____

_____

_____

_____

7 Apply What are you doing this week? Fill in the calendar with activities or plans you have for this week and next. Do any events occur periodically? Explain.

_____

_____

_____

What does the periodic table have in common with a calendar? They both show a periodic pattern. On a calendar, the days of the week repeat in the same order every 7 days.

Sunday	Monday	Tuesday	Wednesday	Thursday	Friday	Saturday

The Periodic Table of Elements

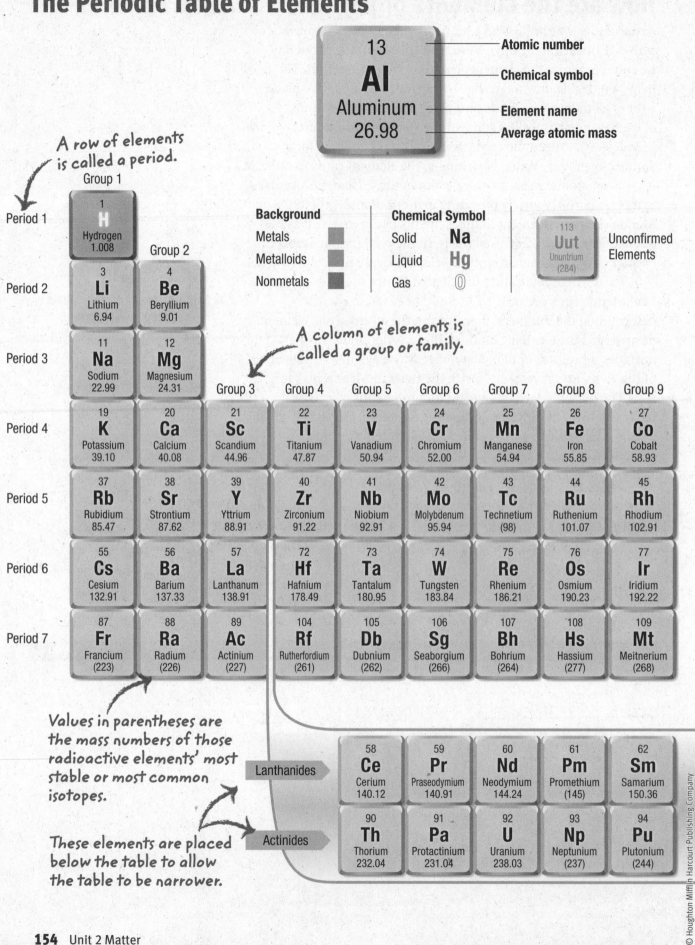

13
Al
Aluminum
26.98

— Atomic number
— Chemical symbol
— Element name
— Average atomic mass

A row of elements is called a period.

Group 1

Period 1 — **1** H Hydrogen 1.008

Group 2

Period 2 — **3** Li Lithium 6.94 | **4** Be Beryllium 9.01

Background
Metals
Metalloids
Nonmetals

Chemical Symbol
Solid **Na**
Liquid **Hg**
Gas ◌

113 Uut Ununtrium (284)
Unconfirmed Elements

A column of elements is called a group or family.

Period 3 — **11** Na Sodium 22.99 | **12** Mg Magnesium 24.31

Group 3	Group 4	Group 5	Group 6	Group 7	Group 8	Group 9

Period 4 — **19** K Potassium 39.10 | **20** Ca Calcium 40.08 | **21** Sc Scandium 44.96 | **22** Ti Titanium 47.87 | **23** V Vanadium 50.94 | **24** Cr Chromium 52.00 | **25** Mn Manganese 54.94 | **26** Fe Iron 55.85 | **27** Co Cobalt 58.93

Period 5 — **37** Rb Rubidium 85.47 | **38** Sr Strontium 87.62 | **39** Y Yttrium 88.91 | **40** Zr Zirconium 91.22 | **41** Nb Niobium 92.91 | **42** Mo Molybdenum 95.94 | **43** Tc Technetium (98) | **44** Ru Ruthenium 101.07 | **45** Rh Rhodium 102.91

Period 6 — **55** Cs Cesium 132.91 | **56** Ba Barium 137.33 | **57** La Lanthanum 138.91 | **72** Hf Hafnium 178.49 | **73** Ta Tantalum 180.95 | **74** W Tungsten 183.84 | **75** Re Rhenium 186.21 | **76** Os Osmium 190.23 | **77** Ir Iridium 192.22

Period 7 — **87** Fr Francium (223) | **88** Ra Radium (226) | **89** Ac Actinium (227) | **104** Rf Rutherfordium (261) | **105** Db Dubnium (262) | **106** Sg Seaborgium (266) | **107** Bh Bohrium (264) | **108** Hs Hassium (277) | **109** Mt Meitnerium (268)

Values in parentheses are the mass numbers of those radioactive elements' most stable or most common isotopes.

These elements are placed below the table to allow the table to be narrower.

Lanthanides — **58** Ce Cerium 140.12 | **59** Pr Praseodymium 140.91 | **60** Nd Neodymium 144.24 | **61** Pm Promethium (145) | **62** Sm Samarium 150.36

Actinides — **90** Th Thorium 232.04 | **91** Pa Protactinium 231.04 | **92** U Uranium 238.03 | **93** Np Neptunium (237) | **94** Pu Plutonium (244)

8 Analyze According to the periodic table, how many elements are a liquid at room temperature?

_____

9 Analyze According to the periodic table, how many elements are metalloids?

_____

Group 18

| 2 |
| **He** |
| Helium |
| 4.003 |

The zigzag line separates metals from nonmetals.

Group 13	Group 14	Group 15	Group 16	Group 17
5 **B** Boron 10.81	6 **C** Carbon 12.01	7 **N** Nitrogen 14.01	8 **O** Oxygen 16.00	9 **F** Fluorine 19.00	10 **Ne** Neon 20.18
13 **Al** Aluminum 26.98	14 **Si** Silicon 28.09	15 **P** Phosphorus 30.97	16 **S** Sulfur 32.07	17 **Cl** Chlorine 35.45	18 **Ar** Argon 39.95

Group 10	Group 11	Group 12					
28 **Ni** Nickel 58.69	29 **Cu** Copper 63.55	30 **Zn** Zinc 65.41	31 **Ga** Gallium 69.72	32 **Ge** Germanium 72.64	33 **As** Arsenic 74.92	34 **Se** Selenium 78.96	35 **Br** Bromine 79.90	36 **Kr** Krypton 83.80
46 **Pd** Palladium 106.42	47 **Ag** Silver 107.87	48 **Cd** Cadmium 112.41	49 **In** Indium 114.82	50 **Sn** Tin 118.71	51 **Sb** Antimony 121.76	52 **Te** Tellurium 127.6	53 **I** Iodine 126.9	54 **Xe** Xenon 131.29
78 **Pt** Platinum 195.08	79 **Au** Gold 196.97	80 **Hg** Mercury 200.59	81 **Tl** Thallium 204.38	82 **Pb** Lead 207.2	83 **Bi** Bismuth 208.98	84 **Po** Polonium (209)	85 **At** Astatine (210)	86 **Rn** Radon (222)
110 **Ds** Darmstadtium (271)	111 **Rg** Roentgenium (272)	112 **Cn** Copernicium (285)	113 **Uut** Ununtrium (284)	114 **Uuq** Ununquadium (289)	115 **Uup** Ununpentium (288)	116 **Uuh** Ununhexium (292)		118 **Uuo** Ununoctium (294)

63 **Eu** Europium 151.96	64 **Gd** Gadolinium 157.25	65 **Tb** Terbium 158.93	66 **Dy** Dysprosium 162.5	67 **Ho** Holmium 164.93	68 **Er** Erbium 167.26	69 **Tm** Thulium 168.93	70 **Yb** Ytterbium 173.04	71 **Lu** Lutetium 174.97
95 **Am** Americium (243)	96 **Cm** Curium (247)	97 **Bk** Berkelium (247)	98 **Cf** Californium (251)	99 **Es** Einsteinium (252)	100 **Fm** Fermium (257)	101 **Md** Mendelevium (258)	102 **No** Nobelium (259)	103 **Lr** Lawrencium (262)

Ma**K**ing Arrangements

What information is contained in each square on the periodic table?

The periodic table is not simply a list of element names. The table contains useful information about each of the elements. The periodic table is usually shown as a grid of squares. Each square contains an element's chemical name, atomic number, chemical symbol, and average atomic mass.

Atomic Number

The number at the top of the square is the atomic number. The atomic number is the number of protons in the nucleus of an atom of that element. All atoms of an element have the same atomic number. For example, every aluminum atom has 13 protons in its nucleus. So the atomic number of aluminum is 13.

Chemical Symbol

The **chemical symbol** is an abbreviation for the element's name. The first letter is always capitalized. Any other letter is always lowercase. For most elements, the chemical symbol is a one- or two-letter symbol. However, some elements have temporary three-letter symbols. These elements will receive a permanent one- or two-letter symbol once it has been reviewed by an international committee of scientists.

```
   13
   Al
 Aluminum
  26.98
```

Chemical Name

The names of the elements come from many sources. Some elements, such as mendelevium, are named after scientists. Others, such as californium, are named after places.

Average Atomic Mass

All atoms of a given element contain the same number of protons. But the number of neutrons in those atoms can vary. So different atoms of an element can have different masses. The **average atomic mass** of an atom is the weighted average of the masses of all the naturally occurring isotopes of that element. A weighted average accounts for the percentages of each isotope. The unit for atomic mass is u.

Active Reading

10 Apply What is the average atomic mass of aluminum?

_____

© Houghton Mifflin Harcourt Publishing Company

How are the elements arranged on the periodic table?

Have you ever noticed how items in a grocery store are arranged? Each aisle contains a different kind of product. Within an aisle, similar products are grouped together on shelves. Because the items are arranged in categories, it is easy to find your favorite brand of cereal. Similarly, the elements are arranged in a certain order on the periodic table. If you understand how the periodic table is organized, you can easily find and compare elements.

Metals, Nonmetals, and Metalloids Are Found in Three Distinct Regions

Elements on the periodic table can be classified into three major categories: metals, nonmetals, and metalloids. The zigzag line on the periodic table can help you identify where these three classes of elements are located. Except for hydrogen, the elements to the left of the zigzag line are metals. **Metals** are elements that are shiny and conduct heat and electricity well. Most metals are solid at room temperature. Many metals are *malleable,* or able to be formed into different shapes. Some metals are *ductile,* meaning that they can be made into wires. The elements to the right of the zigzag line are nonmetals. **Nonmetals** are poor conductors of heat and electricity. Nonmetals are often dull and brittle. Metalloids border the zigzag line on the periodic table. **Metalloids** are elements that have some properties of metals and some properties of nonmetals. Some metalloids are used to make semiconductor chips in computers.

---

11 Identify Fill in the blanks below with the word *metal, nonmetal,* or *metalloid.*

Iron is a good conductor of thermal energy.

Silicon has some properties of metals and some properties of nonmetals. Silicon is used in solar panels.

Graphite is brittle, meaning that it breaks easily. Graphite is made of carbon.

Elements in Each Column Have Similar Properties

The periodic table groups elements with similar properties together. Each vertical column of elements (from top to bottom) on the periodic table is called a **group**. Elements in the same group often have similar physical and chemical properties. For this reason, a group is sometimes called a *family*.

The properties of elements in a group are similar because the atoms of these elements have the same number of *valence electrons*. Valence electrons are found in the outermost portion of the electron cloud of an atom. Because they are far from the the attractive force of the nucleus, valence electrons are able to participate in chemical bonding. The number of valence electrons helps determine what kind of chemical reactions the atom can undergo. For example, all of the atoms of elements in Group 1 have a single valence electron. These elements are very reactive. The atoms of elements in Group 18 have a full set of valence electrons. The elements in Group 18 are all unreactive gases.

Active Reading **12 Explain** Why do elements within a group have similar chemical properties?

_____

_____

_____

Alkali metals, found in Group 1, share the property of reactivity with water.

Sodium has 1 valence electron.

Potassium has 1 valence electron.

Just as this family is made up of members that have similar characteristics, families in the periodic table are made up of elements that have similar properties.

Groups of Elements Have Similar Properties

Observe the similarities of elements found in Group 1 and in Group 18.

Elements in Each Row Follow Periodic Trends

Each horizontal row of elements (from left to right) on the periodic table is called a **period**. The physical and chemical properties of elements change in predictable ways from one end of the period to the other. For example, within any given period on the periodic table, atomic size decreases as you move from left to right. The densities of elements also follow a pattern. Within a period, elements at the left and right sides of the table are the least dense, and the elements in the middle are the most dense. The element osmium has the highest known density, and it is located at the center of the table. Chemists cannot predict the exact size or density of an atom of elements based on that of another. However, these trends are a valuable tool in predicting the properties of different substances.

Elements Are Arranged in Order of Increasing Atomic Number

As you move from left to right within a period, the atomic number of each element increases by one. Once you've reached the end of the period, the pattern resumes on the next period. You might have noticed that two rows of elements are set apart from the rest of the periodic table. These rows, the lanthanides and actinides, are placed below the table to allow it to be narrower. These elements are also arranged in order of increasing atomic number.

Think Outside the Book Inquiry

13 Apply Imagine that you have just discovered a new element. Explain where this element would appear on the periodic table and why. Describe the element's properties and propose a chemical symbol and name for the element.

Noble gases, found in Group 18, glow brightly when an electric current is passed through them.

Neon has 8 valence electrons.

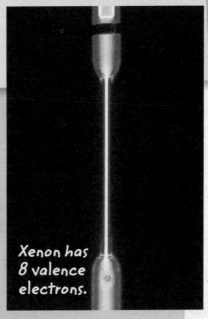

Xenon has 8 valence electrons.

14 Analyze List three other elements that have 1 valence electron. (Hint: Refer to the periodic table.)

_____

_____

_____

15 Analyze List three other elements that have 8 valence electrons. (Hint: Refer to the periodic table.)

_____

_____

_____

Visual Summary

To complete this summary, fill in the blanks with the correct word or phrase. Then use the key below to check your answers. You can use this page to review the main concepts of the lesson.

The periodic table arranges elements in columns and rows.

16 Elements in the same

_____

have similar properties.

17 Rows on the periodic table are known as

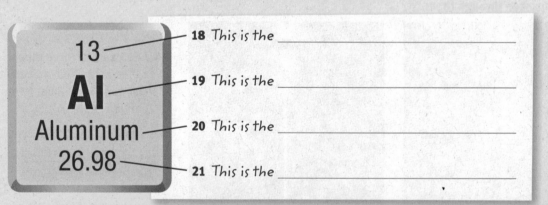

The **Periodic** Table

The periodic table contains information about each element.

13

Al

Aluminum

26.98

18 This is the _____

19 This is the _____

20 This is the _____

21 This is the _____

Answers: 16 group; 17 periods; 18 atomic number; 19 chemical symbol; 20 chemical name; 21 average atomic mass

22 Describe Some elements are highly unstable and break apart within seconds, making them difficult to study. How can the periodic table help scientists infer the properties of these elements?

Lesson Review

Vocabulary

Draw a line to connect the following terms to their definitions.

1 metal

2 nonmetal

3 metalloid

A an element that has properties of both metals and nonmetals

B an element that is shiny and that conducts heat and electricity well

C an element that conducts heat and electricity poorly

Key Concepts

4 Identify Elements in the same _____ on the periodic table have the same number of valence electrons.

5 Identify Properties of elements within a _____ on the periodic table change in a predictable way from one side of the table to the other.

6 Describe What is the purpose of the zigzag line on the periodic table?

_____

_____

7 Apply Thorium (Th) has an average atomic mass of 232.0 and an atomic number of 90. In the space below, draw a square from the periodic table to represent thorium.

Critical Thinking

Use this graphic to answer the following questions.

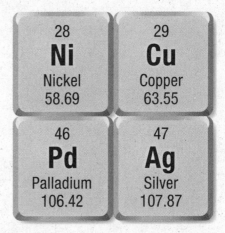

8 Infer What can you infer about copper and silver based on their position relative to each other?

_____

_____

9 Apply How does the nucleus of a copper atom compare to the nucleus of a nickel atom?

_____

_____

10 Explain Explain how chemists can state with certainty that no one will discover an element that would appear on the periodic table between sulfur (S) and chlorine (Cl).

_____

_____

_____

_____

_____

_____

My Notes

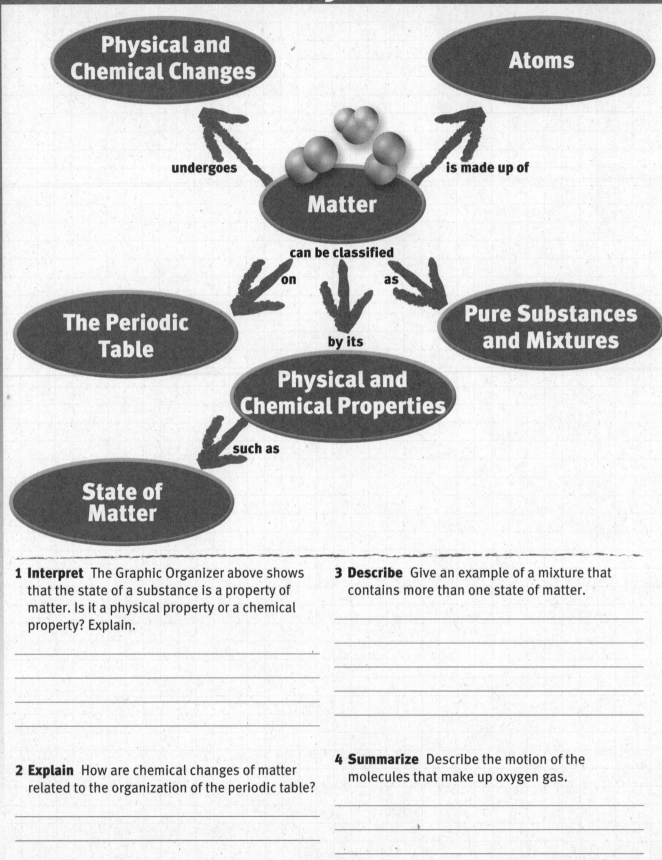

Physical and Chemical Changes

Atoms

undergoes

is made up of

Matter

can be classified

on

as

by its

The Periodic Table

Pure Substances and Mixtures

Physical and Chemical Properties

such as

State of Matter

1 Interpret The Graphic Organizer above shows that the state of a substance is a property of matter. Is it a physical property or a chemical property? Explain.

_____

_____

_____

_____

2 Explain How are chemical changes of matter related to the organization of the periodic table?

_____

_____

_____

_____

3 Describe Give an example of a mixture that contains more than one state of matter.

_____

_____

_____

_____

4 Summarize Describe the motion of the molecules that make up oxygen gas.

_____

_____

_____

_____

Name _____

Multiple Choice

Identify the choice that best completes the statement or answers the question.

1 Marcus wants to use two objects to compare the sizes of a proton and an electron. If he uses a basketball for a proton, which object would **best** represent an electron?

    A. a pea

    B. a bowling ball

    C. a beach ball

    D. a soccer ball

2 Tyson draws a model to show how the particles in a liquid appear.

Which model (or models) above could be Tyson's drawing of particles in a liquid?

    F. Model 1

    G. Model 3

    H. Model 1 and Model 2

    I. Model 1, Model 2, and Model 3

3 Some compounds are classified as acids or bases. The pH scale shows how acidic or how basic these compounds are. The lower the pH, the more acidic a compound is. The higher the pH, the more basic it is. Sodium hydroxide, a compound commonly found in drain cleaners, has a pH of about 13.

pH Scale

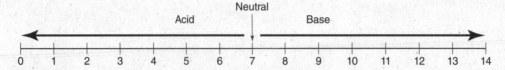

Which of these phrases describes sodium hydroxide?

A. highly basic

B. highly acidic

C. slightly basic

D. slightly acidic

4 Gordon places a piece of solid zinc metal in a beaker containing hydrochloric acid. He identifies the products as zinc chloride and hydrogen gas. Which process took place in the beaker?

F. evaporation

G. condensation

H. a physical change

I. a chemical change

5 Rita wants to make some toast for breakfast. She puts a slice of bread in the toaster. After 3 min, Rita notices that the sides of the bread are black. What has happened?

A. The bread has undergone a change of state.

B. The bread has undergone a change in density.

C. Some of the matter in the bread was destroyed.

D. New substances have formed as the result of a chemical change.

6 Trini adds 10 g of baking soda to 100 g of vinegar. The mixture begins to bubble. When the bubbling stops, Trini finds the mass of the resulting mixture. She determines its mass is 105 g. Why has the mass changed?

F. A gas has formed and left the mixture.

G. Vinegar evaporated during the experiment.

H. Mixtures are always less massive than their parts.

I. Matter was destroyed when vinegar reacted with baking soda.

7 Density is the ratio of mass to volume. Troy listed the density of four metals at 20 °C.

Material	Density (g/cm³)
Brass	8.9
Gold	19.3
Iron	7.8
Lead	11.3

If Troy has a 4-cm cube of each of these metals, which cube will have the **greatest** mass?

A. brass

B. gold

C. iron

D. lead

8 Raul and Bonnie are trying to classify several objects that they found during a field trip to the beach. They collected a sample of seawater, a piece of driftwood, and several smooth pebbles. How are the particles that make up the driftwood similar to those of the pebbles but not to those of the seawater?

F. They move freely in all directions.

G. They vibrate, but are locked in place.

H. They continually collide with one another.

I. They slide past one another.

9 Water freezes at 0 °C. If a temperature drop is causing a glass of water to freeze, how would a thermometer in the water most likely change as the water freezes?

A. The temperature would keep rising steadily.

B. The temperature would keep falling steadily.

C. The temperature would fall to 0 °C and stay there until all the water froze.

D. The temperature would not change or would change unpredictably.

10 It is important to understand the differences between chemical and physical changes. Chemical changes result in new substances, but physical changes do not. Which process is an example of a physical change?

F. Water turns to steam when boiled over a Bunsen burner.

G. Carbon combines with oxygen to form carbon dioxide gas.

H. Water breaks down into hydrogen and oxygen gases.

I. Limestone breaks down into lime and carbon dioxide when heated.

11 Alexandra knows that the atomic number of the element potassium, K, is 19. She also knows that one particular isotope of potassium has a mass number of 39. How many neutrons can be found in the nucleus of this isotope of potassium?

    A. 19

    B. 20

    C. 39

    D. 58

12 Atoms of different elements can join together in arrangements to produce a variety of substances that are found on Earth. There are more than a hundred known elements. Which of the following best describes these elements?

    F. Most of these elements are metals.

    G. Most of these elements are metalloids.

    H. Most of these elements are nonmetals.

    I. Most of the these elements are noble gases.

13 All matter has both physical and chemical properties. A physical property can be observed without changing the identity of the substance. Which of these choices is a physical property?

    A. density

    B. flammability

    C. ability to rust

    D. reactivity with water

14 Dr. Suri placed a dog on the scale at the veterinary clinic. Then she recorded a reading of 8 lb. What does this reading mean?

    F. The dog's mass is equal to 8 lb.

    G. The dog has an average density of 8 lb/ft³.

    H. The volume of the dog is exactly 8 lb.

    I. The weight of the dog as measured by the scale is 8 lb.

15 The row and the column where each element on the periodic table is located are useful in determining the properties of an element.

H																	He
Li	Be											B	C	N	O	F	Ne
Na	Mg											Al	Si	P	S	Cl	Ar
K	Ca	Sc	Ti	V	Cr	Mn	Fe	Co	Ni	Cu	Zn	Ga	Ge	As	Se	Br	Kr
Rb	Sr	Y	Zr	Nb	Mo	Tc	Ru	Rh	Pd	Ag	Cd	In	Sn	Sb	Te	I	Xe
Cs	Ba	La	Hf	Ta	W	Re	Os	Ir	Pt	Au	Hg	Tl	Pb	Bi	Po	At	Rn
Fr	Ra	Ac	Rf	Db	Sg	Bh	Hs	Mt	Ds	Rg	Cn						

Metals
Metalloids
Nonmetals

Ce	Pr	Nd	Pm	Sm	Eu	Gd	Tb	Dy	Ho	Er	Tm	Yb	Lu
Th	Pa	U	Np	Pu	Am	Cm	Bk	Cf	Es	Fm	Md	No	Lr

Which of these statements best describes the elements Mn and Fe?

A. They are in the same group.

B. They are in the same period.

C. They are in the same family.

D. They are in the same group and the same period.

16 Any atom that has 13 protons is an aluminum atom. Which statement **best** describes what would happen if a proton were added to an aluminum atom?

F. The atom would lose electrons.

G. The atom would have a negative charge.

H. The atom would no longer be aluminum.

I. The atom would have a smaller atomic number.

17 Esther is studying the physical and chemical properties of a solid object. She subjects the object to a number of tests and observations. Which of these statements describes a chemical property of the object?

A. The object is white in color.

B. The object has a powdery texture.

C. The object's density is 2.11 g/cm³.

D. The object reacts with acid to form water.

18 A magnet was placed near a pile that contained both iron and sulfur. The magnet was moved gradually closer to the pile. As it neared the pile, the magnet started attracting small pieces of iron from the pile.

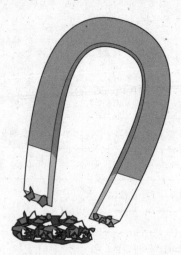

Which of these statements **best** describes the contents of the pile?

F. It is a solution of iron and sulfur that can be separated by magnetism.

G. It is a heterogeneous mixture of iron and sulfur that can be separated by magnetism.

H. It is a compound of iron and sulfur that can be separated by magnetism.

I. It is a suspension of sulfur in iron that can be separated by magnetism.

Waves and Light

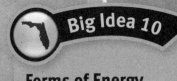

Big Idea 10

Forms of Energy

What do you think?

Waves can travel great distances. This large radio telescope gathers radio waves from space. Other telescopes use mirrors to gather light waves. What have people learned about space from light waves?

Unit 3
Waves and Light

CITIZEN SCIENCE

Looking Into Space

The first telescopes were refracting telescopes, which used a pair of lenses to gather light. Today, astronomers also use reflecting telescopes, which gather light with large mirrors, to observe distant objects.

Galileo observing space

1609
Galileo Galilei used a refracting telescope to observe phases of Venus, the moons of Jupiter, the surface of the moon, sunspots, and a supernova.

List other tools that use lenses and think of a use for each one.

_____

_____

_____

_____

_____

Telescope similar to Isaac Newton's

Skylab image of the sun

1973
Telescopes that operate from space, like the sun-observing telescope that was aboard Skylab, can see all kinds of things we can't see from Earth.

1668
Isaac Newton built a reflecting telescope that used a curved mirror to gather light. Newton's mirror did not split light into colors like the lenses in early refracting telescopes did.

Hubble Space Telescope

1990
The orbiting Hubble Space Telescope can capture detailed images of objects very far from Earth. The Hubble Space Telescope has taken images of the most distant galaxies astronomers have ever seen.

Take It Home   Eyes to the Sky

Use a pair of binoculars or a telescope to look at the night sky. Compare what you can see with magnification to what you can see when looking at the same part of the sky without magnification. Draw or write your observations in the chart.

Unmagnified Night Sky	Magnified Night Sky

Waves

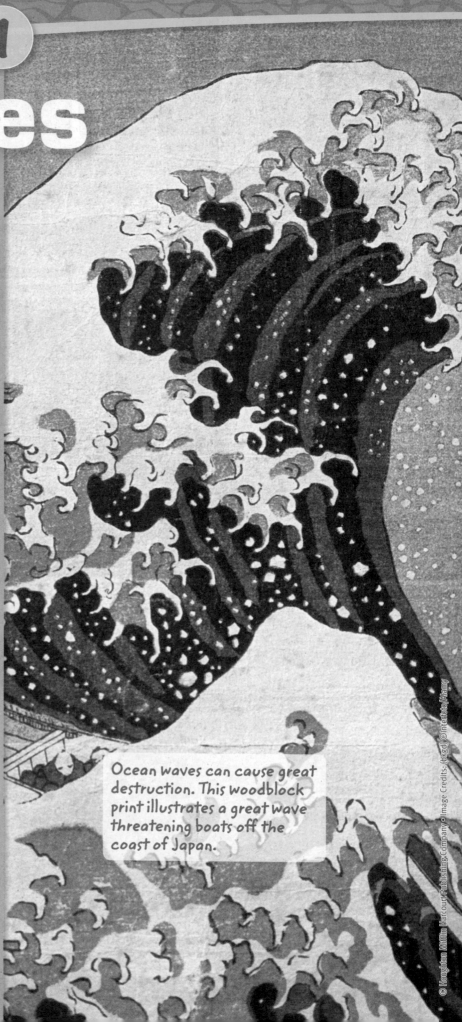

ESSENTIAL QUESTION

What are waves?

By the end of this lesson, you should be able to distinguish between types of waves, based on medium and direction of motion.

Ocean waves can cause great destruction. This woodblock print illustrates a great wave threatening boats off the coast of Japan.

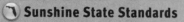 **Sunshine State Standards**

SC.7.N.1.1 Define a problem from the seventh grade curriculum, use appropriate reference materials to support scientific understanding, plan and carry out scientific investigation of various types, such as systematic observations or experiments, identify variables, collect and organize data, interpret data in charts, tables, and graphics, analyze information, make predictions, and defend conclusions.

SC.7.P.10.3 Recognize that light waves, sound waves, and other waves move at different speeds in different materials.

Engage Your Brain

1 Predict Check T or F to show whether you think each statement is true or false.

T   F

☐ ☐ The air around you is full of waves.

☐ ☐ Ocean waves carry water from hundreds of miles away.

☐ ☐ Sound waves can travel across outer space.

☐ ☐ Visible light is a wave.

2 Identify Make a list of items in the classroom that are making waves. Next to each item, write what kind of waves you think it is making.

 ## Active Reading

3 Distinguish Which of the following definitions of *medium* do you think is most likely to be used in the context of studying waves?

A of intermediate size

B the matter in which a physical phenomenon takes place

C between two extremes

Vocabulary Terms

- **wave**
- **medium**
- **longitudinal wave**
- **transverse wave**
- **mechanical wave**
- **electromagnetic wave**

4 Apply As you learn the definition of each vocabulary term in this lesson, write your own definition or sketch to help you remember the meaning of the term.

What are waves?

The world is full of waves. Water waves are just one of many kinds of waves. Sound and light are also waves. A **wave** is a disturbance that transfers energy from one place to another.

Waves Are Disturbances

Many waves travel by disturbing a material. The material then returns to its original place. A **medium** is the material through which a wave travels.

You can make waves on a rope by shaking the end up and down. The rope is the medium and the wave is the up-and-down disturbance. As the part nearest your hand moves, it causes the part next to it to move up and down too. The motion of this part of the rope causes the next part to move. In this way, the wave moves as a disturbance down the whole length of the rope.

Each piece of the rope moves up and down as a wave goes by. Then the piece returns to where it was before. A wave transfers energy from one place to another. It does not transfer matter.

The points where the wave is highest are called crests. The points where the wave is lowest are called troughs. In other types of waves, the maximum disturbances are called peaks.

Active Reading

5 Identify Underline the names for the highest and lowest points of a wave.

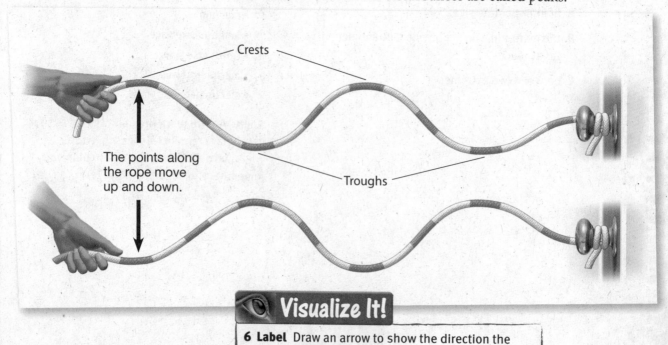

Crests

The points along the rope move up and down.

Troughs

Visualize It!

6 Label Draw an arrow to show the direction the wave energy travels.

Waves Are a Transfer of Energy

A wave is a disturbance that transfers energy. Waves that need a medium to transfer energy include ocean waves, which move through water, and waves that are carried on guitar or cello strings when they vibrate. Some waves can transfer energy without a medium. One example is visible light. Light waves from the sun transfer energy to Earth across empty space.

 **Visualize It!**

Each snapshot below shows the passage of a wave. The leaf rises and falls as crests and troughs carry it.

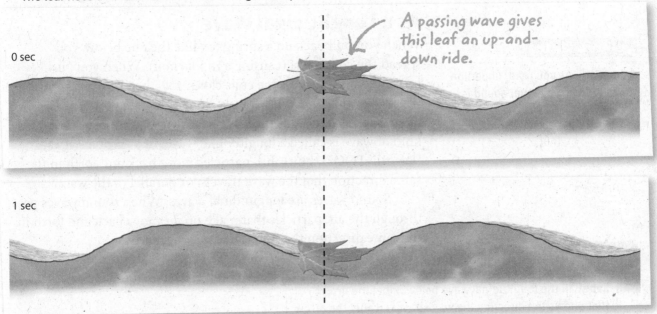

0 sec

A passing wave gives this leaf an up-and-down ride.

1 sec

7 Illustrate In the picture below, draw the leaf in the location it will be in after 2 seconds.

2 sec

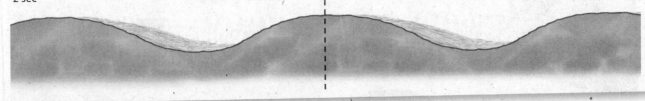

8 Model In the space below, draw the leaf and wave as they will appear after 3 seconds.

3 sec

How does a wave transfer energy?

A wave transfers energy in the direction it travels. However, the disturbance can be in different directions. Waves can be classified by comparing the direction that they cause particles in the medium to move with the direction in which the wave moves.

As a Longitudinal Wave

9 Identify As you read, underline the type of wave that sound is.

When you pull back on a spring toy like the one below, you spread the coils apart (causing a *rarefaction*). When you push forward, you compress the coils closer together. The compression you make when you push travels along the spring toy. The coils move back and forth as the wave passes along the spring toy. This kind of wave is called a longitudinal wave. In a **longitudinal wave** (lawn•ji•TOOD• ehn•uhl), particles move back and forth in the same direction that the wave travels, or parallel to the wave.

Sound waves are longitudinal waves. When sound waves pass through the air, particles that make up air move back and forth in the same direction that the sound waves travel.

Visualize It!

10 Label In the longitudinal wave below, label the arrow that shows the direction the wave travels. Label the arrow that shows how the spring is disturbed.

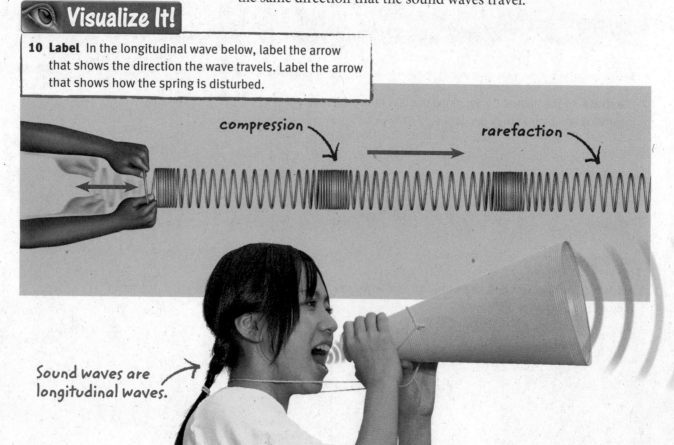

compression

rarefaction

Sound waves are longitudinal waves.

As a Transverse Wave

The same spring toy can be used to make other kinds of waves. If you move the end of the spring toy up and down, a wave also travels along the spring. In this wave, the spring's coils move up and down as the wave passes. This kind of wave is called a **transverse wave**. In a transverse wave, particles move perpendicularly to the direction the wave travels.

Transverse waves and longitudinal waves often travel at different speeds in a medium. In a spring toy, longitudinal waves are usually faster. An earthquake sends both longitudinal waves (called P-waves) and transverse waves (called S-waves) through Earth's crust. In this case, the longitudinal waves are also faster. During an earthquake, the faster P-waves arrive first. A little while later the S-waves arrive. The S-waves are slower but usually more destructive.

A transverse wave and a longitudinal wave can combine to form another kind of wave called a surface wave. Ripples on a pond are an example of a surface wave.

11 Categorize Is the stadium wave at right a transverse or longitudinal wave?

_____

When these fans do "The Wave" in a stadium, they are modeling the way a disturbance travels through a medium.

Visualize It!

12 Label In the transverse wave below, label which arrow shows the direction the wave travels in, and which shows the direction the spring is disturbed.

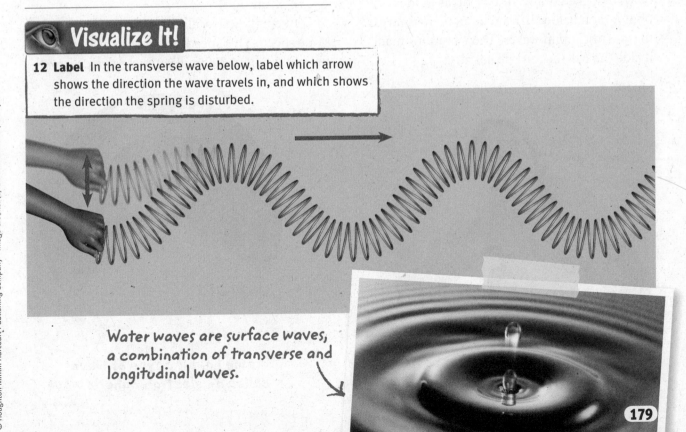

Water waves are surface waves, a combination of transverse and longitudinal waves.

Making Waves

What are some types of waves?

As you have learned, waves are disturbances that transfer energy. Waves can be classified by the direction of disturbance. But they can also be classified by what they are disturbing.

Mechanical Waves

Most of the waves we have talked about so far are waves in a medium. For water waves, water is the medium. For earthquake waves, Earth's crust is the medium. Waves that require a medium are called **mechanical waves**.

Some mechanical waves can travel through more than one medium. For example, sound waves can move through air, through water, or even through a solid wall. The waves travel at different speeds in the different media. Sound waves travel much faster in a liquid or a solid than in air.

Mechanical waves can't travel without a medium. Suppose all the air is removed from beneath a glass dome, or bell jar, as in the photograph below. In a vacuum, there is no air to transmit sound waves. The vibrations made inside the bell jar can't be heard.

Electromagnetic Waves

Are there any waves that can travel without a medium? Yes. Sunlight travels from the sun to Earth through empty space. Although light waves can travel through a medium, they can also travel without a medium. Light and similar waves are called electromagnetic (EM) waves. **Electromagnetic waves** are disturbances in electric and magnetic fields. They are considered transverse waves.

Examples of EM waves include
- visible light
- radio waves
- microwaves
- ultraviolet (UV) light
- x-rays

In empty space, all these waves travel at the same speed. This speed, referred to as the speed of light, is about 300 million meters per second!

The sound from the toy cannot be heard because there is no air to transmit the sound.

Visible light is a type of wave called an electromagnetic wave.

Visualize It!

13 Classify Identify each example of waves in these three photographs as mechanical or electromagnetic.

Sunlight is a(n)
_____

Water waves are
_____

A towel waving displays a(n)
_____

Vocal sounds are
_____

Music is a(n)
_____

Firelight is a(n)
_____

Visual Summary

To complete this summary, read the statements in the boxes below. Circle any that are true. Cross out any that are false, and correct the statement so that it is true. You can use this page to review the main concepts of the lesson.

Waves are disturbances that transport energy.

14 The water particles in the wave move to the right, along with the wave.

_____
_____
_____

Waves can be longitudinal or transverse.

15 The toy above and the toy below both show longitudinal waves.

_____
_____
_____

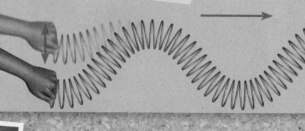

Waves

Waves can be mechanical or electromagnetic.

16 This picture shows only examples of mechanical waves.

_____
_____
_____

17 Support Use an example to support the following statement: Waves transfer energy but not matter.

Lesson Review

Vocabulary

Circle the term that best completes the following sentences.

1 A wave is a disturbance that transfers (*matter* / *energy*).

2 In a (*longitudinal* / *transverse*) wave, particles move parallel to the direction the wave travels.

3 (*Mechanical* / *Electromagnetic*) waves require a medium in which to travel.

Key Concepts

4–6 Identify Identify the medium for each of the following types of waves.

Type of wave	Medium
ocean waves	**4**
earthquake waves	**5**
sound waves from a speaker	**6**

7 Describe Describe how transverse waves can be produced on a rope. Then describe how pieces of the rope move as waves pass.

_____

_____

_____

_____

8 Analyze Are the sun's rays mechanical waves or electromagnetic waves? How do you know?

_____

_____

_____

9 Contrast Mechanical waves travel as disturbances in a physical medium. How do electromagnetic waves travel?

_____

_____

_____

Critical Thinking

Use this photo to answer the following questions.

10 Infer Even though the phone is ringing, no sound comes out of the jar. What does this tell you about what is in the jar?

_____

_____

_____

_____

11 Infer What does this same experiment tell you about light waves?

_____

_____

_____

Properties of Waves

ESSENTIAL QUESTION

How can we describe a wave?

By the end of this lesson, you should be able to identify characteristics of a wave and describe wave behavior.

🌞 Sunshine State Standards

SC.7.P.10.3 Recognize that light waves, sound waves, and other waves move at different speeds in different materials.

MA.6.A.3.6 Construct and analyze tables, graphs, and equations to describe linear functions and other simple relations using both common language and algebraic notation.

LA.6.4.2.2 The student will record information (e.g., observations, notes, lists, charts, legends) related to a topic, including visual aids to organize and record information and include a list of sources used.

A heartbeat monitor displays a wave, the characteristics of which contain information about a patient's heartbeat.

Engage Your Brain

1 Describe Fill in the blank with the word that you think correctly completes the following sentences.

A guitar amplifier makes a guitar sound

_____

FM radio frequencies are measured in mega- _____

The farther you are from a sound source, the _____ the sound is.

 Active Reading

3 Predict Some scientific terms have meanings close to their meanings in everyday use. For each of the following terms, write in your own words what it means in common use. Then try writing a definition of what it might mean when applied to waves.

length:

_____

_____

_____

_____

speed:

_____

_____

period (of time):

_____

_____

frequency:

_____

_____

2 Illustrate Draw a diagram of a wave in the space below. How would you describe your wave so that a friend on the phone could duplicate your drawing?

Vocabulary Terms

- amplitude
- hertz
- wavelength
- wavefront
- wave period
- wave speed
- frequency

4 Compare As you read the lesson, compare the definitions in the text to the definitions that you made in the previous exercise. If the definitions differ, read that passage with extra care to make sure you understand the concepts.

Amp It UP!

How can we describe a wave?

Suppose you are talking to a friend who had been to the beach. You want to know what the waves were like. Were they big or small? How often did they come? How far apart were they? Were they moving fast? Each of these is a basic property that can be used to describe waves.

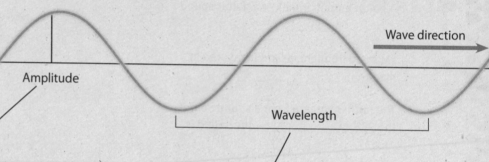

Wave direction

Amplitude

Wavelength

By Its Amplitude

As a wave passes, particles in the medium move up and down or back and forth. The points of maximum displacement are called peaks. A wave's **amplitude** is a measure of how far particles in the medium move away from their normal rest position. For a water wave, amplitude is the height of a crest. For other waves, it is the displacement at a peak. You can also use a graph of the wave, as shown below. The amplitude is half of the difference between the highest and lowest values on the graph.

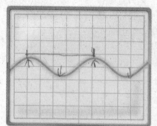 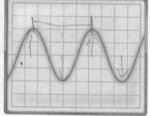

👁 **Visualize It!**

5 Label Mark the amplitude in each graph above. Which wave has the greater amplitude?

Second graph

By Its Wavelength

You can use amplitude to describe the height of an ocean wave. You might also want to describe how long it is. **Wavelength** is the distance over which the wave's shape repeats. Wavelength is measured by the distance from one point on a wave to an identical point later on the wave. For example, wavelength can be measured as the distance from one crest or peak to the next, from one trough to the next, or between any other two corresponding points. Wavelength measures the length of one cycle, or repetition.

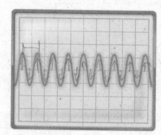 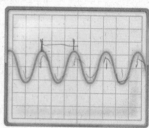

6 Label Mark the wavelength in each graph above. Which wave has the greater wavelength?

The first graph

By Its Frequency

Wavelength and amplitude tell you about the size of a wave. Another property tells you how much time a wave takes to repeat. **Wave period** (usually just "period") is the time required for one cycle. You can measure the period by finding the time for one full pattern of a wave to pass a given point. For example, you could start timing when one crest passes you and stop when the next crest passes. The time between two crests is the period.

Another way to express the time of a wave is frequency. **Frequency** tells you how many cycles occur in an amount of time, most commonly 1 s. Frequency is measured in **hertz** (Hz). One hertz is equal to one cycle per second. If ten peaks pass each second, the frequency is 10 Hz.

Frequency and period are closely related. Frequency is the inverse of period:

$$frequency = \frac{1}{period}$$

Suppose the time from one peak to another—the period—is 5 s. The frequency is then 1/5 Hz, or 0.2 Hz. In other words, one-fifth (0.2) of a wave passes each second.

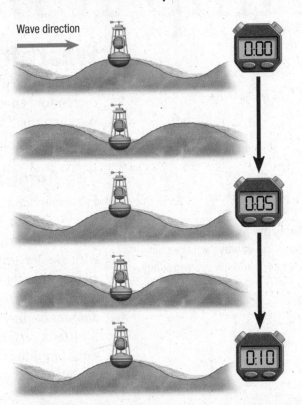

The buoy moves down and back up every five seconds as waves pass.

Wave direction

Frequency is equal to the number of cycles per unit of time:

$$frequency = \frac{number\ of\ cycles}{time}$$

Visualize It!

7 Illustrate On the grid below, draw a wave, and then draw another wave with twice the amplitude.

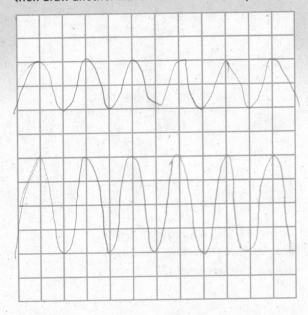

8 Illustrate On the grid below, draw a wave, and then draw another wave with half the wavelength.

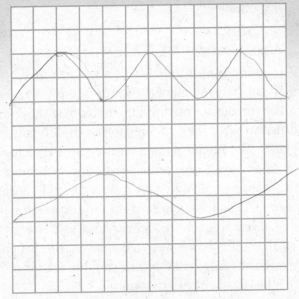

Amp It Down

What affects the energy of a wave?

All waves carry energy from one place to another, but some waves carry more energy than others. A leaf falling on water produces waves so small they are hard to see. An earthquake under the ocean can produce huge waves that cause great destruction.

The Amplitude or Frequency

For a mechanical wave, amplitude is related to the amount of energy the wave carries. For two similar waves, the wave with greater amplitude carries more energy. For example, sound waves with greater amplitude transfer more energy to your eardrum and so they sound louder.

Greater frequency can also mean greater energy in a given amount of time. If waves hit a barrier three times in a minute, they transfer a certain amount of energy to the barrier. If waves of the same amplitude hit nine times in a minute, they transfer more energy in that minute.

For most electromagnetic (EM) waves, energy is most strongly related to frequency. Very high-frequency EM waves, such as x-rays and gamma rays, carry enough energy to damage human tissue. Lower-frequency EM waves, such as visible light waves, can be absorbed safely by your body.

Active Reading

9 Identify As you read, underline the kind of wave whose energy depends mostly on frequency.

Energy Loss to a Medium

A medium transmits a wave. However, a medium may not transmit all of the wave's energy. As a wave moves through a medium, particles may move in different directions or come to rest in different places. The medium may warm up, shift, or change in other ways. Some of the wave's energy produces these changes. As the wave travels through more of the medium, more energy is lost to the medium.

Often, higher-frequency waves lose energy more readily than lower-frequency waves. When you stand far from a concert, you might hear only the low-frequency (bass) sounds.

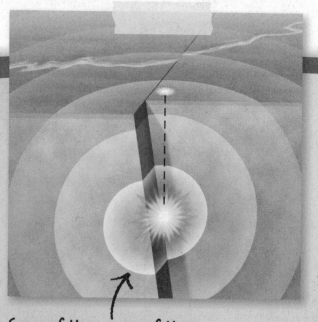

Some of the energy of these waves is lost to the medium when the ground shifts.

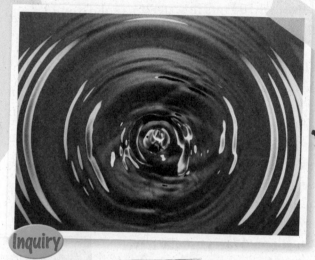

Sound waves expand in three dimensions.

Energy Loss Due to Spreading

So far, we have mostly talked about waves moving in straight lines. But waves usually spread out in more than one dimension. The peaks can be drawn as shapes, such as circles or spheres, called **wavefronts**. As each wavefront moves farther from the source, it becomes larger. The energy is spread over a greater area. Less energy is available at any one point on the wavefront. If you measure a wave at a point farther from the source, you measure less energy. But the total energy of the wavefront stays the same.

Inquiry

Ripples on a water surface expand in two dimensions.

10 Predict Which type of wave spreading do you think causes faster energy loss—two-dimensional or three-dimensional? Explain.

Two dimesional because it expands into two dimensions

As the student on the left knocks on the table, the students further away feel the resulting waves less strongly.

Visualize It! Inquiry

11 Synthesize If these students repeated their experiment using a longer table, what differences would they observe? Why?

They would feel the same

189

A Happy Medium

What determines the speed of a wave?

Waves travel at different speeds in different media. For example, sound waves travel at about 340 m/s in air at room temperature, but they travel at nearly 1,500 m/s in water. In a solid, sound waves travel even faster.

The Medium in Which It Travels

The speed at which a wave travels—called **wave speed**—depends on the properties of the medium. Specifically, wave speed depends on the interactions of the atomic particles of the medium. In general, waves travel faster in solids than in liquids, and faster in liquids than in gases. This is because solids generally have the fastest interactions between particles and gases have the slowest.

The speed of interactions depend on many factors. For example, wave speed depends on the density of the medium. Waves usually travel slower in the denser of two solids or the denser of two liquids. When the particles are more densely packed, they resist motion more, so they transfer waves more slowly.

In a gas, wave speed depends on temperature as well as density. Particles in hot air move faster than particles in cold air, so particles in hot air collide more often. This faster interaction allows waves to pass through hot air more quickly than through cold air, even though hot air may be less dense. The speed of sound in air at 20 °C is about 340 m/s. The speed of sound in air at 0 °C is slower, about 330 m/s.

Electromagnetic waves don't require a medium, so they can travel in a vacuum. All electromagnetic waves travel at the same speed in empty space. This speed, called the speed of light, is about 300,000,000 m/s. While passing through a medium such as air or glass, EM waves travel more slowly than they do in a vacuum.

Active Reading **12 Identify** Does sound travel faster or slower when the air gets warmer?

<u>faster</u>

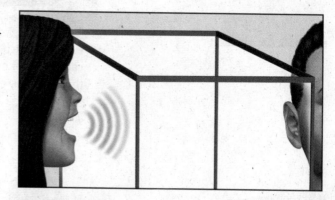

Visualize It!

13 Diagram The diagram above shows sound traveling through an air-filled tank. Draw a medium in the tank below in which sound will travel faster than in the air-filled tank.

As a person bounces on a trampoline, they model a particle being moved by a wave.

Imagine if the tension on the trampoline were much lower: each bounce would take longer, because the person would sink much lower.

The more flexible a medium is, the slower it transmits waves.

Its Frequency and Wavelength

Wave speed can be calculated from frequency and wavelength. To understand how, it helps to remember that speed is defined as distance divided by time.

$$speed = \frac{distance}{time}$$

So, if a runner runs 8 m in 2 s, then the runner's speed is 8 m ÷ 2 s = 4 m/s. For a wave, a peak moves a distance of one wavelength in one cycle. The time for the cycle to occur is one period. Use wavelength and period as the distance and time:

$$wave\ speed = \frac{wavelength}{wave\ period}$$

So, if a peak moves one wavelength of 8 m in one period of 2 s, the wave speed is calculated just like the runner's speed: 8 m ÷ 2 s = 4 m/s.

Frequency is the inverse of the wave period. So the relationship can be rewritten like this:

$$wave\ speed = frequency \times wavelength$$
or
$$wavelength = \frac{wave\ speed}{frequency}$$

If you already know the wave speed, you can use this equation to solve for frequency or wavelength.

 **Do the Math** You Try It

14 Calculate Complete this table relating wave speed, frequency, and wavelength.

Wave speed (m/s)	Frequency (Hz)	Wavelength (m)
20		5
75	15	
386	23	16
625		25
	38	20

(handwritten: 38)

(handwritten:
23
×16
138
230
368)

Visual Summary

To complete this summary, fill in the blanks with the correct word or phrase. Then use the key below to check your answers. You can use this page to review the main concepts of the lesson.

Amplitude tells the amount of displacement of a wave.

Wavelength tells how long a wave is.

Wave period is the time required for one cycle.

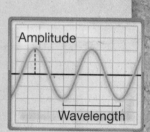

Wave energy depends on amplitude and frequency.

Most waves lose energy over time as they travel and spread.

18 Some of the wave's energy stays in the _____

15 _____ = $\dfrac{1}{\text{wave period}}$

16 Hertz are used to measure _____

17 One hertz is equal to _____

Wave Properties

Wave speed depends on the properties of the medium.

In a vacuum, electromagnetic waves all move at the speed of light.

19 wave speed = frequency × _____

Answers: 15 frequency; 16 frequency; 17 one cycle per second; 18 medium; 19 wavelength

20 Synthesize Describe how the properties of sound waves change as they spread out in a spherical pattern.

JOB BOARD

Dispensing Optician

What You'll Do: Help select and then fit eyeglasses and contact lenses.

Where You Might Work: Medical offices, or optical, department, or club stores

Education: Most training is on the job or through apprenticeships that last two years or longer. Some employers prefer graduates of postsecondary training programs in opticianry.

Other Job Requirements: A good eye for fashion, face shape, and color is a plus, as opticians help people find glasses they like.

Lighting Designer

What You'll Do: Work in theater, television, or film to make what happens on stage or on set visible to audiences. Lighting designers also use lighting and shadow to create the right tone or mood.

Where You Might Work: Theaters, television and film studios and sets, concerts and other special events

Education: A diploma or certificate in lighting design or technical stage management from a college or performing arts institute

Other Job Requirements: Experience lighting stage productions, the ability to work in a team

ELY Stone

A New Light on Microscopy

Doctors and medical researchers use fluorescent microscopes to see colored or fluorescent dyes in medical research. These microscopes use expensive and dangerous mercury light bulbs to illuminate the dyes. But Ely Stone, a retired computer programmer and inventor in Florida, found a less expensive source of light.

When the mercury bulb on his microscope died, Ely replaced it with many differently colored light-emitting diodes (LEDs). Each inexpensive LED emits light of a different wavelength. The LEDs cost only a couple of dollars each and are much safer than mercury bulbs. Yet they still provide the light needed to view the fluorescent dyes. Now, researchers can use the LED microscopes to really light up their dyes!

The Electromagnetic Spectrum

ESSENTIAL QUESTION

What is the relationship between various EM waves?

By the end of this lesson, you should be able to distinguish between the parts of the electromagnetic spectrum.

This iron glows with EM radiation that we normally can't see. The brighter areas represent hotter parts of the iron.

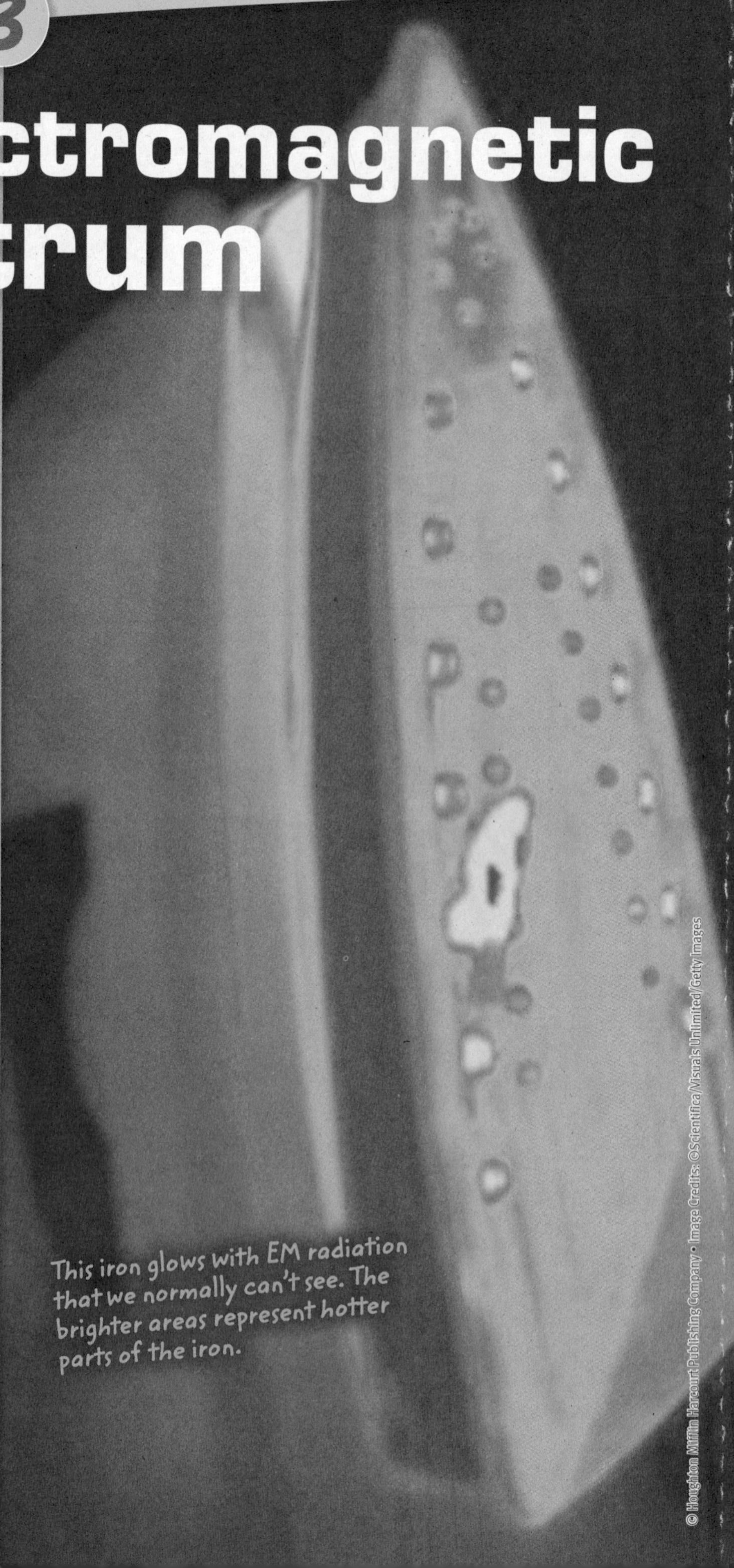

Sunshine State Standards

SC.7.P.10.1 Illustrate that the sun's energy arrives as radiation with a wide range of wavelengths, including infrared, visible, and ultraviolet, and that white light is made up of a spectrum of many different colors.

1 Select Circle the word or phrase that best completes each of the following sentences:

Radio stations transmit (*radio waves*/*gamma rays*).

The dentist uses (*infrared light*/*x-rays*) to examine your teeth.

Intense (*visible light*/*ultraviolet light*) from the sun can damage your skin.

2 Predict Imagine that humans had not realized there are other parts of the electromagnetic spectrum besides visible light. How would your day today have been different without technology based on other parts of the EM spectrum?

_____

_____

_____

_____

_____

_____

Active Reading

3 Synthesize You can often define an unknown word if you know the meaning of its word parts. Use this table of word parts to make an educated guess about the meanings given.

Word part	Meaning
ultra-	beyond
infra-	below
electro-	related to electricty
-magnetic	related to magnetism

What word means "beyond violet"?

_____

What word means "below red"?

_____

What word means "related to electricity and magnetism"?

_____

Vocabulary Terms

- **Radiation**
- **Electromagnetic spectrum**
- **Infrared**
- **Ultraviolet**

4 Apply As you learn the definition of each vocabulary term in this lesson, think of an example of a real-world use. Practice writing the term and its definition, and then writing or drawing a sketch of the example next to the definition.

What is the nature of light?

Light is a type of energy that travels as waves, but light waves are not disturbances in a medium. Light waves are disturbances in electric and magnetic fields. If you have felt the static cling of fabric and the pull of a magnet, then you have experienced electric and magnetic fields. Because these fields can exist in empty space, light does not need a medium in which to travel.

When an electrically charged particle vibrates, it disturbs the electric and magnetic fields around it. These disturbances, called electromagnetic (EM) waves, carry energy away from the charged particle. The disturbances are perpendicular to each other and to the direction the wave travels. **Radiation** (ray•dee•AY•shuhn) is the transfer of energy as EM waves.

In a vacuum, all EM waves move at the same speed: 300,000,000 m/s, called the speed of light. That's fast enough to circle Earth more than seven times in one second!

Although light and other EM waves do not need a medium, they can travel through many materials. EM waves travel more slowly in a medium such as air or glass than in a vacuum.

5 Identify Underline what produces EM waves.

6 Synthesize Why do we see lightning before we hear the accompanying thunder?

_____

_____

_____

_____

Visualize It!

7 Label Mark and label the wavelength and amplitude of the disturbances in the fields.

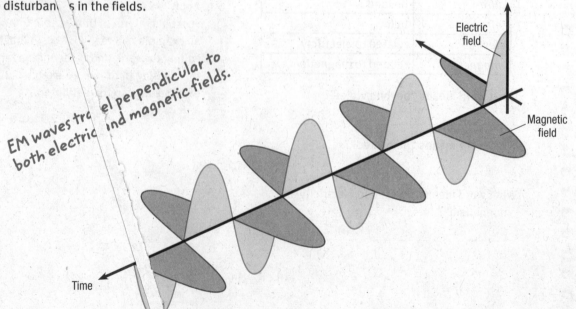

EM waves travel perpendicular to both electric and magnetic fields.

Electric field

Magnetic field

Time

The color with the shortest wavelengths is violet. Violet light has the highest frequencies.

The color with the longest wavelengths is red. Red light has the lowest frequencies.

What determines the color of light?

Light comes in many colors, from red to violet. But what is different about each color of light? Like all waves, light has wavelengths. Different wavelengths of light are interpreted by our eyes as different colors. The shortest wavelengths are seen as violet. The longest wavelengths are seen as red. Even the longest wavelengths we can see are still very small—less than one ten-thousandth of a centimeter.

White light is what we perceive when we see all the wavelengths of light at once, in equal proportions. A prism can split white light into its component colors, separating the colors by wavelength. The various wavelengths of light can also be combined to produce white light.

Our eyes only register three color ranges of light, called the primary colors—red, green, and blue. All other colors we see are a mixture of these three colors. A television or computer screen works by sending signals to make small dots, called pixels, give off red, green, and blue light.

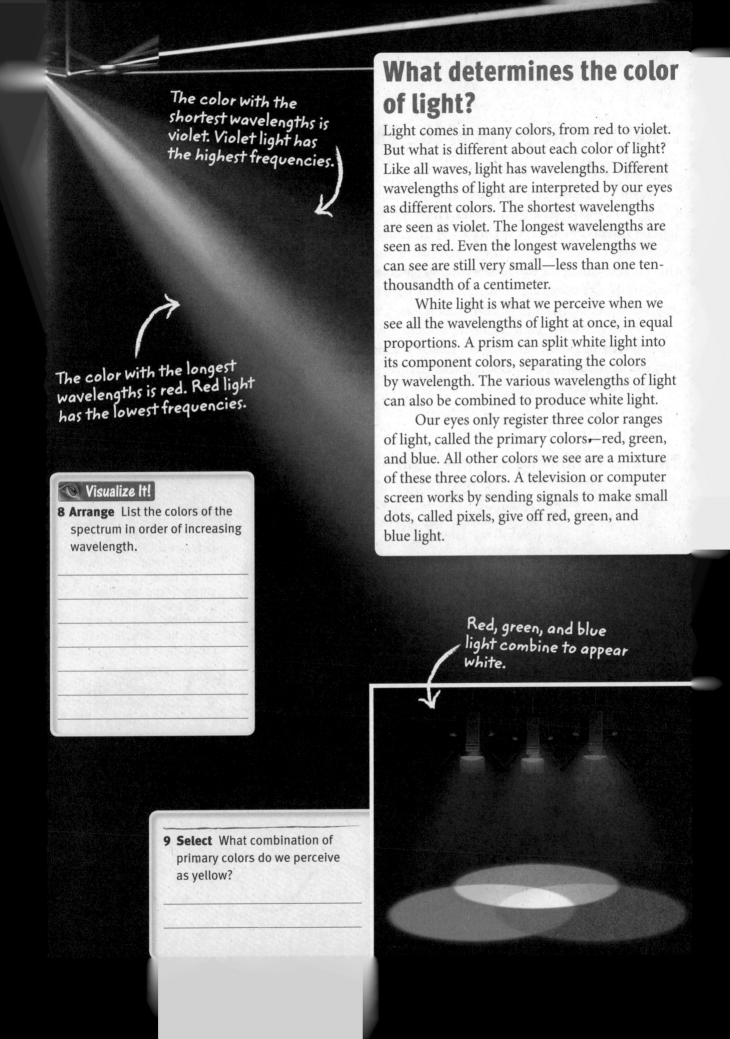

Visualize It!

8 Arrange List the colors of the spectrum in order of increasing wavelength.

_____

_____

_____

_____

_____

_____

Red, green, and blue light combine to appear white.

9 Select What combination of primary colors do we perceive as yellow?

_____

_____

Invisible Colors

What are the parts of the EM spectrum?

EM waves are measured by frequency or by wavelength. The light waves we see are EM waves. However, visible light represents only a very small part of the range of frequencies (or wavelengths) that an EM wave can have. This range is called the **electromagnetic (EM) spectrum**. These other EM waves are the same type of wave as the light we're used to. They're just different frequencies.

Two parts of the spectrum are close to visible light. **Infrared**, or IR, light has slightly longer wavelengths than red light. **Ultraviolet**, or UV, light has slightly shorter wavelengths than violet light.

The Electromagnetic Spectrum

Microwaves
Despite their name, microwaves are not the shortest EM waves. Besides heating food, microwaves are used in cellular phones.

Infrared Light
Infrared means "below red." The amount of infrared light an object gives off depends on its temperature. Below, colors indicate different amounts of infrared light.

Radio Waves
Radio waves have the longest wavelengths. They are used to broadcast many signals, including radio, television, and alarm systems.

Frequency in hertz (1 hertz = 1 cycle/second)

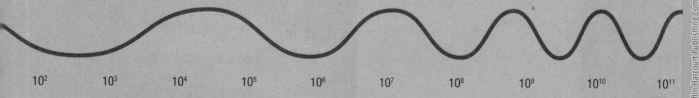

10^2	10^3	10^4	10^5	10^6	10^7	10^8	10^9	10^{10}	10^{11}

Radio Waves

Microwaves

The inner part of these flowers reflects UV light differently than the outer part. A bee's eyes are sensitive to UV light, and the bee can see the difference. However, human eyes cannot detect UV light. Our eyes can detect yellow light, and the center and edges of the flower reflect yellow light equally, so we see an all-yellow flower.

Human eyes see the flowers as entirely yellow.

A bee's eyes see a pattern in UV light.

Think Outside the Book

10 **Incorporate** The flower shows designs that are visible to bees, which can see light in the ultraviolet range. Research and explain how this adaptation leads to a symbiotic relationship between the flowers and bees.

Visible Light
Visible light is all the colors of the EM spectrum we can see. It is the narrowest part of the EM spectrum.

Ultraviolet Light
Ultraviolet means "beyond violet." Some animals can see ultraviolet light.

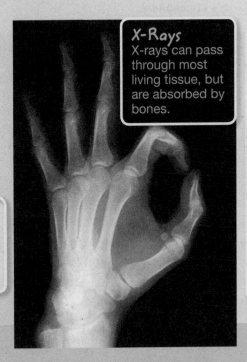

X-Rays
X-rays can pass through most living tissue, but are absorbed by bones.

Gamma Rays
Gamma rays can be used to treat illnesses and in making medical images.

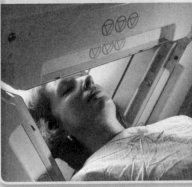

10^{12} 10^{13} 10^{14} 10^{15} 10^{16} 10^{17} 10^{18} 10^{19} 10^{20}

Infrared Light   **Ultraviolet Light**   **Gamma Rays**

Visible Light   **X-Rays**

Star Light,

How much of the sun's energy reaches us?

The sun gives off huge amounts of energy in the form of EM radiation. More of this energy is in the narrow visible light range than any other part of the spectrum, but the sun gives off some radiation in every part of the spectrum.

 **Active Reading** **11 Identify** What prevents most of the sun's gamma rays from reaching us?

_____

Visualize It!

The illustration shows how far down each part of the EM spectrum penetrates Earth's atmosphere.

The Earth Shields Us From Some EM Radiation

Between the sun and us lies Earth's atmosphere. In order to see anything, some of the sun's light must make it through the atmosphere. However, not all wavelengths of light penetrate the atmosphere equally. The atmosphere blocks most of the higher-frequency radiation like x-rays and gamma rays from reaching us at the ground level, while allowing most of the visible light to reach us. There is a "window" of radio frequencies that are barely blocked at all, and this is why the most powerful ground-based telescopes are radio telescopes.

Radio   Microwave   Infrared   Visible   Ultraviolet   X-ray   Gamma rays

Radio and visible light penetrate all the way to the ground. Most ultraviolet light is blocked high in the atmosphere.

12 Apply Why do we keep some telescopes in space?

_____

_____

_____

_____

Star Bright

© Houghton Mifflin Harcourt Publishing Company • Image Credits: (bkgd) ©NASA; (l) ©Ryan McVay/Photodisc/Getty Images; (r) ©NASA

Inquiry

13 Hypothesize Why might it be less dangerous to wear no sunglasses than to wear sunglasses that do not block UV light?

_____

_____

_____

_____

Astronauts need extra protection from EM radiation in space.

We Shield Ourselves From Some Radiation

The atmosphere blocks much of the sun's radiation, but not all. Some EM radiation can be dangerous to humans, so we take extra steps to protect ourselves. Receiving too much ultraviolet (UV) radiation can cause sunburn, skin cancer, or damage to the eyes, so we wear sunscreen and wear UV-blocking sunglasses to protect us from the UV light that passes through the atmosphere. Hats, long-sleeved shirts, and long pants can protect you, too.

You need this protection even on overcast days because UV light can travel through clouds. Even scientists in Antarctica, one of the coldest places on Earth, need to wear sunglasses, because fresh snow reflects about 80% of UV light back up where it might strike their eyes.

Outer space is often thought of as being cold, but despite this, one of the biggest dangers to astronauts is from overheating! Outside of Earth's protective atmosphere, the level of dangerous EM radiation is much higher. Also, in the vacuum of space, it's much harder to dispose of any unwanted energy, because there's no surrounding matter (like air) to absorb the extra energy. This is why astronauts' helmets are made to be highly reflective, using a thin layer of pure gold to reflect back unwanted EM radiation.

Frequency
Asked Questions

How much energy does EM radiation have?

What makes some EM waves safe, and some dangerous? The answer is that different frequencies of EM waves carry different amounts of energy.

Higher Frequency Means More Energy

The energy of an EM wave depends on its frequency. High-frequency, short-wavelength EM waves have more energy than low-frequency, long-wavelength waves.

More Energy Means More Dangerous

A high-frequency EM wave carries a lot of energy, so it has the possibility of damaging living tissue. But a low-frequency wave carries much less energy, and is safer. This is why radio waves (which have the lowest frequencies) are used so often, such as in walkie-talkies and baby monitors. In contrast, UV light causes sunburn unless you have protection, and when working with even higher-energy waves like x-rays, special precautions must be taken, such as wearing a lead apron to block most of the rays.

> **Active Reading** **14 Conclude** What kind of EM waves are most dangerous to humans?

Think Outside the Book

15 Apply On a separate sheet of paper, write a short story where the main character needs protection from two different kinds of EM radiation.

Radio waves pass through humans safely.

UV waves can cause damage to living tissue.

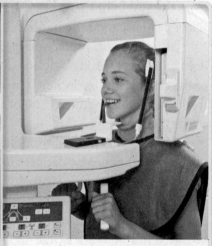

X-rays require extra safety.

Fire in the Sky

The sun constantly streams out charged particles. Earth has a strong magnetic field. When particles from the sun strike Earth, the magnetic field funnels them together, accelerating them. When these particles collide with the atmosphere, they give off electromagnetic radiation in the form of light, and near the poles where they usually come together, a beautiful display called an *aurora* (uh•RAWR•uh) sometimes lights up the sky.

Winds of Change
The stream of electrically charged particles from the sun is called the *solar wind*.

What a Gas!
An aurora produced by nitrogen atoms may have a blue or red color, while one produced by oxygen atoms is green or brownish-red.

Pole Position
At the North Pole, this phenomenon is called the *aurora borealis* (uh•RAWR•uh bawr•ee•AL•is), or northern lights. At the south pole, is it called the *aurora australis* (uh•RAWR•uh aw•STRAY•lis), or southern lights.

Extend

16 Relate Which color of aurora gives off higher-energy light, green or red?

17 Explain Why don't we see auroras on the moon?

18 Hypothesize Based on what you have learned about auroras, do you think auroras occur on other planets? Why or why not?

Visual Summary

To complete this summary, fill in the blanks with the correct word or phrase. Then use the key below to check your answers. You can use this page to review the main concepts of the lesson.

The Electromagnetic Spectrum

Different wavelengths of light appear as different colors.

19 The color of the longest visible wavelength is _____

20 The color of the shortest visible wavelength is _____

Higher frequency waves carry more energy. This makes them more dangerous.

21 The energy of an electromagnetic (EM) wave is proportional to its _____ .

EM waves exist along a spectrum.

22 The waves with the longest wavelengths are _____ waves.

23 The wavelengths with the shortest wavelengths are _____

10^0 10^{19}

Radio Waves   **Gamma Rays**

Answers: 19. red; 20. violet; 21. frequency; 22. radio; 23. gamma rays

24 Synthesize Suppose you are designing a device to transmit information without wires. What part of the EM spectrum will your device use, and why?

You Try It!

The data table below shows the data collected for rooms in three halls in the school.

Illuminance (lux)				
	Room 1	**Room 2**	**Room 3**	**Room 4**
Science Hall	150	250	500	400
Art Hall	300	275	550	350
Math Hall	200	225	600	600

① **Using Formulas** Find the mean, median, mode, and range of the data for the school.

② **Analyzing Methods** The school board is looking into complaints that some areas of the school are too poorly lit. They are considering replacing the lights. If you were in favor of replacing the lights, which representative value for the school's data would you use to support your position? If you were opposed to replacing the lights, which representative value for the school's data would you choose to support your position? Explain your answer.

_____

_____

_____

_____

_____

_____

_____

_____

_____

_____

_____

Language Arts Connection

On flashcards, write sentences that use the keywords *mean, median, mode,* and *range.* Cover the keywords with small sticky notes. Review each sentence, and determine if it provides enough context clues to determine the covered word. If necessary, work with a partner to improve your sentences.

Interactions of Light

ESSENTIAL QUESTION

How does light interact with matter?

By the end of this lesson, you should be able to explain how light and matter can interact.

These windows allow different colors of light to pass through. The colorful pattern is then reflected off the floor inside.

Sunshine State Standards

SC.7.N.1.1 Define a problem from the seventh grade curriculum, use appropriate reference materials to support scientific understanding, plan and carry out scientific investigation of various types, such as systematic observations or experiments, identify variables, collect and organize data, interpret data in charts, tables, and graphics, analyze information, make predictions, and defend conclusions.

SC.7.P.10.2 Observe and explain that light can be reflected, refracted, and/or absorbed.

SC.7.P.10.3 Recognize that light waves, sound waves, and other waves move at different speeds in different materials.

© Houghton Mifflin Harcourt Publishing Company • Image Credits: ©Philippe Renault/Hemis/Corbis

Engage Your Brain

1 Predict Check T or F to show whether you think each statement is true or false.

T   F

☐   ☐   Light cannot pass through solid matter.

☐   ☐   A white surface absorbs every color of light.

☐   ☐   Light always moves at the same speed.

2 Identify Unscramble the letters below to find words about interactions between light and matter. Write your words on the blank lines.

OCRLO   _____

RIORMR   _____

NABORIW   _____

TTRACSE   _____

CENFOLRETI   _____

Active Reading

3 Synthesize You can often define an unknown word if you know the meaning of its word parts. Use the word parts and sentence below to make an educated guess about the meanings of the words *transmit*, *transparent*, and *translucent*.

Word part	Meaning
trans-	through
-mit	send
-par	show
-luc	light

transmit: _____

_____

transparent: _____

_____

translucent: _____

Vocabulary Terms

- transparent
- translucent
- opaque
- absorption
- reflection
- refraction
- scattering

4 Apply As you learn the definition of each vocabulary term in this lesson, create your own definition or sketch to help you remember the meaning of the term.

Shedding Light

How can matter interact with light?

Interactions between light and matter produce many common but spectacular effects, such as color, reflections, and rainbows. Three forms of interaction play an especially important role in how people see light.

Matter Can Transmit Light

Recall that light and other electromagnetic waves can travel through empty space. When light encounters a material, it can be passed through the material, or transmitted. The medium can transmit all, some, or none of the light.

Matter that transmits light is **transparent** (tranz•PAHR•uhnt). Air, water, and some types of glass are transparent materials. Objects can be seen clearly through transparent materials.

Translucent (tranz•LOO•suhnt) materials transmit light but do not let the light travel straight through. The light is scattered into many different directions. As a result, you can see light through translucent materials, but objects seen through a translucent material look distorted or fuzzy. Frosted glass, some lamp shades, and tissue paper are examples of translucent materials.

Active Reading

5 Identify As you read, underline three words that describe how well matter transmits light.

Objects can be seen clearly through transparent glass.

Objects look distorted when seen through translucent glass.

Think Outside the Book

6 Discuss Write a short story in which it is important that a piece of glass is translucent or transparent.

on the Matter

Matter Can Absorb Light

Opaque (oh•PAYK) materials do not let any light pass through them. Instead, they reflect light, absorb light, or both. Many materials, such as wood, brick, or metal, are opaque. When light enters a material but does not leave it, the light is absorbed. **Absorption** is the transfer of light energy to matter.

The shirt at right absorbs the light that falls on it, and so the shirt is opaque. However, absorption is not the only way an object can be opaque.

The shirt is opaque, because light does not pass through it. We can't see the table underneath.

> **Visualize It!**

7 Explain Is the table in the photo at right transparent, translucent, or opaque? Explain how you know.

_____

_____

_____

Matter Can Reflect Light

You see an object only when light from the object enters your eye. However, most objects do not give off, or emit, light. Instead, light bounces off the object's surface. The bouncing of light off a surface is called **reflection**.

Most objects have a surface that is at least slightly rough. When light strikes a rough surface, such as wood or cloth, the light reflects in many different directions. Some of the reflected light reaches your eyes, and you see the object.

Light bounces at an angle equal to the angle at which it hit the surface. When light strikes a smooth or shiny surface such as mirror, it reflects in a uniform way. As a result, a mirror produces an image. Light from a lamp might be reflected by your skin, then be reflected by a mirror, and then enter your eye. You look at the mirror and see yourself.

> **Visualize It!**

8 Identify What is the difference between the way light interacts with the shirt above and the way light interacts with the mirror at right?

_____

_____

Light is reflected by the girl's face and by the mirror.

Color Me Impressed!

What determines the color of objects we see?

Visible light includes a range of colors. Light that includes all colors is called white light. When white light strikes an object, the object can transmit some or all of the colors of light, reflect some or all of the colors, and absorb some or all of the colors.

The Light Reflected or Absorbed

The perceived color of an object is determined by the colors of light reflected by the object. For example, a frog's skin absorbs most colors of light, but reflects most of the green light. When you look in the direction of the frog, the green light enters your eyes, so the frog appears green.

An object that reflects every color appears white. An object that absorbs every color appears black.

The frog's body is green because it reflects green light while absorbing other colors of light.

> **Think Outside the Book**
>
> **9 Diagram** Use colored pencils, crayons, or markers to draw light shining on an object. Draw arrows showing the colors of incoming light and arrows showing which colors are reflected.

The Light Transmitted

The color of a transparent or translucent object works differently than it does for opaque objects. Some materials may absorb some colors but let other colors pass through. Green plastic, for example, does not appear green because it reflects green light, but rather, because it transmits green light while absorbing other colors of light. When you look toward a bottle made of green plastic, the transmitted green light reaches your eyes. Therefore, the bottle looks green.

Some matter can absorb visible light but let other kinds of electromagnetic waves pass through. For example, radio waves can easily pass through walls that are opaque to visible light. X-rays pass through skin and muscle, but are stopped by denser bone.

The bottle is green because it allows green light to pass through while absorbing other colors of light.

The Available Light

Sometimes the perceived color of an object depends on the light available in the area. You may have been in a room with a red light bulb. The glass around the bulb filters out all colors except red, plus some orange and yellow. An object that reflects red light would still appear red under such a light bulb. But an object that absorbed all red, orange, and yellow light would appear gray or black. We can't see colors of light that aren't there to be reflected to our eyes!

Filtered Light

Below, the light from the bulb is being filtered before shining on a frog.

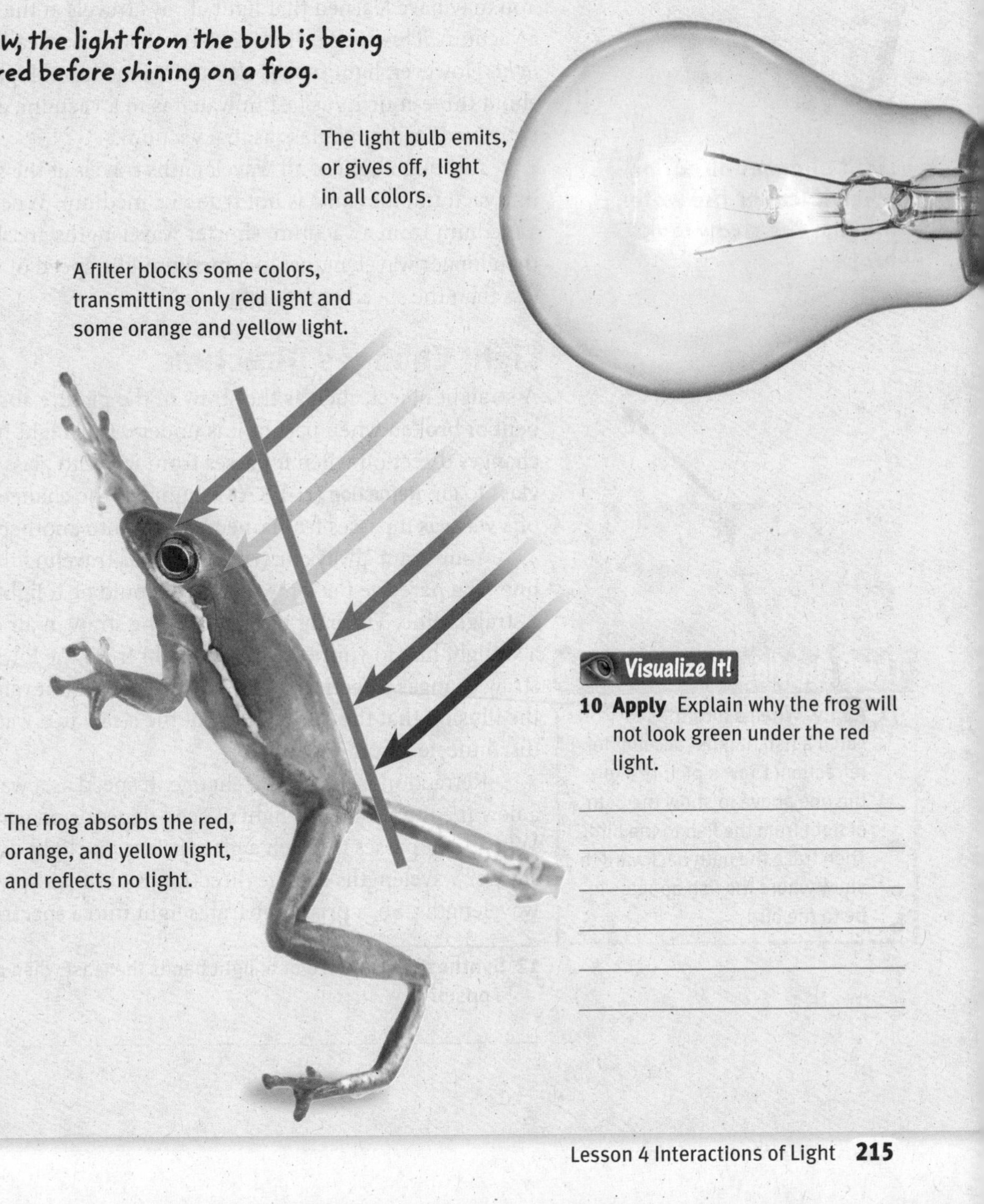

The light bulb emits, or gives off, light in all colors.

A filter blocks some colors, transmitting only red light and some orange and yellow light.

The frog absorbs the red, orange, and yellow light, and reflects no light.

Visualize It!

10 Apply Explain why the frog will not look green under the red light.

_____

_____

_____

_____

_____

_____

Matter Scatter

What happens when light waves interact with matter?

You have already learned that light can pass through a transparent medium. But when light waves pass through a medium, the medium can change properties of the light.

Light Slows When It Passes Through Matter

You may have learned that light always travels at the same speed in a vacuum. This speed, about 300,000,000 m/s, is called the *speed of light*. However, light travels slower in a medium. Light travels only about three-fourths as fast in water as in a vacuum, and only about two-thirds as fast in glass as in a vacuum.

Although light of all wavelengths travels at the same speed in a vacuum, the same is not true in a medium. When light enters a medium from a vacuum, shorter wavelengths are slowed more than longer wavelengths. In a medium, the speed of violet light is less than the speed of red light.

Light Changes Direction

A straight object, such as the straw in the picture above, looks bent or broken when part of it is underwater. Light from the straw changes direction when it passes from water to glass and from glass to air. **Refraction** (ri•FRAK•shuhn) is the change in direction of a wave as it passes from one medium into another at an angle.

Your brain always interprets light as traveling in a straight line. You perceive the straw where it would be if light traveled in a straight line. The light reflected by the straw in air does travel in a straight line to your eye. But the light from the lower part of the straw changes direction when it passes into air. It refracts, causing the illusion that the bottom part of the straw in a water glass is disconnected from the top part.

Refraction is due to the change in speed as a wave enters a new medium. In glass, light's speed depends on wavelength. When light passes through a glass prism, the light waves with shorter wavelengths change direction more than waves with longer wavelengths. So, a prism separates light into a spectrum of colors.

Light changes direction when it leaves the water, making the straw look broken.

Think Outside the Book

11 Apply When a bird tries to catch a fish, it must account for refraction. Draw a picture like the one above to show the path of light from the fish to the bird. Then trace the path backward to show where the fish appears to be to the bird.

12 Synthesize Which color of light bends the least when passing through a prism?

Light Scatters

You don't see a beam of light shining through clear air. But if the beam of light shines through fog, some of the light is sent in many different directions. Some enters your eye, and you see the beam. **Scattering** occurs when light is sent in many directions as it passes through a medium. Dust and other small particles can scatter light.

The color of the sky is due to scattered light. Particles of air scatter short wavelengths—blue and violet light—more than long wavelengths. As sunlight passes through air, blue light is scattered first. The blue light appears to come from all directions, and so the sky appears blue. When the sun is near the horizon in the sky, sunlight passes through more of the atmosphere. As the light passes through more and more air, almost all light of short wavelengths is scattered. Only the longest wavelengths are left. The sun and the sky appear yellow, orange, or red.

 **Active Reading**

13 Identify What color of light is scattered most easily by the atmosphere?

We can see the light beam coming out of the lighthouse because the fog scatters the light.

In the diagram below, the red lines represent paths of light from the sun. The white brackets show the amount of atmosphere the light must pass through to reach our eyes.

Not to scale

In the evening, sunlight travels through a lot of air. The blue light scatters, leaving only redder light.

The daytime sky appears blue because air scatters blue light more than it does other colors.

Visual Summary

To complete this summary, circle the correct word to complete each statement. Then, use the key below to check your answers. You can use this page to review the main concepts of the lesson.

Interactions of Light and Matter

Matter can transmit, reflect, or absorb light.

14 Matter that transmits no light is (transparent/translucent/opaque).

The color of an object depends on what colors of light it reflects or transmits.

15 A frog in white light appears green because it

(reflects/absorbs/transmits)

green light and

(reflects/absorbs/transmits) other colors of light.

A transparent medium can bend, scatter, or change the speed of light.

16 The bending of light is called (reflection/refraction/scattering).

Answers: 14. opaque; 15. reflects, absorbs; 16. refraction

17 **Synthesize** Suppose you are looking at a yellow fish in a fish tank. The tank is next to a window. Describe the path that light takes in order for you to see the fish, starting at the sun and ending at your eyes.

Lesson Review

Vocabulary

Fill in the blank with the term that best completes the following sentences.

1 An object appears fuzzy when seen through a(n) _____ material.

2 A(n) _____ material lets light pass through freely.

3 The bouncing of light off a surface is called _____

4 The bending of light when it changes media is called _____

5 _____ occurs when light changes direction after colliding with particles of matter.

Key Concepts

6 **Identify** For each picture below, identify the material enclosing the sandwich as transparent, translucent, or opaque.

a. _____

b. _____

c. _____

d. _____

7 **Identify** Which material in the pictures above reflects the most light?

8 **Identify** Which material in the pictures above absorbs the most light?

Critical Thinking

9 **Infer** Is a mirror's surface transparent, translucent, or opaque? How do you know?

10 **Apply** Why does a black asphalt road become hotter than a white cement sidewalk in the same amount of sunlight?

11 **Explain** Why is the sky blue?

12 **Explain** Red, green, and blue light rays each enter a drop of water from the same direction. Which light ray's path through the drop will bend the most, and which will bend the least? Why?

My Notes

Unit 3 **Summary**

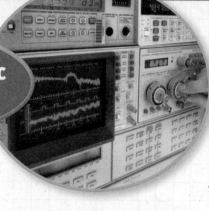

The Electromagnetic Spectrum

is arranged based on the energy of

Waves

are influenced by

Properties of Waves

are influenced by

Interactions of Light

---

1 Interpret The Graphic Organizer above shows that the properties of waves are influenced by the energy of waves. Name two properties of waves that affect the energy of waves.

_____

_____

_____

2 Predict When you look in a mirror, you see the reflection of visible light. Would you expect that ultraviolet light would be reflected by a mirror? Explain.

_____

_____

_____

3 Relate Compare the energy and wavelength of a microwave to the energy of a gamma ray.

_____

_____

_____

_____

_____

_____

4 Synthesize Is a radio wave a longitudinal wave or a transverse wave?

_____

_____

_____

Name _____

Multiple Choice

Identify the choice that best completes the statement or answers the question.

1 The visible part of the electromagnetic spectrum consists of the colors that we see in a rainbow. Each color we see corresponds to a different wavelength of light. Which color of visible light has the shortest wavelength?

   A. red

   B. green

   C. violet

   D. yellow

2 Heather puts a straw into a glass of water. She notices that when she looks through the glass and the water from the side, the straw appears to be broken. Which term **best** explains why the straw looks like it is broken?

   F. absorption

   G. refraction

   H. scattering

   I. transmission

3 The diagram below shows a wave. The features of the wave are labeled A, B, C, and D.

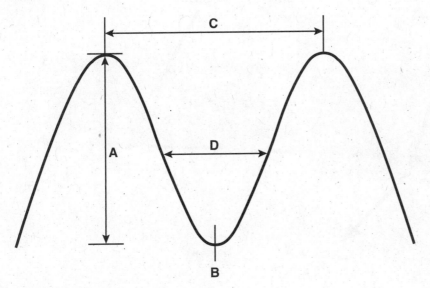

Which label identifies the wavelength?

   A. A

   B. B

   C. C

   D. D

4 The energy generated by the sun travels to Earth as electromagnetic waves. Because the radiation from the sun travels to Earth in varying wavelengths, scientists consider them to be a spectrum. Which statement describes an electromagnetic wave with a long wavelength?

F. It has a high frequency and low energy.

G. It has a high frequency and high energy.

H. It has a low frequency and can travel through a vacuum.

I. It has a low frequency and needs a medium to travel through.

5 Calvin shines a thin beam of light onto a material, and the light refracts. Which diagram **best** shows what happens to the light?

A.
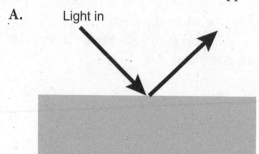

C.
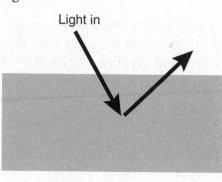

B.
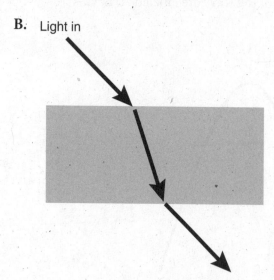

D.
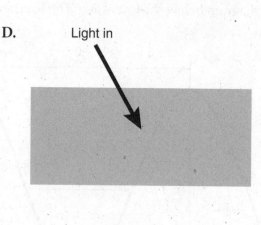

6 Kana shines a light onto paper as shown in the figure below. The light contains both blue and red wavelengths of light.

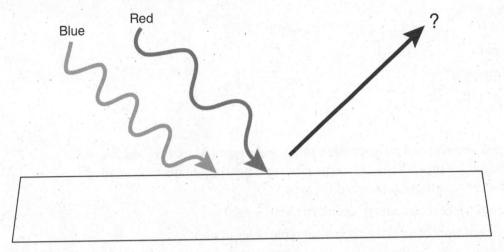

If the paper is blue, what color (or colors) of light bounces off the paper?

F. only red

G. only blue

H. both red and blue

I. neither red nor blue

7 Habib looks around his classroom at different objects. Which object reflects almost all of the light that strikes it?

A. white poster board

B. clear window glass

C. bright overhead light

D. black construction paper

8 Electromagnetic energy travels through space as waves. The electromagnetic spectrum includes all electromagnetic waves, arranged according to frequency and wavelength. Which of these is an example of an electromagnetic wave?

F. radio wave

G. sound wave

H. ocean wave

I. gravitational pull

9 Emma measured the maximum displacement of a wave that she made by moving the end of a string up and down. What property of a wave was she measuring?

- A. period
- B. frequency
- C. amplitude
- D. wavelength

10 Sonia tapped one end of a long wooden table. Sanjay and Marc listened for the sounds. Sanjay pressed his ear to the table and heard the taps that seemed louder than the taps that Marc heard. Why?

- F. More energy reached Sanjay's ear than Marc's ear.
- G. Particles of wood are farther apart than particles of air.
- H. Sound travels through air and wood at different speeds..
- I. The taps only made the table vibrate, they did not make the air vibrate.

11 Ava covers a flashlight with a piece of thick, black paper. Why doesn't she see the light when she turns on the flashlight?

- A. The paper absorbs most of the light.
- B. The paper refracts most of the light.
- C. The paper reflects most of the light.
- D. The paper transmits most of the light.

12 Caleb counts the number of ocean waves that pass the end of a pier in one minute. What property of waves does Caleb measure?

- F. wave speed
- G. frequency
- H. amplitude
- I. wavelength

Energy and Heat

Big Idea 11

Energy Transfer and Transformations

A thermogram is a special type of image that shows the relative temperatures of objects.

Sealing windows keeps the warmth inside.

What do you think?

See all the red areas in this thermogram? These areas show where energy (in the form of heat) is escaping through gaps around windows and doors. Why is it important to reduce this loss of energy from a home?

Saving Energy

Humans use many sources of energy in our everyday lives. For example, we need electricity to see at night, fuel to keep our cars running, and food to nourish our bodies. But we need to be careful in our use of energy resources. And you can help!

① Ask a Question

How can individuals avoid wasting energy resources at home?

Make a list of all the sources of energy, such as electricity or natural gas, used in your home. Then, write down what those energy sources are used for, and estimate how much your family uses them each week. For example: "We use natural gas for cooking on our stove approximately three hours each week." Can your family reduce energy consumption in any areas? Work with your family to develop your ideas.

Using a programmable thermostat can help conserve energy.

② Think About It

What is one source of energy used in your home?

_____

_____

Where is energy used most often in your school?

_____

_____

_____

_____

Where is energy used most often in your home?

_____

_____

_____

_____

What are some possible areas in the home and at school where energy usage can be easily reduced?

_____

_____

_____

_____

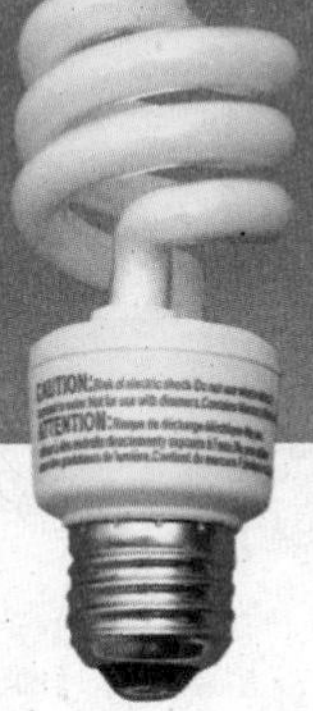

Solar panels can convert energy from the sun into a form that can be used in a home.

③ Apply Your Knowledge

A Choose some of the places you identified in your home. Develop strategies for reducing the amount of energy your family uses in those areas.

Area	Strategy

B Apply the strategies you listed above. Track how your energy usage changes as you conserve energy. Examine your utility bill if you have access to it.

_____

_____

_____

Take It Home

As a class, create an energy conservation plan for your school. Implement it in your class and track how much energy you have saved. Share your results with your school.

Energy Conversion and Conservation

ESSENTIAL QUESTION

How is energy conserved?

By the end of this lesson, you should be able to analyze how energy is conserved through transformations between different forms.

Sunshine State Standards

SC.7.P.11.2 Investigate and describe the transformation of energy from one form to another.

SC.7.P.11.3 Cite evidence to explain that energy cannot be created nor destroyed, only changed from one form to another.

MA.6.A.3.6 Construct and analyze tables, graphs, and equations to describe linear functions and other simple relations using both common language and algebraic notation.

LA.6.4.2.2 The student will record information (e.g., observations, notes, lists, charts, legends) related to a topic, including visual aids to organize and record information and include a list of sources used.

The energy in rocket fuel is changed into energy that allows this rocket to blast off.

Engage Your Brain

1 Explain Draw a diagram that shows what you think happens when a light bulb is turned on. When making your diagram, think about what happens to the energy.

2 Describe What do you know about energy? Using the first letters of the word *energy*, make an acrostic poem that describes energy.

E _____

N _____

E _____

R _____

G _____

Y _____

Active Reading

3 Apply Many scientific terms, such as *transformation* and *efficiency*, also have everyday meanings. Use context clues to write your own definition for each underlined word.

Example sentence
After she learned how to play soccer, she went through a complete <u>transformation</u>. Now she practices every day.

transformation:

_____

_____

Example sentence
He finished all of his homework in two hours, and he got everything correct. I wish that I could work with such <u>efficiency</u>.

efficiency:

_____

_____

Vocabulary Terms

- energy transformation
- law of conservation of energy
- efficiency

4 Apply As you learn the definition of each vocabulary term in this lesson, create your own definition or sketch to help you remember the meaning of the term.

What are some forms of energy?

Remember that energy is the ability to cause change. Energy is measured in joules (J). Energy can come in many different forms. Some common forms of energy are discussed below.

> **Active Reading** **5 Identify** As you read, underline examples of energy provided in the text.

Mechanical Energy

Mechanical energy is the sum of an object's kinetic energy and potential energy. The energy that a car has while moving is mechanical energy, as is the energy a book has on top of a desk.

Sound Energy

Sound energy results from the vibration of particles. People are able to detect these tiny vibrations with structures in their ears that vibrate due to the sound. When you hear a car, you are detecting vibrations in the air that transfer sound energy. Sound cannot travel through empty space. If there were no air or other substance between you and the car, then you would not hear sounds from the car.

Electromagnetic Energy

Electromagnetic (ee•LEK•troh•mag•NEH•tik) energy is transmitted through space in the form of electromagnetic waves. Electromagnetic waves can be produced by the vibration of electrically-charged particles. Unlike sound, electromagnetic waves can travel through empty space. Light energy is a form of electromagnetic energy. Some examples of electromagnetic energy are visible light, x-rays, and microwaves. X-rays are high-energy waves used by doctors to look at your bones. Microwaves can be used to cook food. The sun releases a large amount of electromagnetic energy, some of which is absorbed by Earth.

The piccolo player is producing sound energy.

Microwaves use electromagnetic energy to warm food.

This solar flare is an example of many forms of energy. The solar flare releases electromagnetic energy and heat energy produced by nuclear energy in the sun.

Chemical Energy

Chemical energy is the energy stored in chemical bonds that hold chemical compounds together. If a molecule's bonds are broken or rearranged, energy is released or absorbed. Chemical energy can be stored in food and in matches.

Thermal Energy and Heat

Thermal energy is the energy an object has due to the motion of its molecules. The faster the molecules in an object move, the more thermal energy the object has. Heat is the energy transferred from an object at a higher temperature to an object at a lower temperature.

Nuclear Energy

The nucleus of an atom is the source of nuclear (NOO•klee•uhr) energy. When an atom's nucleus breaks apart, or when the nuclei of two small atoms join together, energy is released. The energy given off by the sun comes from nuclear energy. In the sun, hydrogen nuclei join to make a helium nucleus. This reaction gives off a huge amount of energy. The sun's light and heat come from these reactions. Without nuclear energy from the sun, life would not exist on Earth.

7 Categorize Fill in the blank parts of the chart below.

Example	Type of Energy
Bicycle going up a hill	
	Electromagnetic
Orchestra music	

ghton Mifflin Harcourt Publishing Company • Image Credits: (bkgd) ©NASA

Think Outside the Book

6 Apply Keep a journal of ten examples of energy that you see throughout the day. Classify each example as mechanical, sound, electromagnetic, chemical, thermal, or nuclear.

Transformers

What is an energy transformation?

An **energy transformation** takes place when energy changes from one form into another form. Any form of energy can change into any other form of energy. Often, one form of energy changes into more than one form. For example, when you rub your hands together, you hear a sound and your hands get warm. The kinetic energy of your moving hands was transformed into both sound energy and thermal energy.

Another example of an energy transformation is when chemical energy is converted in the body. Why is eating breakfast so important? Eating breakfast gives your body the energy needed to help you start your day. Your chemical potential energy comes from the food you eat. Your body breaks down the components of the food to access the energy contained in them. This energy is then changed to the kinetic energy in your muscles. Some of the chemical energy is converted into thermal energy that allows your body to stay warm.

 Visualize It!

Some examples of energy transformation are illustrated in this flashlight. Follow the captions to learn how energy is transformed into the light energy that you rely on when you turn on a flashlight!

Batteries

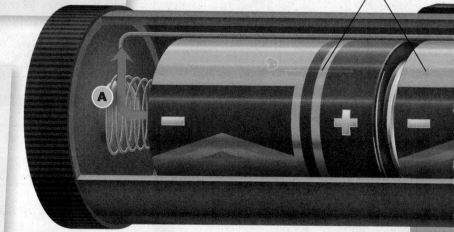

A The chemical energy from the batteries is transformed into electrical energy.

8 Describe Give two other examples of chemical energy being transformed into electrical energy.

_____

_____

_____

_____

Is energy conserved?

A closed system is a group of objects that transfer energy only to one another. For example, a roller coaster can be considered a closed system if it includes everything involved, such as the track, the cars, and the air around them. Energy is conserved in all closed systems. The **law of conservation of energy** states that energy cannot be created or destroyed. It can only change forms. All of the different forms of energy in a closed system always add up to the same total amount of energy. It does not matter how many energy conversions take place.

For example, on a roller coaster some mechanical energy gets transformed into sound and thermal energy as it goes down a hill. The total of the coaster's reduced mechanical energy at the bottom of the hill, the increased thermal energy, and the sound energy, is the same amount of energy as the original amount of mechanical energy. In other words, total energy is conserved.

Active Reading 10 **Relate** How are energy transformations related to the law of conservation of energy?

_____

_____

_____

_____

Think Outside the Book **Inquiry**

11 **Apply** Have you ever thought about how a music player works? What form of energy is used to power a music player? What form of energy do you use from a music player? Can you think of any other forms of energy that may be used inside of a music player?

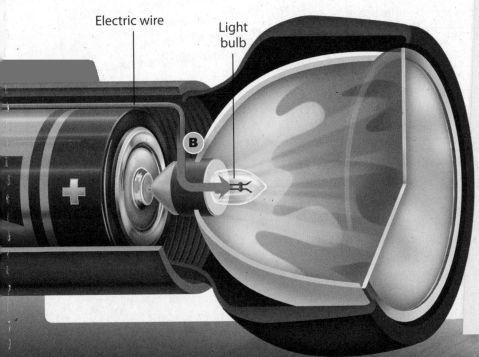

Electric wire

Light bulb

B

B The electrical energy in the wire is transformed into light energy in the light bulb. Some of the electrical energy is also transferred to the surroundings as heat.

9 **Describe** Give another example of electrical energy being transformed into light energy.

_____

_____

_____

_____

Efficiency Expert!

How is efficiency measured?

When energy is transformed from one form to another form, some energy is turned into useful energy, but some energy is always transformed into an unintended form. One of the most common unintended forms of energy in an energy transformation is heat. No transformation can ever be 100% efficient. **Efficiency** (ee•FIH•shuhn•see) is the ratio of useful output energy to input energy. Energy efficiency is a comparison of the amount of useful energy after a conversion with the amount of energy before a conversion. Energy efficiency is highly desirable in any system. An efficient process means that as much energy as possible is converted to useful forms of energy. You may have heard that a car is energy efficient if it gets good gas mileage, and that your home may be energy efficient if it is well insulated. Energy conversions that are more efficient waste fewer resources.

Active Reading **12 Explain** How does the scientific use of the word *efficiency* differ from the everyday use of the word?

_____

_____

_____

unwanted sound energy

unwanted heat energy

The chemical energy in a laptop battery is converted into electrical energy that runs the machine. However, some of the energy is converted into unwanted heat and sound energy.

Using a Ratio

Efficiency is the ratio of useful output energy to input energy.

$$\text{Percent efficiency} = \frac{\text{Energy out}}{\text{Energy in}} \times 100\%$$

Energy efficiency is expressed as a percentage. Improving the efficiency of machines is important because greater efficiency results in less waste. If less energy is wasted, less energy is needed to operate a machine. We can use calculations of efficiency to compare different machines to see which is more efficient.

Do the Math

Sample Problem

An old refrigerator required 400 J of energy to give out 50 J of energy. What is its efficiency?

Identify

A. What do you know?

Energy in = 400 J, Energy out = 50 J

B. What do you want to find out? Efficiency

Plan

C. Draw and label a sketch:

400 J ⟶ [ ] ⟶ 50 J

D. Write the formula:

Efficiency = (Energy out / Energy in) × 100%

E. Substitute into the formula:

Efficiency = (50 J / 400 J) × 100%

Solve

F. Calculate and simplify: Efficiency =
(50 J / 400 J) × 100% = 12.5%

G. Check that your units agree:

Answer is a percentage. Efficiency is also a percentage. Units agree.

Answer: 12.5%

You Try It

13 Calculate You would like to replace the refrigerator from the previous problem with a more efficient model. One option requires 300 J of energy and gives out 50 J of energy. What is this refrigerator's efficiency? Is it more efficient than the refrigerator in the previous problem?

Identify

A. What do you know?

B. What do you want to find out?

Plan

C. Draw and label a sketch:

D. Write the formula:

E. Substitute into the formula:

Solve

F. Calculate and simplify:

G. Check that your units agree:

Answer:

This old refrigerator is not as efficient as many new refrigerators that are made today.

Visual Summary

To complete this summary, fill in the blanks with the correct word or phrase. Then, use the key below to check your answers. You can use this page to review the main concepts of the lesson.

Energy Conversions

Energy can come in many different forms such as mechanical energy, sound energy, electromagnetic energy, thermal energy, chemical energy, and nuclear energy.

14 A dog running through the yard is an example of _____ energy.

15 Energy is measured in units called _____

One form of energy can transform into another form of energy.

16 Energy cannot be _____ or _____

17 Energy in a flashlight's battery changes from _____ energy to electrical energy.

Efficiency is a ratio of useful output energy to input energy.

$$\text{Percent efficiency} = \left(\frac{\text{Energy out}}{\text{Energy in}} \right) \times 100\%$$

18 No energy transformation can ever be _____ efficient.

19 A common form of unwanted energy in an energy transformation is _____

unwanted sound energy

unwanted heat energy

20 **Apply** Describe a process in which energy changes forms at least twice. Are there any unwanted forms of energy that are produced during the energy transformations?

Lesson Review

Vocabulary

In your own words, define the following terms.

1 Law of conservation of energy:

_____

_____

2 Efficiency:

_____

_____

Key Concepts

3 Contrast Describe the difference between nuclear energy and light energy.

_____

_____

4 Provide Give an example of an energy conversion. Make sure to discuss which forms of energy are involved.

_____

_____

5 Describe Give an example of an energy conversion that produces an unwanted form of energy.

_____

_____

6 Calculate Suppose a vacuum cleaner uses 120 J of electrical energy. If 45 J are used to pull air into the vacuum cleaner, how efficient is the vacuum cleaner?

_____

_____

_____

_____

_____

_____

Use this photo to answer the following questions.

7 Analyze List one example of each of the following forms of energy found in the photo.

sound energy:

_____

chemical energy:

_____

mechanical energy:

_____

8 Analyze List two examples of energy transformations necessary for the sporting event to take place.

_____

_____

_____

Critical Thinking

9 Relate Consider the statement "You can move parts of your body because of energy from the sun." Describe a series of energy conversions that supports this idea.

_____

_____

_____

_____

Temperature

ESSENTIAL QUESTION

How is temperature related to kinetic energy?

By the end of this lesson, you should be able to relate the temperature of a substance to the kinetic energy of its particles.

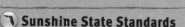

Sunshine State Standards

SC.7.P.11.1 Recognize that adding heat to or removing heat from a system may result in a temperature change and possibly a change of state.

SC.7.P.11.4 Observe and describe that heat flows in predictable ways, moving from warmer objects to cooler ones until they reach the same temperature.

What does it mean to be hot or cold? You can tell that this environment is cold because there is ice and because the person is in a hat and coat.

Engage Your Brain

1 Predict Check T or F to show whether you think each statement is true or false.

T F

☐ ☐ Solids and liquids are made of particles, but gases are made of air, which is not made of particles.

☐ ☐ Kinetic energy is the energy of motion.

☐ ☐ Kinetic energy depends on mass and speed.

2 Illustrate Think about a time when you were very cold. Then draw a picture of a time when you were very hot. Write a caption about the differences between the two situations.

Active Reading

3 Synthesize Many English words have their roots in other languages. Use the Greek words below to make an educated guess about the meaning of the word *thermometer*. A context sentence is provided for help. Then, write a sentence using the word correctly.

Greek word	Meaning
thermos	warm
metron	to measure

Example sentence
This <u>thermometer</u> indicates that it is 72 °F in this room.

Define thermometer:

_____

_____

Sentence with thermometer:

_____

_____

_____

Vocabulary Terms

- **kinetic theory of matter**
- **temperature**
- **degree**
- **thermometer**

4 Identify This list contains the key terms you'll learn in this lesson. As you read, circle the definition of each term.

Particle Party

What is the kinetic theory of matter?

All matter is made of atoms. These particles are always moving, even if it doesn't look like they are. The **kinetic theory of matter** states that all of the particles that make up matter are constantly in motion. Because the particles are in motion, they have kinetic energy. The faster the particles are moving, the more kinetic energy they have.

While the particles of matter are constantly moving, the particles move in different directions and at different speeds. This motion is random. Therefore, the individual particles of matter have different amounts of kinetic energy. The average kinetic energy of all these particles takes into account their different random movements. As seen in this picture, solids, liquids, and gases have different average kinetic energies.

This bridge is a solid, so its particles are close together and vibrate.

In this hot pool, the liquid particles are moving around.

The particles in the gas in the air are far apart and moving quickly.

The particles in this cold river water are moving freely.

How do particles move in solids, liquids, and gases?

The kinetic theory of matter explains the motion of particles in solids, liquids, and gases.

- The particles in a solid, such as concrete, are not free to move around very much. They vibrate back and forth in the same position and are held tightly together by forces of attraction.
- The particles in a liquid, such as water in a pool, move much more freely than particles in a solid. They are constantly sliding around and tumbling over each other as they move.
- In a gas, such as the air around you, particles are far apart and move around at high speeds. Particles collide with one another, but otherwise they do not interact much.

Active Reading **5 Describe** In your own words, describe the difference between the movement of particles in liquids and the movement of particles in gases.

_____
_____
_____
_____

Visualize It!

6 Illustrate Locate another solid, liquid, or gas in this photo. Sketch a representation of the particles that make up the solid, liquid, or gas. Make sure to indicate how fast you think the particles might be moving based on temperature. Then, write a caption describing the particle movement.

_____
_____
_____
_____

Mercury Rising

How does temperature relate to kinetic energy?

Temperature (TEM•per•uh•chur) is a measure of the average kinetic energy of all the particles in an object. In the picture on the previous page, the particle diagrams for two different liquids are shown. For the colder liquid, the particles are moving slower. For the warmer liquid, the particles are moving faster. If an iron is hot, the particles in the solid are vibrating very fast and have a high average kinetic energy. If the iron has a low temperature, the particles in the solid are vibrating more slowly and have a lower average kinetic energy.

How is temperature measured?

You know that the particles in a substance have a greater kinetic energy at a warmer temperature. How is temperature measured and what does that measurement mean? Suppose you hear on the radio that the temperature outside is 30 degrees. Do you need to wear a warm coat to spend the day outside? The answer depends on the temperature scale being used. There are three common temperature scales, all of which measure the average kinetic energy of particles. These scales are called Celsius, Fahrenheit, and Kelvin. However, 30 degrees on one scale is quite different from 30 degrees on the other scales.

To establish a temperature scale, two known values and the number of units between the values are needed. The freezing and boiling points of pure water are often used as the standard values. These points are always the same under the same conditions, and they are easy to reproduce. In the Celsius and Fahrenheit scales, temperature is measured in units called degrees. **Degrees** (°) are equally spaced units between two points. The space between degrees can vary from scale to scale. In the Kelvin scale, no degree sign is used. Instead, the unit is just called a kelvin. Temperature is measured using an instrument called a **thermometer**.

Active Reading **7 Explain** How does a substance's temperature change when the average kinetic energy of its particles increases? When it decreases?

_____

_____

_____

Think Outside the Book **Inquiry**

8 Produce Write a story about someone who travels from one extreme temperature to another. Make sure to talk about how your character adjusts to the change in temperature. How are the character's daily activities or decisions affected?

Celsius Scale

The temperature scale most commonly used around the world, and often used by scientists, is the Celsius (SEL•see•uhs) scale (°C). This scale was developed in the 1740s by Anders Celsius. On the Celsius scale, pure water freezes at 0 °C and boils at 100 °C, so there are 100 degrees—100 equal units—between these two temperatures.

Fahrenheit Scale

The scale used most commonly in the United States for measuring temperature is the Fahrenheit scale (°F). It was developed in the early 1700s by Gabriel Fahrenheit. On the Fahrenheit scale, pure water freezes at 32 °F and boils at 212 °F. Thus, there are 180 degrees—180 equal units— between the freezing point and the boiling point of water.

Kelvin Scale

A temperature scale used commonly by physicists is the Kelvin scale. This scale was not officially developed until the 20th century. The equal units in the Kelvin scale are called kelvins, not degrees. On the kelvin scale, pure water freezes at 273 K and boils at 373 K. There are 100 kelvins—100 equal units—between these two temperatures.

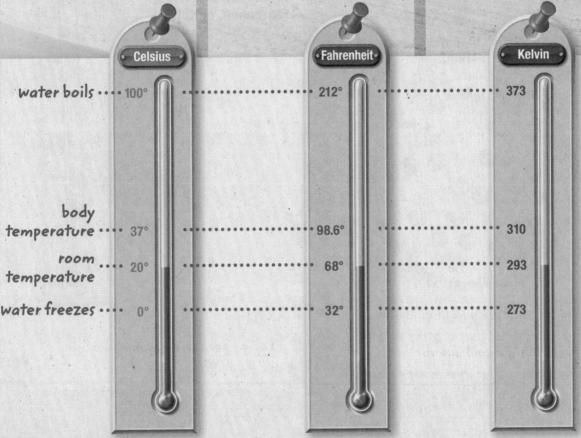

	Celsius	Fahrenheit	Kelvin
water boils	100°	212°	373
body temperature	37°	98.6°	310
room temperature	20°	68°	293
water freezes	0°	32°	273

Visualize It!

9 Identify What is body temperature in the Celsius scale? In the Fahrenheit scale? In the Kelvin scale?

_____

_____

_____

_____

10 Apply The water in swimming pools is typically about 80 °F. Mark this temperature on the Fahrenheit thermometer above. Estimate what temperature this is in the Celsius and Kelvin scales.

_____

_____

_____

Visual Summary

To complete this summary, fill in the blanks with the correct word. Then use the key below to check your answers. You can use this page to review the main concepts of the lesson.

Temperature

Temperature is a measure of the average kinetic energy of all the particles in an object. Temperature is measured using one of three scales: Celsius, Fahrenheit, or Kelvin.

Fahrenheit

212°

98.6°

68°

32°

All of the particles that make up matter are constantly in motion.

11 The particles in a hot liquid move _____ than the particles in a cold liquid.

12 Temperature is measured using a _____ .

13 Infer If a puddle of water is frozen, do particles in the ice have kinetic energy? Explain.

Lesson Review

Vocabulary

For each pair of terms, write a sentence using both words that demonstrates the definition of each word.

1 Kinetic theory of matter and temperature

_____

_____

_____

_____

2 Thermometer and degree

_____

_____

_____

_____

_____

Key Concepts

3 Relate Describe the relationship between temperature and kinetic energy.

_____

_____

_____

4 Apply Particles in a warmer substance have a _____ average kinetic energy than particles in the substance when it is cooler.

5 Identify What are the three scales used to measure temperature? What are the units of each scale?

_____

_____

_____

_____

Critical Thinking

Use the art below to answer the following questions.

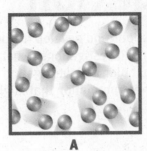 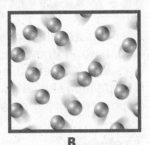

A　　　　　　　　B

6 Observe Which illustration represents the substance at a higher temperature? Explain.

_____

_____

_____

7 Predict What would happen to the particles in illustration A if the substance were chilled? What would happen if the particles in illustration B were warmed?

_____

_____

_____

_____

_____

8 Apply Using your knowledge of the difference between the three different temperature scales, what do you think would happen if a human's body temperature was 98.6 °C? Why do doctors worry more about a fever of a couple of degrees Celsius than a fever of a couple of degrees Fahrenheit?

_____

_____

_____

_____

_____

Planning an Investigation

Scientists ask many questions and develop hypotheses about the natural world. They conduct investigations to help answer these questions. A scientist must plan an investigation carefully. The investigation should gather information that might support or disprove the hypothesis.

Tutorial

Use the following steps to help plan an investigation.

① Write a hypothesis.
The hypothesis should offer an explanation for the question that you are asking. The hypothesis must also be testable. If it is not testable, rewrite the hypothesis.

② Identify and list the possible variables in your experiment.
Select the independent variable and the dependent variable. In your investigation, you will change the independent variable to see any effect it may have on the dependent variable.

③ List the materials that you will need to perform the experiment.
This list should also include equipment that you need for safety.

④ Determine the method you will use to test your hypothesis.
Clearly describe the steps you will follow. If you change any part of the procedure while you are conducting the investigation, record the change. Another scientist should be able to follow your procedure to repeat your investigation.

⑤ Analyze the results.
Your data and observations from all of your experiments should be recorded carefully and clearly to maintain credibility. Record how you analyze your results so others can review your work and spot any problems or errors in your analysis.

⑥ Draw conclusions.
Describe what the results of the investigation show. Tell whether the results support your hypothesis.

Sunshine State Standards

SC.7.N.1.1 Define a problem from the seventh grade curriculum, use appropriate reference materials to support scientific understanding, plan and carry out scientific investigation of various types, such as systematic observations or experiments, identify variables, collect and organize data, interpret data in charts, tables, and graphics, analyze information, make predictions, and defend conclusions.

LA.6.4.2.2 The student will record information (e.g., observations, notes, lists, charts, legends) related to a topic, including visual aids to organize and record information and include a list of sources used.

You Try It!

You are a member of a research team that is trying to design and test a system that can protect an ice cube from melting. The system also has to be small enough to fit inside a milk carton. Therefore, you need to find an answer to the following question: What type of material will minimize the rate of melting of the ice cube?

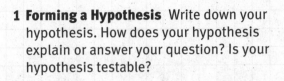

1 Forming a Hypothesis Write down your hypothesis. How does your hypothesis explain or answer your question? Is your hypothesis testable?

_____

_____

_____

_____

2 Identifying Variables List the possible variables in this experiment. Identify which variable you will be changing and which variable you will look at to see the effect.

_____

_____

_____

_____

3 Selecting Materials What equipment and tools will you need to test this variable? What might happen if you select inappropriate tools?

_____

_____

_____

_____

4 Testing Your Hypothesis What will your system look like? Will it support your testing? You may sketch the system below or on a separate page.

_____

_____

5 Planning Your Procedure What steps will you need to follow in order to test your hypothesis? What kinds of measurements will you collect? What kind of graphic organizer will you use to record your information?

_____

_____

_____

_____

_____

6 Drawing Conclusions What conclusions can you draw from your data? Was your hypothesis useful?

_____

_____

_____

_____

Take It Home

Look closely at objects and materials in your home. Write a list of things that help to prevent the transfer of thermal energy. Design an investigation using one or more of these items to learn more about the job they do. Record your observations. Evaluate your results to see if they might point to a further investigation or an improvement to a product. Present your results in a pamphlet.

Thermal Energy and Heat

ESSENTIAL QUESTION

What is the relationship between heat and temperature?

By the end of this lesson, you should be able to analyze the relationship between heat, temperature, and thermal energy.

Sunshine State Standards

SC.7.N.1.1 Define a problem from the seventh grade curriculum, use appropriate reference materials to support scientific understanding, plan and carry out scientific investigation of various types, such as systematic observations or experiments, identify variables, collect and organize data, interpret data in charts, tables, and graphics, analyze information, make predictions, and defend conclusions.

SC.7.P.11.1 Recognize that adding heat to or removing heat from a system may result in a temperature change and possibly a change of state.

SC.7.P.11.4 Observe and describe that heat flows in predictable ways, moving from warmer objects to cooler ones until they reach the same temperature.

LA.6.2.2.3 The student will organize information to show understanding (e.g., representing main ideas within text through charting, mapping, paraphrasing, summarizing, or comparing/contrasting).

The Afar Depression, in Eastern Africa, is one of the hottest places on Earth. In the summer, temperatures average over 100 °F!

Engage Your Brain

1 Describe Fill in the blanks with the words that you think correctly complete the following sentences.

When you put your hands on a cold object, like a glass of ice water, your hands become _____ The glass of water becomes _____ if you leave your hands on it for a long time. If you leave the glass of ice water out in the sun, the ice will start to _____

2 Describe Write your own caption for this photo.

_____
_____
_____
_____

3 Apply Many scientific words, such as *conductor*, also have everyday meanings. Use context clues to write your own definition for each meaning of the word *conductor*.

Example Sentence
That school's band is very good because their <u>conductor</u> is a great teacher.

Conductor:

_____
_____

Example Sentence
That metal spoon is a good <u>conductor</u>, so it will get hot if you put it into boiling soup.

Conductor:

_____
_____

Vocabulary Terms

- **thermal energy**
- **heat**
- **calorie**
- **conduction**
- **conductor**
- **insulator**
- **convection**
- **radiation**

4 Apply As you learn the definition of each vocabulary term in this lesson, create your own definition or sketch to help you remember the meaning of the term.

There are more water molecules in this lake than in the glass of water on the right.

What is thermal energy?

Thermal energy is the total kinetic energy of all particles in a substance. In the SI system, thermal energy is measured in joules (J). Remember that temperature is not energy, but it does give a measure of the average kinetic energy of all the particles in a substance. If you have two identical glasses of water and one is at a higher temperature than the other, the particles in the hotter water have a higher average kinetic energy. The water at a higher temperature will have a higher amount of thermal energy.

What is the difference between thermal energy and temperature?

Temperature and thermal energy are different from each other. Temperature is related to the average kinetic energy of particles, while thermal energy is the total kinetic energy of all the particles. A glass of water can have the same temperature as Lake Superior, but the lake has much more thermal energy because the lake contains many more water molecules.

After you put ice cubes into a pitcher of lemonade, energy is transferred from the warmer lemonade to the colder ice. The lemonade's thermal energy decreases and the ice's thermal energy increases. Because the particles in the lemonade have transferred some of their energy to the particles in the ice, the average kinetic energy of the particles in the lemonade decreases. Thus, the temperature of the lemonade decreases.

Active Reading **5 Explain** What are two factors that determine the thermal energy of a substance?

_____

_____

Under Where?

There are fewer water molecules in this glass than in the lake.

6 Apply For each object pair in the table below, circle the object that has more thermal energy. Assume that both objects are at the same temperature.

bowl of soup	small balloon	tiger
pot of soup	large balloon	house cat

Heat It Up!

What is heat?

You might think of the word *heat* as having to do with things that feel hot. But heat also has to do with things that feel cold. Heat causes objects to feel hot or cold or to get hot or cold under the right conditions. You probably use the word *heat* every day to mean different things. However, in science, **heat** is the energy transferred from an object at a higher temperature to an object at a lower temperature.

When two objects at different temperatures come into contact, energy is always transferred from the object that has the higher temperature to the object that has the lower temperature. Energy in the form of heat always flows from hot to cold. For example, if you put an ice cube into a glass of water, energy is transferred from the warmer water to the colder ice cube.

Energy in the form of heat flows from the warm drinks to the cold ice. The ice melts.

---

7 Apply For each object pair in the table below, draw an arrow in the direction in which energy in the form of heat would flow.

Object 1	Direction of heat flow	Object 2
metal rod		fire
hat		snowman
ice cube		glass of warm water

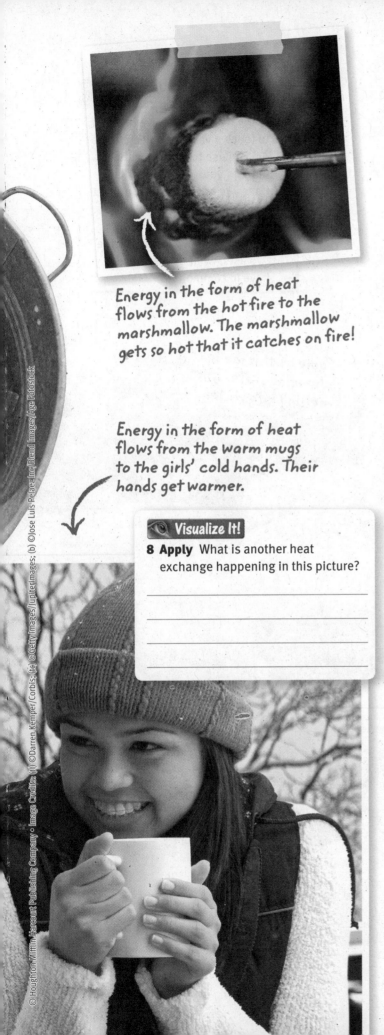

Energy in the form of heat flows from the hot fire to the marshmallow. The marshmallow gets so hot that it catches on fire!

Energy in the form of heat flows from the warm mugs to the girls' cold hands. Their hands get warmer.

Visualize It!

8 Apply What is another heat exchange happening in this picture?

_____

_____

_____

_____

How is heat measured?

Heat is measured in two ways. One way is the calorie (cal). One **calorie** is equal to the amount of energy needed to raise the temperature of 1 g of water by 1 °C. Heat can also be measured in joules (J) because heat is a form of energy. One calorie is equal to 4.18 J.

You probably think of calories in terms of food. However, in nutrition, one Calorie—written with a capital C—is actually one kilocalorie, or 1,000 calories. This means that one Calorie (Cal) contains enough energy to raise the temperature of 1 kg of water by 1 °C. Each Calorie in food contains 1,000 cal of energy.

To find out how many Calories are in an apple, the apple is burned inside an instrument called a calorimeter. A thermometer measures the increase in temperature, which is used to calculate how much energy is released. This amount is the number of Calories.

How is heat related to thermal energy?

Adding or removing heat from a substance will affect its temperature and thermal energy. Heat, however, is not the same as thermal energy and temperature. These are properties of a substance. Heat is the energy involved when these properties change.

Think of what happens when two objects at different temperatures come into contact. Energy as heat flows from the object at the higher temperature to the object at the lower temperature. When both objects come to the same temperature, no more energy as heat flows. Just because the temperature of the two objects is the same does not mean they have the same thermal energy. One object may be larger than the other and thus have more particles in motion.

Active Reading **9 Relate** What will happen if two objects at different temperatures come into contact?

_____

_____

_____

How can heat affect the state of an object?

The matter that makes up a frozen juice bar is the same whether the juice bar is frozen or has melted. The matter is just in a different form, or state. Remember that the kinetic theory of matter states that the particles that make up matter move around at different speeds. The state of a substance depends on the speed of its particles. Adding energy in the form of heat to a substance may result in a change of state. The added energy may cause the bonds between particles to break. This is what allows the state to change. Adding energy in the form of heat to a chunk of glacier may cause the ice to melt into water. Removing energy in the form of heat from a substance may also result in a change of state.

Active Reading **11 Predict** What are two ways to change the state of a substance?

_____

_____

© Houghton Mifflin Harcourt Publishing Company • Image Credits: ©Arcticphoto /Alamy

Think Outside the Book **Inquiry**

10 Compare Have you ever needed to touch a very hot object? What did you use to touch it without burning yourself? Make a list. Have you ever needed to protect yourself from being cold? What sorts of things did you use? Make a list. Now, looking at the two lists, what do the things have in common?

Some of this ice is changing state. It is melting into water.

How do polar bears stay warm?

Keep Your Cool

What is conduction?

There are three main ways to transfer energy as heat: conduction, convection, and radiation. **Conduction** is the transfer of energy as heat from one substance to another through direct contact. It occurs any time that objects at different temperatures come into contact with each other. The average kinetic energy of particles in the warmer object is greater than the average kinetic energy of the particles in the cooler object. As the particles collide, some of the kinetic energy of the particles in the warmer object is transferred to the cooler object. As long as the objects are in contact, conduction continues until the temperatures of the objects are equal.

Conduction can also occur within a single object. In this case, energy in the form of heat is transferred from the warmer part of the object to the cooler part of the object. Imagine you put a metal spoon into a cup of hot cocoa. Energy will be conducted from the warm end of the spoon to the cool end until the temperature of the entire spoon is the same.

Conductors

Some materials transfer the kinetic energy of particles better than others. A **conductor** is a material that transfers heat very well. Metals are typically good conductors. You know that when one end of a metal object gets hot, the other end quickly becomes hot as well. Consider pots or pans that have metal handles. A metal handle becomes too hot to touch soon after the pan is placed on a hot stove.

Insulators

An **insulator** (IN•suh•lay•ter) is a material that is a poor conductor of heat. Some examples of insulators are wood, paper, and plastic foam. Plastic foam is a good insulator because it contains many small spaces that are filled with air. A plastic foam cup will not easily transfer energy in the form of heat by conduction. That is why plastic foam is often used to keep hot drinks hot. Think about the metal pan handle mentioned above. It can be dangerous to have handles get hot so quickly. Instead, pot handles are often made of an insulator, such as wood or plastic. Although a plastic handle will also get hot when the pot is on the stove, it takes a much longer time for it to get hot than it would for a metal handle.

---

12 Classify Decide whether each object below is a conductor or an insulator. Then check the correct box.

Flannel shirt	☐ Conductor ☐ Insulator
Iron skillet	☐ Conductor ☐ Insulator
Copper pipe	☐ Conductor ☐ Insulator
Oven mitt	☐ Conductor ☐ Insulator

This is a photo of polar bear hair magnified about 350 times! Notice that it is hollow inside. The air inside is a good insulator.

13 Identify As you read, underline examples of heat transfer.

This pot of boiling water shows how convection currents move.

What is convection?

Energy in the form of heat can also be transferred through the movement of gases or liquids. **Convection** (kuhn•VEK•shuhn) is the transfer of energy as heat by the movement of a liquid or gas. In most substances, as temperature increases, the density of the liquid or gas decreases. Convection occurs when a cooler, denser mass of a gas or liquid replaces a warmer, less dense mass of a gas or liquid by pushing it upward.

When you boil water in a pot, the water moves in roughly circular patterns because of convection. The water at the bottom of the pot gets hot because there is a source of heat at the bottom. As the water heats, it becomes less dense. The warmer water rises through the denser, cooler water above it. At the surface, the warm water begins to cool. The particles move closer together, making the water denser. The cooler water then sinks back to the bottom, is heated again, and the cycle repeats. This cycle causes a circular motion of liquids or gases. The motion is due to density differences that result from temperature differences. The motion is called a *convection current*.

What is radiation?

Radiation is another way in which heat can be transferred. **Radiation** is the transfer of energy by electromagnetic waves. Some examples of electromagnetic waves include visible light, microwaves, and infrared light. The sun is the most significant source of radiation that you experience on a daily basis. However, all objects—even you—emit radiation and release energy.

When radiation is emitted from one object and then absorbed by another, the result is often a transfer of heat. Like conduction and convection, radiation can transfer heat from warmer to cooler objects. However, radiation differs from conduction and convection in a very significant way. Radiation can travel through empty space, as it does when it moves from the sun to Earth.

14 Classify Fill in the blanks in the chart below.

Example	Conduction, Convection, or Radiation
When you put some food in the microwave, it gets hot.	
	Conduction
A heater on the first floor of the school makes the air on the second floor warm.	

Practical Uses of Radiation

Do you think that you could cook your food using the energy from the sun? Using a device called a solar cooker, you could! A solar cooker works by concentrating the radiation from the sun into a small area using mirrors. Solar cookers aren't just fun to use—they also help some people eat clean food!

As a hobby
This woman demonstrates how her solar cooker works. Many people like to use solar cookers because they do not require any fuel. They also do not release any emissions that are harmful to the planet.

In a refugee camp
This woman, who lives in a refugee camp in Sudan, is making tea with water that she boiled in a solar cooker. For many people living far from electricity or a source of clean water, a solar cooker provides a cheap and portable way to sterilize their water. This helps to prevent disease.

Extend

Inquiry

15 Identify Two examples of radiation are shown in the photos above. What is the source of the radiation in the examples?

16 Relate Research other places throughout the world where solar cookers are being used.

17 Produce Explain how solar cookers are useful to society by doing one of the following:
• Make a solar cooker and demonstrate how it works.
• Write a story about a family who uses a solar cooker to stay healthy and safe.

Visual Summary

To complete this summary, circle the correct word or phrase. Then use the key below to check your answers. You can use this page to review the main concepts of the lesson.

Thermal energy is the total kinetic energy of all particles in a substance.

18 If two objects are at the same temperature, the one with more / fewer / the same amount of particles will have a higher thermal energy.

Heat is the energy transferred from an object at a higher temperature to an object at a lower temperature.

19 Heat always flows from cold to hot / hot to cold / left to right.

Heat can change the state of a substance.

20 Adding heat to an object causes bonds between particles to form / break / combine. This is what allows the state change.

Heat

There are three main ways to transfer energy as heat: conduction, convection, and radiation.

conduction

convection

radiation

21 Conduction is the transfer of energy from a warmer object to a cooler object through a gas / empty space / direct contact.

22 Energy from the sun travels to Earth through conduction / convection / radiation.

Answers: 18 more; 19 hot to cold; 20 break; 21 direct contact; 22 radiation

23 Conclude Suppose you are outside on a hot day and you move into the shade of a tree. Which form of energy transfer are you avoiding? Explain.

Lesson Review

Vocabulary

In your own words, define the following terms.

1 heat

_____

_____

_____

2 thermal energy

_____

_____

_____

3 conduction

_____

_____

_____

4 convection

_____

_____

_____

5 radiation

_____

_____

_____

Key Concepts

6 Compare What is the difference between heat and temperature?

_____

_____

_____

_____

7 Predict If two objects at different temperatures are in contact with each other, what happens to their temperatures?

_____

_____

_____

_____

Use this photo to answer the following questions.

8 Classify Which type of energy transfer is occurring at each lettered area?

A _____

B _____

C _____

Critical Thinking

9 Synthesize Describe the relationships among temperature, heat, and thermal energy.

_____

_____

_____

_____

10 Synthesize Do you think that solids can undergo convection? Explain.

_____

_____

_____

_____

_____

My Notes

Unit 4 **Summary**

Heat

is transferred and changes

↓

Thermal Energy

of objects that differ in

↙

Temperature

which observes

↘

Energy Conservation

---

1 Interpret The Graphic Organizer above shows that thermal energy observes energy conservation. Give an example of energy conservation involving thermal energy.

_____

_____

_____

_____

2 Compare Describe conductors and insulators in terms of energy.

_____

_____

_____

_____

3 Apply Describe the movement of particles in a cold glass as thermal energy is transferred to it from warm hands.

_____

_____

_____

4 Explain Can you use a thermometer to measure thermal energy? Why or why not?

_____

_____

_____

_____

_____

Name _____

Multiple Choice
Identify the choice that best completes the statement or answers the question.

1 During science class, Sophie measures the temperature of water every minute as it is heating. After a few minutes, the temperature is 82 °C. How far below the boiling point of water is this?

A. 8 °C

B. 18 °C

C. 130 °C

D. 191 °C

2 Sarah heated two cubes of aluminum to 50 °C. Cube A has a volume of four cubic centimeters. Cube B has a volume of two cubic centimeters. If the cubes do not touch each other, which of these statements is **true**?

F. Cube A has a higher temperature than cube B.

G. Cube B has a higher temperature than cube A.

H. Cube A has more thermal energy than cube B.

I. Cube B has more thermal energy than cube A.

3 These two beakers contain the same liquid substance at the same temperature.

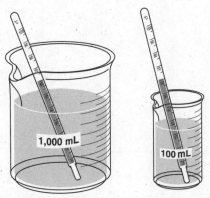

1,000 mL

100 mL

How does the thermal energy of the liquid in the larger beaker compare or contrast with the thermal energy of the liquid in the smaller beaker?

A. The liquid in the larger beaker has less thermal energy than the liquid in the smaller beaker.

B. The liquid in the larger beaker has more thermal energy than the liquid in the smaller beaker.

C. The liquid in the larger beaker has the same amount of thermal energy as the liquid in the smaller beaker.

D. The exact volume of liquid in each beaker must be known to compare the thermal energy of the liquids.

4   Deval drew the models of particles in a substance shown below. Which model **best** represents the particles in a solid?

F.

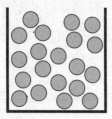

G.

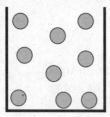

H.

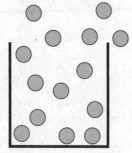

I.

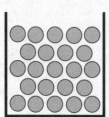

5   Ms. Lewis is a chemist mixing two solutions together. A chemical reaction takes place, and the solution becomes warm. Which statement **best** describes what has happened?

A.   Energy has been created in the form of thermal energy.

B.   Energy has been transformed from one form to another.

C.   More energy has been created than has been destroyed.

D.   The chemical energy of the solution has been destroyed.

6 A group of sheep are grazing in a field. As they eat, the sheep break down the molecules in the grass, which releases energy. Which form of energy is stored in the grass?

    F. chemical energy

    G. elastic energy

    H. nuclear energy

    I. thermal energy

7 Laith notices that the air in his science classroom is much warmer than the air in his math classroom. Which statement describes how the air particles are different in his colder math classroom?

    A. They move faster on average.

    B. They are vibrating.

    C. They have less average energy.

    D. They move more freely.

8 Kito puts his metal spoon into a helping of fresh, hot, mashed potatoes as shown in the figure below.

Metal spoon 20 °C

Mashed potatoes 50 °C

Which process takes place when the two objects come together?

    F. The temperature of the spoon increases, but its thermal energy does not change.

    G. Energy in the form of heat is transferred from the warmer mashed potatoes to the cooler spoon.

    H. The thermal energy of both the mashed potatoes and the spoon increases as heat flows between them.

    I. The average temperature of the spoon does not change.

9 Gordon throws a baseball into the air. It rises, stops momentarily when it reaches its greatest height, and then falls back to the ground. At what point does kinetic energy convert to potential energy?

A. when the baseball is rising

B. when the baseball is falling

C. just after the baseball hits the ground

D. while the baseball is at the highest point

10 Liang is warming a pot of soup on the stove. How is the motion of the particles in the soup different after the temperature of the soup increases?

F. They move faster on average.

G. They have less average energy.

H. They move less freely.

I. They vibrate and are close together.

11 Ella holds an ice cream cone in her hand. She soon notices that her hand begins to feel cold. What is different about the particles that make up her hand?

A. They are getting larger.

B. They are gaining average energy.

C. They are moving slower on average.

D. They are joining together.

12 Damon is a musician playing in a band. At the end of a song, he plucks a single guitar string. The string moves rapidly back and forth as shown in the figure below.

Which of these statements explains what happens to the kinetic energy of the moving string?

F. The kinetic energy is changed into potential energy and stored.

G. The kinetic energy is converted to sound energy and thermal energy.

H. The kinetic energy is slowly destroyed until no energy remains.

I. Some of the energy is converted to sound energy, but the rest is destroyed.

Energy, Motion, and Forces

The parachute helps slow the shuttle down.

n Harcourt Publishing Company • Image Credits: (bkgd) ©Gary I. Rothstein/epa/Corbis; (br) ©Eliot J. Schechter/Getty Images

Big Idea 11

Energy Transfer and Transformations

Big Idea 12

Motion of Objects

Big Idea 13

Forces and Changes in Motion

What do you think?

How do you change the direction in which an object is moving? By applying force, of course. Can you tell what force helps the shuttle slow down? What allows the rocket in the photo to lift off?

CITIZEN SCIENCE

What's in a Vane?

For hundreds of years, people have used the wind to do work, such as grind flour and pump water.

① Define the Problem

We need electricity to do work, such as power the lights and appliances that we use daily. As our need for electricity grows, many people are becoming more interested in new ways to generate electricity. Have you heard of using windmills to generate electricity?

A windmill sail or vane is a large structure that is attached to a rotating axle. The vane catches the wind and turns around. This turning motion can be used to generate electricity.

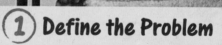

© Houghton Mifflin Harcourt Publishing Company • Image Credits: ©Jim Howard/The Image Bank/Getty Images

② Think About It

Designing a windmill vane

What characteristics of a windmill vane help it to catch the most wind? Create two different designs for windmill vanes that you can test to see which characteristics are the most beneficial.

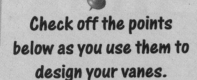

Check off the points below as you use them to design your vanes.

☐ The size of the vanes.

☐ The shape of the vanes.

☐ Materials used to build the vane.

— Windmill vane

Take It Home

With the help of an adult, research windmills that are used to generate electricity for homes. Study the different designs and decide which would be best for your family.

③ Plan and Test Your Design

A In the space below, sketch the two designs to be tested. Use four vanes in each design.

B To test your designs, you will have to:
- Attach your windmill vanes to a straw or wooden spindle. The straw or spindle will be the axle.
- Mount your axle so that it can spin freely during the test.
- Identify what you will use as a wind source and the variables you must control in the space below.

_____

_____

_____

C Conduct your test and briefly state your findings below.

_____

_____

_____

_____

_____

Kinetic and Potential Energy

ESSENTIAL QUESTION

How is mechanical energy conserved?

By the end of this lesson, you should be able to describe how mechanical energy is conserved through the transformation between kinetic and potential energy.

As this girl juggles, the balls fly up and down. As each ball moves, one type of energy changes into another.

 Sunshine State Standards

SC.6.N.3.3 Give several examples of scientific laws.

SC.6.P.11.1 Explore the Law of Conservation of Energy by differentiating between potential and kinetic energy. Identify situations where kinetic energy is transformed into potential energy and vice versa.

Engage Your Brain

1 Describe Fill in the blank with the word or phrase that you think correctly completes the following sentences.

A running cat has _____ energy than a walking cat.

A balloon in the air has more energy than

_____

_____

Conservation of energy means that energy is

_____

_____

2 Explain Draw a sketch that shows two uses of energy. Write a caption to go with your sketch.

Active Reading

3 Apply Many scientific words, such as *energy*, also have everyday meanings. Use context clues to write your own definition for each meaning of the word *energy*.

Example Sentence
I am tired today and don't have much <u>energy</u>.

Energy:

_____

_____

_____

Example Sentence
Make sure to turn off the lights when you're done to save <u>energy</u>.

Energy:

_____

_____

_____

Vocabulary Terms

- energy
- kinetic energy
- potential energy
- mechanical energy
- law of conservation of energy

4 Identify This list contains the vocabulary terms you'll learn in this lesson. As you read, circle the definition of each term.

Exciting Energy!

What is energy?

Energy is the ability to cause change. It is measured in units called joules. Energy takes many different forms and has many different effects. For example, you use energy provided by the food you eat to do different activities. Your body uses energy by converting it to other forms. If you are exercising, sitting, or even thinking, then you are using energy. All forms of energy have one thing in common—they can cause changes to occur.

Just about everything that you see happening around you involves energy. In the photo of the amusement park below, there are many examples of energy uses. The lights on the Ferris wheel use energy. The rides use energy as they move. The speakers use energy as they broadcast music.

Think Outside the Book

5 Discuss You have probably used the word *energy* before. With a partner or as a class, discuss how the scientific definition of *energy* relates to the daily use of the word.

The lights on the Ferris wheel use energy.

The rides use energy as they move.

Visualize It!

6 Identify List four examples of energy being used in this photo.

_____

_____

_____

_____

© Houghton Mifflin Harcourt Publishing Company • Image Credits: ©Doug Armand/Getty Images

What are two types of energy?

Imagine that you are biking up a hill. You would be using many different types of energy. You would use one type of energy to go up the hill. As the bike goes up the hill, it gains a second type of energy that you can use to go down the hill. These two types of energy are called kinetic energy and potential energy.

Kinetic Energy

Kinetic energy (kuh•NET•ik) is the energy of motion. All moving objects have kinetic energy. Like all forms of energy, kinetic energy has the ability to cause change. For example, as a hammer moves toward a nail, it has kinetic energy. This kinetic energy can be used to move the nail into a piece of wood. A change has occurred. First, the nail was outside of the wood. Then it was inside of the wood.

The amount of kinetic energy that an object has depends on two things: mass and speed. The more mass a moving object has, the more kinetic energy it has. If there are two objects moving at the same speed, then the one with more mass will have more kinetic energy. For example, if a car and a bike are both moving at the same speed, then the car will have more kinetic energy because it has more mass.

Kinetic energy also depends on speed. The faster an object moves, the more kinetic energy it has. If there are two objects with the same mass, then the one going faster will have more kinetic energy. For example, a cheetah has more kinetic energy when it is running than it does when it is walking.

![Active Reading] **7 Apply** A bowling ball and a soccer ball are both moving at the same speed. Which one has more kinetic energy? Why?

_____

_____

_____

_____

This running cheetah has more kinetic energy than the walking cheetah because it is moving faster.

Potential Energy

Not all energy has to do with motion. Some energy is stored energy, or potential energy. **Potential energy** is the stored energy that an object has due to its position, condition, or chemical composition. Like kinetic energy, stored potential energy has the ability to cause change. For example, a book held in your hands has potential energy. If you drop it, its position will change.

One type of potential energy is called gravitational potential energy. Gravity is the force that pulls objects toward Earth's center. When you lift an object, you transfer energy to the object and give the object gravitational potential energy. Any object above the ground has gravitational potential energy. The skydivers in this photo have gravitational potential energy as they ride in the plane.

The amount of gravitational potential energy that an object has depends on its mass and its height above the ground. Gravitational potential energy increases as an object's distance from the ground, or from its lowest possible position, increases. A skydiver has more gravitational potential energy on the plane than she does after she jumps out and gets closer to the ground. Gravitational potential energy also increases as mass increases. If there are two skydivers on the plane, the one with more mass will have more gravitational potential energy.

There are other types of potential energy. Energy can be stored in springs or elastic bands. Chemical potential energy, such as the energy stored in food, depends on chemical composition. It results from the bonds between atoms. When chemical bonds of molecules are broken, and their atoms are rearranged through a series of chemical changes, energy is released.

Active Reading **8 Apply** Which has more gravitational potential energy: a bird on the ground or the same bird in a tree? Why?

_____

_____

_____

_____

As these skydivers fall, their gravitational potential energy decreases.

How are kinetic energy and potential energy different?

Kinetic energy and potential energy both have the ability to cause change. But they have some important differences. Kinetic energy is the energy of motion, but potential energy is stored energy that can be converted into motion. It is easy to know whether an object has kinetic energy because it is moving. It may not be easy to know how much potential energy an object has, because there are many kinds of potential energy. It is hard to see how much chemical energy an object has. However, you can usually know if an object has gravitational potential energy because it will be above the ground and can fall.

Many objects have both kinetic and potential energy. For example, an object can be both moving and above the ground. There are many examples of this: a helicopter flying through the air, a bumblebee whizzing past your head, or a baseball thrown to a catcher. The skydivers in the air have both kinetic and potential energy. They have kinetic energy because they are moving as they fall through the air. They also have gravitational potential energy because they are above the ground and can continue to fall.

9 Classify Determine whether the three scenarios in the chart below are examples of kinetic energy, gravitational potential energy, or both.

Scenario	Kind of energy
Speeding boat	
Flying bird	
Diver at the top of a diving board	

Think Outside the Book Inquiry

10 Classify Keep a journal of ten examples of kinetic and potential energy that you see in one day. Are they examples of kinetic energy, gravitational potential energy, or both?

Add It Up!

What is mechanical energy?

The skater in the picture has both kinetic energy and potential energy. There are many times when these two types of energy are found together. **Mechanical energy** (meh•KAN•ih•kuhl) is the kinetic energy plus the potential energy due to position.

Gravitational potential energy is one type of energy of position. An object compressing a spring also has potential energy of position. Both of these are mechanical potential energies. Add together an object's mechanical potential energies and its kinetic energy to get its mechanical energy. Often, you can add just the object's kinetic and gravitational potential energies.

At any point on the half-pipe shown in the photograph, the mechanical energy of the skater is equal to the sum of his kinetic energy and his gravitational potential energy. At any point where his kinetic energy is zero, then his mechanical energy is equal to potential energy. When he is both moving and above his lowest point, his mechanical energy is the sum of both kinds of energy.

As the skater moves up the ramp, he gains height but loses speed. The kinetic energy he loses is equal to the potential energy that he gains.

D

At the bottom of the ramp, the skater's kinetic energy is greatest because he is going the fastest. His potential energy is at its lowest because he is closer to the ground than at any other point on the ramp.

C

What is the law of conservation of energy?

The **law of conservation of energy** states that energy can be neither created nor destroyed. It can only be transformed. The mechanical energy of an object always remains the same unless some of it is transformed into other forms of energy, such as heat through friction. If no energy is transformed, the mechanical energy of an object stays the same.

As a skater rolls down the ramp, the amounts of kinetic and potential energy change. However, the law of conservation of energy requires that the total—or mechanical energy—stays the same, assuming no energy is converted into other forms. In order for the mechanical energy to stay the same, some potential energy changes into kinetic energy. At other times, some kinetic energy changes into potential energy. The picture below shows the skater's mechanical energy at four key places: the top of the ramp, between the top and the bottom of the ramp, the bottom of the ramp, and between the bottom and top of the ramp.

Active Reading

11 Identify As you read, underline examples in the text where kinetic energy changes into potential energy or where potential energy changes into kinetic energy.

At the top of the ramp, the skater has potential energy because gravity can pull him downward. He has no speed, so he has no kinetic energy.

Ⓐ

As the skater moves closer to the ground, he loses potential energy, but gains the same amount of kinetic energy. As he rolls down the ramp, his potential energy decreases because his distance from the ground decreases. His kinetic energy increases because his speed increases.

Ⓑ

12 Analyze Do you think that the skater has any gravitational potential energy at point C? Why?

_____

_____

_____

_____

_____

_____

_____

_____

Visual Summary

To complete this summary, fill in the blanks with the correct word or phrase. Then, use the answer key to check your answers. You can use this page to review the main concepts of the lesson.

Energy is the ability to cause change.

13 Kinetic energy is the energy of

_____

14 Potential energy is the energy of

_____

Kinetic and Potential Energy

Mechanical energy is conserved. Ball A has the most potential energy. As it rolls down the hill, its potential energy is converted to kinetic energy. Ball B has both kinetic and potential energy. At the bottom of the hill, most of the ball's energy is kinetic.

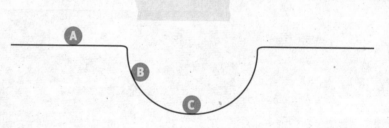

15 Mechanical energy is the sum of

_____

Answers: 13 motion; 14 position or chemical composition; 15 kinetic energy and potential energy

16 Apply Explain how the law of conservation of energy might apply to energy use that you observe in your daily life.

Lesson Review

Vocabulary

Fill in the blank with the term that best completes the following sentences.

1 Energy is the ability to _Cause change_

2 _Mechanical Energy_ is an object's total kinetic and potential energy.

3 The law of conservation of energy states that _energy can be either created or destroyed_

Key Concepts

4 Describe List two ways you use energy. How does each example involve a change?

charging my phone it helps my phone to work better

5 Identify What are two factors that determine an object's kinetic energy?

mass & speed

6 Identify What are two factors that determine an object's gravitational potential energy?

mass & height

7 Describe How does the law of conservation of energy affect the total amount of energy in any process?

the words you speak travel lik waves

Critical Thinking

Use the illustration below to answer the following questions.

8 Apply At which position would the skater have the most kinetic energy?

_1_

9 Apply At which position would the skater have the most potential energy?

_3_

10 Synthesize At which position would the skater's kinetic energy begin to change into potential energy? Explain.

2 & 4 because it always will down to 3rd Position

11 Incorporate How have your ideas about energy and its forms changed after reading this lesson? Provide an example to describe how you would have thought about energy compared to how you think about it now.

Now I know that there are two types of energy Kinetic & Potential. Kinetic is energy of motion. Potential is stored energy

Interpreting Graphs

Sunshine State Standards

SC.6.N.1.1 Define a problem from the sixth grade curriculum, use appropriate reference materials to support scientific understanding, plan and carry out scientific investigation of various types, such as systematic observations or experiments, identify variables, collect and organize data, interpret data in charts, tables, and graphics, analyze information, make predictions, and defend conclusions.

A visual display, such as a graph or table, is a useful way to show data that you have collected in an experiment. The ability to interpret graphs is a necessary skill in science, and it is also important in everyday life. You will come across various types of graphs in newspaper articles, medical reports, and, of course, textbooks. Understanding a report or article's message often depends heavily on your ability to read and interpret different types of graphs.

Tutorial

Ask yourself the following questions when studying a graph.

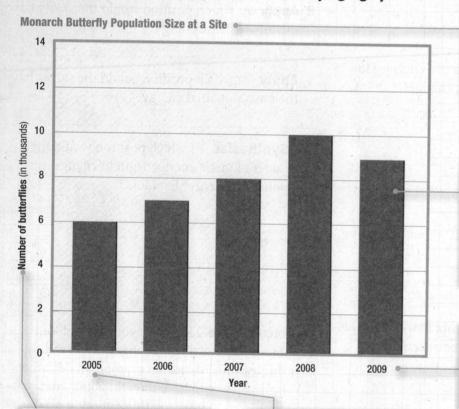

Monarch Butterfly Population Size at a Site

What is the title of the graph? Reading the title can tell you the subject or main idea of the graph. The subject here is monarch butterfly population.

What type of graph is it? Bar graphs, like the one here, are useful for comparing categories or total values. The lengths of the bars are proportional to the value they represent.

Do you notice any trends in the graph? After you understand what the graph is about, look for patterns. For example, here the monarch butterfly population increased each year from 2005 to 2008. But in 2009, the monarch butterfly population decreased.

What are the labels and headings in the graph? What is on each axis of the graph? Here, the vertical axis shows the population in thousands. Each bar represents a different year from 2005 to 2009. So from 2005 to 2009, the monarch butterfly population ranged from 6,000 to 10,000.

Can you describe the data in the graph? Data can be numbers or text. Analyze the information you read at specific data points. For example, the graph here tells us that there were 6,000 monarch butterflies in 2005.

You Try It!

A member of your research group has made the graph shown below about an object in motion. Study the graph, then answer the questions that follow.

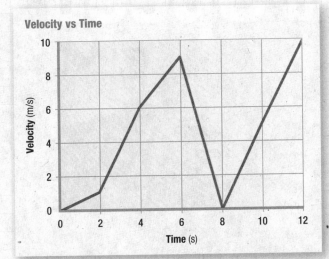

Velocity vs Time

1 Interpreting Graphs Study the graph shown above. Identify the title of this graph, the *x*-axis, the *y*-axis, and the type of graph.

A title of graph _____

B *x*-axis _____

C *y*-axis _____

D type of graph _____

2 Identify Study the graph shown above and record the velocity at the indicated times.

Time (s)	Velocity (m/s)
2	
4	
6	
8	
10	

3 Using Graphs Use the graph to answer the following questions.

A What is the approximate velocity of the object at 5 seconds?

_____

B During what time interval is the object slowing down? Explain how you can tell.

_____

_____

_____

_____

C At what time or times was the velocity of the object about 40 m/s?

_____

4 Communicating Results In a short paragraph, describe the motion of the object.

_____

_____

_____

_____

_____

_____

_____

_____

Take It Home

Find a newspaper or magazine article that has a graph. What type of graph is it? Study the graph and determine its main message. Bring the graph to class and be prepared to discuss your interpretation of the graph.

Motion and Speed

ESSENTIAL QUESTION

How are distance, time, and speed related?

By the end of this lesson, you should be able to analyze how distance, time, and speed are related.

🌀 **Sunshine State Standards**

SC.6.P.12.1 Measure and graph distance versus time for an object moving at a constant speed. Interpret this relationship.

MA.6.A.3.6 Construct and analyze tables, graphs, and equations to describe linear functions and other simple relations using both common language and algebraic notation.

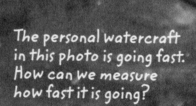

The personal watercraft in this photo is going fast. How can we measure how fast it is going?

Engage Your Brain

1 Predict Circle the correct words in the paragraph below to make true statements.

A dog usually moves faster than a bug. That means that if I watch them move for one minute, then the dog would have traveled a *greater*/ *smaller* distance than the bug. However, a car usually goes *faster*/*slower* than a dog. If the car and the dog both traveled to the end of the road, then the *car*/*dog* would get there first.

2 Explain Draw or sketch something that you might see move. Write a caption that answers the following questions: How would you describe its motion? Is it moving at a constant speed, or does it speed up and slow down?

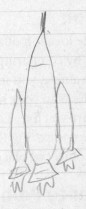

Active Reading

3 Define Fill in the blank with the word that best completes the following sentences.

If an object changes its position, then it is

_____Reference Point_____

The speed of a car describes

_____velocity_____

Vocabulary Terms

- position
- reference point
- motion
- speed
- vector
- velocity

4 Apply As you learn the definition of each vocabulary term in this lesson, make your own definition or sketch to help you remember the meaning of the term.

Location, location,

How can you describe the location of an object?

Have you ever gotten lost while looking for a specific place? If so, you probably know that the description of the location can be very important. Imagine that you are trying to describe your location to a friend. How would you explain where you are? You need two pieces of information: a position and a reference point.

With a Position

Position describes the location of an object. Often, you describe where something is by comparing its position with where you currently are. For example, you might say that a classmate sitting next to you is two desks to your right, or that a mailbox is two blocks south of where you live. Each time you identify the position of an object, you are comparing the location of the object with the location of another object or place.

With a Reference Point

When you describe a position by comparing it to the location of another object or place, you are using a reference point. A **reference point** is a location to which you compare other locations. In the example above of a mailbox that is two blocks south of where you live, the reference point is "where you live."

Imagine that you are at a zoo with some friends. If you are using the map to the right, you could describe your destination using different reference points. Using yourself as the reference point, you might say that the red panda house is one block east and three blocks north of your current location. Or you might say the red panda house is one block north and one block east of the fountain. In this example, the fountain is your reference point.

![Active Reading] **5 Apply** How would you describe where this question is located on the page? Give two different answers using two different reference points.

_____

_____

_____

_____

location

ZOO MAP

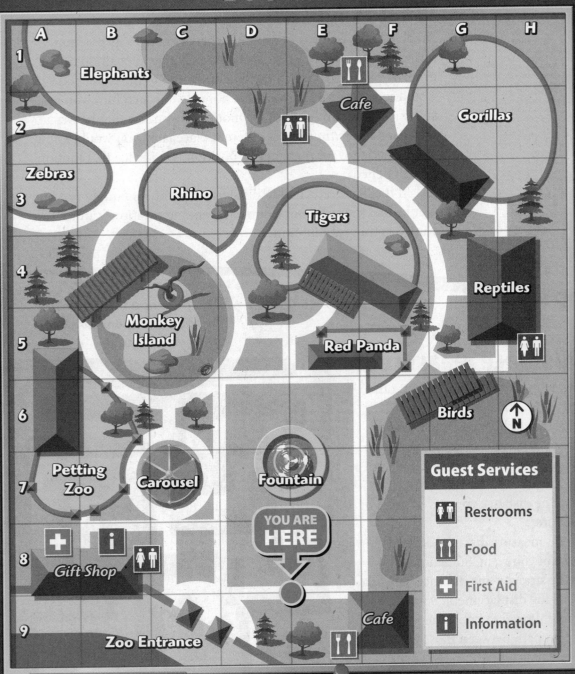

Guest Services

🚻 Restrooms

🍴 Food

➕ First Aid

ℹ️ Information

👁 Visualize It!

6 Apply One of your friends is at the southeast corner of Monkey Island. He would like to meet you. How would you describe your location to him?

I'm at the south of the fountain

7 Apply You need to go visit the first aid station. How would you describe how to get there?

go to Petting zoo and turn around

287

MOVE It!

What is motion?

An object moves, or is in motion, when it changes its position relative to a reference point. **Motion** is a change in position over time. If you were to watch the biker pictured to the right, you would see him move. If you were not able to watch him, you might still know something about his motion. If you saw that he was in one place at one time and a different place later, you would know that he had moved. A change in position is evidence that motion has happened.

If the biker returned to his starting point, you might not know that he had moved. The starting and ending positions cannot tell you everything about motion.

How is distance measured?

Suppose you walk from one building to another building that is several blocks away. If you could walk in a straight line, you might end up 500 meters from where you started. The actual distance you travel, however, would depend on the exact path you take. If you take a route that has many turns, the distance you travel might be 900 meters or more.

The way you measure distance depends on the information you want. Sometimes you want to know the straight-line distance between two positions, or the displacement. Sometimes, however, you might need to know the total length of a certain path between those positions.

When measuring any distances, scientists use a standard unit of measurement. The standard unit of length is the meter (m), which is about 3.3 feet. Longer distances can be measured in kilometers (km), and shorter distances in centimeters (cm). In the United States, distance is often measured in miles (mi), feet (ft), or inches (in).

The distance from point A to point B depends on the path you take.

Visualize It!

8 Illustrate Draw a sample path on the maze that is a different distance than the one in red but still goes from the start point, "A," to the finish point, "B."

This biker is in motion.

What is speed?

A change in an object's position tells you that motion took place, but it does not tell you how quickly the object changed position. The **speed** of an object is a measure of how far something moves in a given amount of time. In other words, speed measures how quickly or slowly the object changes position. In the same amount of time, a faster object would move farther than a slower moving object would.

What is average speed?

The speed of an object is rarely constant. For example, the biker in the photo above may travel quickly when he begins a race but may slow down as he gets tired at the end of the race. *Average speed* is a way to calculate the speed of an object that may not always be moving at a constant speed. Instead of describing the speed of an object at an exact moment in time, average speed describes the speed over a stretch of time.

Active Reading **9 Compare** What is the difference between speed and average speed?

speed is the speed you
are going per second and
average is like per hour

Think Outside the Book Inquiry

10 Analyze Research the top speeds of a cheetah, a race car, and a speed boat. How do they rank in order of speed? Make a poster showing which is fastest and which is slowest. How do the speeds of the fastest human runners compare to the speeds you found?

Speed It Up!

Active Reading

11 Identify As you read, underline sentences that relate distance and time.

How is average speed calculated?

Speed can be calculated by dividing the distance an object travels by the time it takes to cover the distance. Speed is shown in the formula as the letter s, distance as the letter d, and time as the letter t. The formula shows how distance, time, and speed are related. If two objects travel the same distance, the object that took a shorter amount of time will have the greater speed. An object with a greater speed will travel a longer distance in the same amount of time than an object with a lower speed will.

> The following equation can be used to find average speed:
>
> $$\text{average speed} = \frac{\text{distance}}{\text{time}}$$
>
> $$s = \frac{d}{t}$$

The standard unit for speed is meters per second (m/s). Speed can also be given in kilometers per hour (km/h). In the United States, speeds are often given in miles per hour (mi/h or mph). One mile per hour is equal to 0.45 m/s.

Do the Math   Sample Problem

A penguin swimming underwater goes 20 meters in 8 seconds. What is its average speed?

....

Identify

A. What do you know? $d = 20$ m, $t = 8$ s

B. What do you want to find out? average speed

$\dfrac{20}{8}$

2.5

....

Plan

C. Draw and label a sketch: |——— 20 m ———| 8 sec

D. Write the formula: $s = d/t$

E. Substitute into the formula: $s = \frac{20\ \text{m}}{8\ \text{s}}$

....

Solve

F. Calculate and simplify: $s = \frac{20\ \text{m}}{8\ \text{s}} = 2.5$ m/s

G. Check that your units agree: Unit is m/s. Unit of speed is distance/time. Units agree.

Answer: 2.5 m/s

Do the Math **You Try It**

12. Calculate This runner completed a 100-meter race with a time of 13.75 seconds. What was her average speed?

Identify

A. What do you know?

d=100 m
t=13.75

B. What do you want to find out?

average speed

Plan

C. Draw and label a sketch:

|———— 100 m ————|
13.75 s

D. Write the formula:

S = d/t

E. Substitute into the formula:

S = 100/13.75 s

Solve

F. Calculate and simplify:

7.272727272?

G. Check that your units agree:

7.27 m/s

Answer:

Fast Graphs

How is constant speed graphed?

A convenient way to show the motion of an object is by using a graph that plots the distance the object has traveled against time. This type of graph is called a distance-time graph. You can use it to see how both distance and speed change with time.

How far away the object is from a reference point is plotted on the *y*-axis. So the *y*-axis expresses distance in units such as meters, centimeters, or kilometers. Time is plotted on the *x*-axis, and can display units such as seconds, minutes, or hours. If an object moves at a constant speed, the graph is a straight line.

You can use a distance-time graph to determine the average speed of an object. The slope, or steepness, of the line is equal to the average speed of the object. You calculate the average speed for a time interval by dividing the change in distance by the change in time for that time interval.

Suppose that an ostrich is running at a constant speed. The distance-time graph of its motion is shown below. To calculate the speed of the ostrich, choose two data points from the graph below and calculate the slope of the line. The calculation of the slope is shown below. Since we know that the slope of a line on a distance-time graph is its average speed, then we know that the ostrich's speed is 14 m/s.

How can you calculate slope?

$$\text{slope} = \frac{\text{change in } y}{\text{change in } x}$$

$$= \frac{140 \text{ m} - 70 \text{ m}}{10 \text{ s} - 5 \text{ s}}$$

$$= \frac{70 \text{ m}}{5 \text{ s}}$$

$$= 14 \text{ m/s}$$

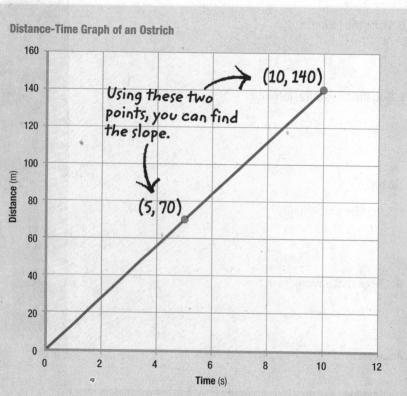

Distance-Time Graph of an Ostrich

Using these two points, you can find the slope.

(10, 140)

(5, 70)

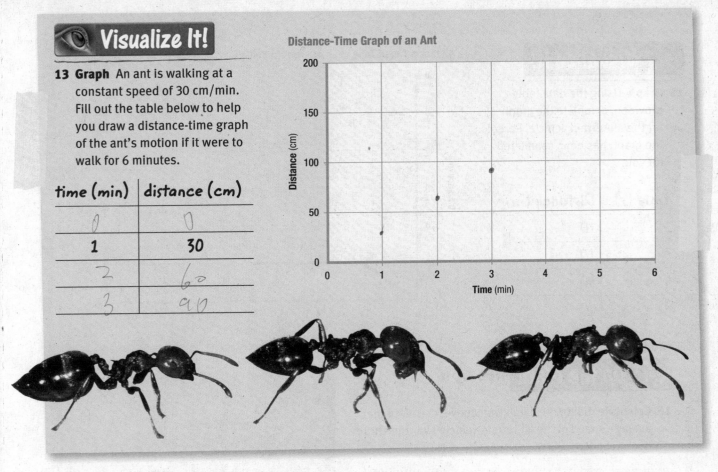

Visualize It!

13 Graph An ant is walking at a constant speed of 30 cm/min. Fill out the table below to help you draw a distance-time graph of the ant's motion if it were to walk for 6 minutes.

Distance-Time Graph of an Ant

time (min)	distance (cm)
0	0
1	30
2	60
3	90

How are changing speeds graphed?

Some distance-time graphs show the motion of an object with a changing speed. In these distance-time graphs, the change in the slope of a line indicates that the object has either sped up, slowed down, or stopped.

As an object moves, the distance it travels increases with time. The motion can be seen as a climbing line on the graph. The slope of the line indicates speed. Steeper lines show intervals where the speed is greater than intervals with less steep lines. If the line gets steeper, the object is speeding up. If the line gets less steep, the object is slowing. If the line becomes flat, or horizontal, the object is not moving. In this interval, the speed is zero meters per second.

For objects that change speed, you can calculate speed for a specific interval of time. You would choose two points close together on the graph. Or, you can calculate the average speed over a long interval of time. You would choose two points far apart on the graph to calculate an average over a long interval of time.

Active Reading **14 Analyze** If a line on a distance-time graph becomes steeper, what has happened to the speed of the object? What if it becomes a flat horizontal line?

steeper it means the ant is getting
slower and the far is that
it is going in a constant speed

15. Graph Using the data table provided, complete the graph for the all-terrain vehicle. Part of the graph has been completed for you.

Time (s)	Distance (m)
1	10
3	10
4	30
5	50

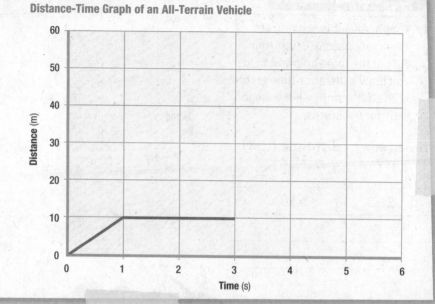

Distance-Time Graph of an All-Terrain Vehicle

 Do the Math **You Try It**

16. Calculate Using the data given above, calculate the average speed of the all-terrain vehicle over the entire five seconds.

Identify

A. What do you know? T= 13 s   D=. 100 m

B. What do you want to find out? average speed

Plan

C. Draw and label a sketch: |‾100m‾|
                                    13 S

D. Write the formula: s= d/t

E. Substitute into the formula: s= 100m / 13 s

Solve

F. Calculate and simplify: 7.69

G. Check that your units agree: 7.69 m pers

Answer:

What would the distance-time graph of this ATV's motion look like?

Follow Directions

What is velocity?

Suppose that two birds start from the same place and fly at 10 km/h for 5 minutes. Why might they not end up at the same place? Because the birds were flying in different directions! There are times when the direction of motion must be included in a measurement. A **vector** is a quantity that has both size and direction.

In the example above, the birds' speeds were the same, but their velocities were different. **Velocity** [vuh•LAHS•ih•tee] is speed in a specific direction. If a police officer gives a speeding ticket for a car traveling 100 km/h, the ticket does not list a velocity. But it would list a velocity if it described the car traveling south at 100 km/h.

Because velocity includes direction, it is possible for two objects to have the same speed but different velocities. In the picture to the right, the chair lifts are going the same speed but in opposite directions: some people are going up the mountain while others are going down the mountain.

Average velocity is calculated in a different way than average speed. Average speed depends on the total distance traveled along a path. Average velocity depends on the straight-line distance from the starting point to the final point, or the displacement. A chair lift might carry you up the mountain at an average speed of 5 km/h, giving you an average velocity of 5 km/h north. After a round-trip ride, your average traveling speed would still be 5 km/h. Your average velocity, however, would be 0 km/h because you ended up exactly where you started.

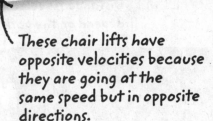

These chair lifts have opposite velocities because they are going at the same speed but in opposite directions.

17. Compare Fill in the Venn diagram to compare and contrast speed and velocity.

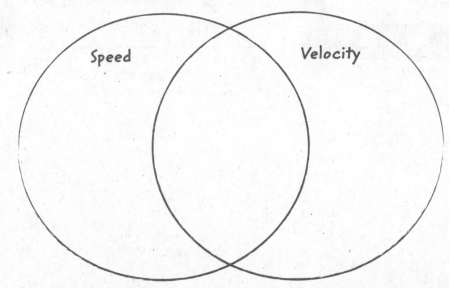

Speed

Velocity

Visual Summary

To complete this summary, check the box that indicates true or false. Then use the key below to check your answers. You can use this page to review the main concepts of the lesson.

Motion is a change in position over time.

Speed measures how far something moves in a given amount of time.

$$s = \frac{d}{t}$$

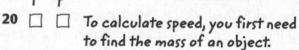

	T	F	
18	☐	☐	A reference point is a location to which you compare other locations.
19	☐	☐	Distance traveled does not depend on the path you take.

	T	F	
20	☐	☐	To calculate speed, you first need to find the mass of an object.
21	☐	☐	Average speed is a way to describe the speed of an object that may not always be moving at a constant speed.

Motion and Speed

A distance-time graph plots the distance traveled by an object and the time it takes to travel that distance.

	T	F	
22	☐	☐	In the graph at the right, the object is moving at a constant speed.

Answers: 18 T; 19 F; 20 F; 21 T; 22 T

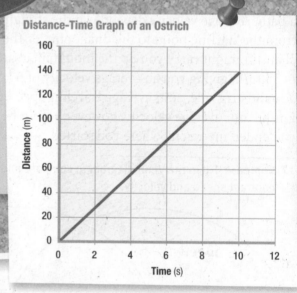

Distance-Time Graph of an Ostrich

23 Predict Amy and Ellie left school at the same time. Amy lives farther away than Ellie, but she and Ellie arrived at their homes at the same time. Compare the girls' speeds.

Lesson Review

Vocabulary

Draw a line to connect the following terms to their definitions.

1 velocity

2 reference point

3 speed

4 position

A describes the location of an object

B speed in a specific direction

C a location to which you compare other locations

D a measure of how far something moves in a given amount of time

Key Concepts

5 Describe What information do you need to describe an object's location?

_____

_____

6 Predict How would decreasing the time it takes you to run a certain distance affect your speed?

_____

_____

_____

_____

7 Calculate Juan lives 100 m away from Bill. What is Juan's average speed if he reaches Bill's home in 50 s?

_____

_____

_____

_____

8 Describe What do you need to know to describe the velocity of an object?

_____

_____

Use this graph to answer the following questions.

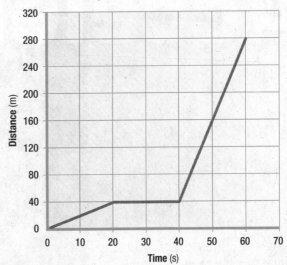

Distance-Time Graph of a Zebra

9 Analyze When is the zebra in motion? When is it not moving?

In motion: _____

Not moving: _____

10 Calculate What is the average speed of the zebra during the time between 0 s and 40 s?

_____

_____

_____

_____

Critical Thinking

11 Apply Look around you to find an object in motion. Describe the object's motion by discussing its position and direction of motion in relation to a reference point. Then explain how you could determine the object's speed.

_____

_____

_____

_____

_____

Acceleration

ESSENTIAL QUESTION

How does motion change?

By the end of this lesson, you should be able to analyze how acceleration is related to time and velocity.

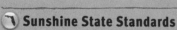

Sunshine State Standards

MA.6.A.3.6 Construct and analyze tables, graphs, and equations to describe linear functions and other simple relations using both common language and algebraic notation.

The riders on this roller coaster are constantly changing direction and speed.

Engage Your Brain

1 Predict Check T or F to show whether you think each statement is true or false.

T   F

☐ ☐ A car taking a turn at a constant speed is accelerating.

☐ ☐ If an object has low acceleration, it isn't moving very fast.

☐ ☐ An accelerating car is always gaining speed.

2 Identify The names of the two things that can change when something accelerates are scrambled together below. Unscramble them!

P E D S E

_____

C D E I I N O R T

_____

Active Reading

3 Synthesize You can often define an unknown word if you know the meaning of its word parts. Use the word parts and sentence below to make an educated guess about the meaning of the word *centripetal*.

Word part	Meaning
centri-	center
pet-	tend toward

Example Sentence:
Josephina felt the <u>centripetal</u> force as she spun around on the carnival ride.

centripetal: _____

_____

_____

Vocabulary Terms

- acceleration
- centripetal acceleration

4 Distinguish As you read, draw pictures or make a chart to help remember the relationship between distance, velocity, and acceleration.

Getting up to

How do we measure changing velocity?

Imagine riding a bike as in the images below. You start off not moving at all, then move slowly, and then faster and faster each second. Your velocity is changing. You are accelerating.

Active Reading **5 Identify** Underline the two components of a vector.

Acceleration Measures a Change in Velocity

Just as velocity measures a rate of change in position, acceleration measures a rate of change in velocity. **Acceleration** (ack•SELL•uh•ray•shuhn) is the rate at which velocity changes. Velocity is a vector, having both a magnitude and direction, and if either of these change, then the velocity changes. So, an object accelerates if its speed, its direction of motion, or both change.

Keep in mind that acceleration depends not only on how much velocity changes, but also on how much time that change takes. A small change in velocity can still be a large acceleration if the change happens quickly, and a large change in velocity can be a small acceleration if it happens slowly. Increasing your speed by 5 m/s in 5 s is a smaller acceleration than to do the same in 1 s.

Each second, the cyclist's southward velocity increases by 1 m/s south.

1 m/s   2 m/s   3 m/s   4 m/s

South

5 m/s

© Houghton Mifflin Harcourt Publishing Company • Image Credits: (bkgd) ©Tim Graham/Getty Images

Speed

How is average acceleration calculated?

Acceleration is a change in velocity as compared with the time it takes to make the change. You can find the average acceleration experienced by an accelerating object using the following equation.

$$average\ acceleration = \frac{(final\ velocity - starting\ velocity)}{time}$$

Velocity is expressed in meters per second (m/s) and time is measured in seconds (s). So acceleration is measured in meters per second per second, or meters per second squared (m/s²).

As an example, consider an object that starts off moving at 8 m/s west, and then 16 s later is moving at 48 m/s west. The average acceleration of this object is found by in the following equation.

$$a = \frac{(48\ m/s - 8\ m/s)}{16\ s}$$
$$a = 2.5\ m/s^2\ west$$

 **Visualize It!**

 **Active Reading**

6 Identify Underline the units of acceleration.

This formula is often abbreviated as

$$a = \frac{(v_2 - v_1)}{t}$$

---

7 Analyze What is the change in velocity of the biker below as he travels from point *B* to point *C*? What is his acceleration from point *B* to point *C*?

_____

_____

8 Calculate Find the average acceleration of the cyclist moving from point *A* to point *B*, and over the whole trip (from point *A* to point *D*).

The cyclist is riding at 4 m/s. One second later, at the bottom of the hill, he is riding at 8 m/s. After going up a small incline, he has slowed to 7 m/s.

A 4 m/s
t = 0 s

B 8 m/s
t = 1 s

C 8 m/s
t = 2 s

D 7 m/s
t = 3 s

What a Drag!

How can accelerating objects change velocity?

Like velocity, acceleration is a vector, with a magnitude and a direction.

Accelerating Objects Change Speed

Although the word *acceleration* is commonly used to mean an increasing speed, in scientific use, the word applies to both increases and decreases in speed.

When you slide down a hill, you go from a small velocity to a large one. An increase in velocity like this is called *positive acceleration*. When a race car slows down, it goes from a high velocity to a low velocity. A decrease in velocity like this is called *negative acceleration*.

What is the acceleration when an object decreases speed? Because the initial velocity is larger than the final velocity, the term $(v_2 - v_1)$ will be negative. So the acceleration $a = \dfrac{(v_2 - v_1)}{t}$ will be a negative.

When acceleration and velocity (rate of motion) are in the same direction, the speed will increase. When acceleration and velocity are in opposing directions, the acceleration works against the initial motion in that direction, and the speed will decrease.

© Houghton Mifflin Harcourt Publishing Company • Image Credits: (l) ©Mel Yates/Photodisc/Getty Images; (r) ©Leo Mason/Corbis

Active Reading

9 Identify Underline the term for an increase in velocity and the term for a decrease in velocity.

The parachute dragging on the air slows the car down, causing a negative acceleration.

Sliding down a hill causes a positive acceleration.

Accelerating Objects Change Direction

An object changing direction of motion experiences acceleration even when it does not speed up or slow down. Think about a car that makes a sharp left turn. The direction of velocity changes from "forward" to "left." This change in velocity is an acceleration, even if the speed does not change. As the car finishes the turn, the acceleration drops to zero.

What happens, however, when an object is *always* turning? An object traveling in a circular motion is always changing its direction, so it always experiences acceleration. Acceleration in circular motion is known as **centripetal acceleration**. (sehn•TRIP•ih•tahl ack•SELL•uh•ray•shuhn)

A skater rounding a curve experiences centripetal acceleration.

Inquiry

10 Conclude An acceleration in the direction of motion increases speed, and an acceleration opposite to the direction of motion decreases speed. What direction is the acceleration in centripetal acceleration, where speed does not change but direction does?

_____

_____

_____

Do the Math

11 Calculate The horse is galloping at 13 m/s. Five seconds later, after climbing the hill, the horse is moving at 5.5 m/s. Find the acceleration that describes this change in velocity.

$$a = \frac{(v_2 - v_1)}{t}$$

5.5 m/s
5 seconds

Running uphill is tough to do without slowing down!

13 m/s
0 seconds

Visual Summary

To complete this summary, complete the statements below by filling in the blanks. You can use this page to review the main concepts of the lesson.

Acceleration

Acceleration measures a change in velocity.

1 m/s 　　　　　　　　5 m/s

12 The formula for calculating average acceleration is

_____

Acceleration can be a change in speed or a change in direction of motion.

13 When acceleration and velocity are in the same direction, the speed will

_____

14 When acceleration and velocity are in opposing directions, the speed will

_____

15 Objects traveling in _____ motion experience centripetal acceleration.

Answers: 12 $a = \dfrac{(v_2 - v_1)}{t}$;
13 increase; 14 decrease; 15 circular

16 Synthesize Explain why a moving object cannot come to a stop instantaneously (in zero seconds). Hint: Think about the acceleration that would be required.

Lesson Review

Vocabulary

Fill in the blank with the term that best completes the following sentences.

1 Acceleration is a change in _____

2 _____ occurs when an object travels in a curved path.

3 A decrease in the magnitude of velocity is called _____

4 An increase in the magnitude of velocity is called _____

Key Concepts

5 State The units for acceleration are

_____

6 Label In the equation $a = \dfrac{(v_2 - v_1)}{t}$, what do v_1 and v_2 represent?

_____

_____

7 Calculate What is the acceleration experienced by a car that takes 10 s to reach 27 m/s from rest?

8 Identify Acceleration can be a change in speed or _____

9 Identify A helicopter flying west begins experiencing an acceleration of 3 m/s² east. Will the magnitude of its velocity increase or decrease?

_____

Critical Thinking

10 Model Describe a situation when you might travel at a high velocity, but with low acceleration.

_____

_____

_____

Use this graph to answer the following questions. Assume Jenny's direction did not change.

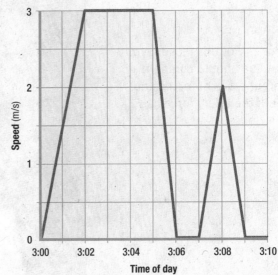

Jenny's Bike Ride

11 Analyze During what intervals was Jenny negatively accelerating?

_____

12 Analyze During what intervals was Jenny positively accelerating?

_____

_____

13 Analyze During what intervals was Jenny not accelerating at all?

_____

_____

_____

Lesson 4

Forces

ESSENTIAL QUESTION

What causes motion?

By the end of this lesson, you should be able to compare different types of forces and explain the effect force has on motion.

Bighorn sheep clash horns with great force in a show of dominance.

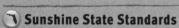

Sunshine State Standards

SC.6.N.3.3 Give several examples of scientific laws.

SC.6.P.13.1 Investigate and describe types of forces including contact forces and forces acting at a distance, such as electrical, magnetic, and gravitational.

SC.6.P.13.3 Investigate and describe that an unbalanced force acting on an object changes its speed, or direction of motion, or both.

MA.6.A.3.6 Construct and analyze tables, graphs, and equations to describe linear functions and other simple relations using both common language and algebraic notation.

Engage Your Brain

1 Identify Draw an example of a force acting on an object.

2 Explain Imagine that you have two marbles on a table. You roll one marble toward another. When the marbles collide, the marble at rest begins to roll. What do you think caused the second marble to move? What do you think causes the marbles to stop rolling?

_____

_____

_____

_____

_____

_____

_____

Active Reading

3 Apply Many scientific words, such as *force*, also have everyday meanings. Use context clues to write your own definition for each underlined word.

Example Sentence
Alena tried to <u>force</u> her brother to leave her bedroom.

force:

_____

_____

_____

Example Sentence
The hammer hit the nail with a great deal of <u>force</u>.

force:

_____

_____

_____

Vocabulary Terms

- force
- net force
- inertia

4 Identify This list contains the key terms you'll learn in this section. As you read, underline the definition of each term.

Force of Nature

What is a force?

You have probably heard the word *force* in everyday conversation. People say things such as, "Our football team is a force to be reckoned with." But what exactly is a force, as it is used in science?

A Force Is a Push or Pull

In science, a **force** is simply a push or a pull. Forces are vectors, meaning that they have both a magnitude and a direction. A force can cause an object to accelerate, and thereby change the speed or direction of motion. In fact, when you see a change in an object's motion, you can infer that one or more forces acted on the object. The unit that measures force is the newton (N). One newton is equal to one kilogram-meter per second squared ($kg \cdot m/s^2$).

All forces act on objects. Forces exist only when there is something for them to act on! However, a force can act on an object without causing a change in motion. For example, when you sit on a chair, the downward force you exert on the chair doesn't cause the chair to move, because the floor exerts a counteracting upward force on the chair.

Active Reading **5 Name** What units are used to measure force?

_____

This athlete's foot exerts force, causing the punching bag to move.

Visualize It!

6 List What are some of the forces affecting each of these rock climbers?

_____
_____
_____
_____
_____

How can forces act?

Forces affect us at all times. Whether you are moving or staying still, many different forces may affect you. How are forces classified, and what do forces do when they act on objects?

Forces Can Act in Direct Contact or at a Distance

It is not always easy to tell what is exerting a force or what is being acted on by a force. Forces can be contact forces, as when one object touches or bumps into another. But forces can also act at a distance. When you jump up, a force called gravity pulls you back to the ground even though you are separated from Earth. Magnetic force is another example of a force that can act at a distance. The magnet does not have to be directly touching the metal to be held to it. This is useful: magnetic force can hold a magnet to a refrigerator even when there is something in the way, like paper or a photograph.

Magnetic force pulls the magnets to the refrigerator, holding the paper in place.

Active Reading **7 Identify** What is the force that holds things to the Earth's surface?

_____

_____

Forces Can Transfer Energy

Forces can be used to transfer energy from one object to another. Unless balanced by another force, when a force acts on an object, it changes the object's motion. The force accelerates the object. If the speed changes, then the kinetic energy of the object is changed by the force. For example, when wind pushes the blades of a windmill, some of the kinetic energy of the moving air is transferred to the blades, which begin to turn.

Sometimes a force slows an object's motion. One such force is called _friction_, which happens when an object moves while touching another object. Friction causes some of the kinetic energy to become heat energy. You can feel the energy as warmth when you rub your hands together quickly. So, a force transfers energy when it converts kinetic energy to heat energy.

A force provides energy for this radio.

Inquiry

8 Explain Describe how force enables the hand-powered radio to work.

_____

_____

_____

In *the* Balance

How do multiple forces interact?

Usually, more than one force is acting on an object. The **net force** is the combination of all the forces acting on an object. How do we determine net force? The answer depends on the directions of the forces involved.

When forces act in the same direction, they are simply added together to determine the net force. When forces act in opposite directions, the smaller force is subtracted from the larger force to determine the net force.

Active Reading

9 **Determine** How do you determine the net force on an object if all forces act in the same direction?

_____

_____

_____

_____

These dogs are pulling with equal force on the toy. The net force is 0 N, and the toy will not move.

Balanced Forces Do Not Change Motion

When the forces on an object produce a net force of 0 N, the forces are balanced. Balanced forces will not cause a change in the motion of a moving object, and will not cause a nonmoving object to start moving. Many objects around you have only balanced forces acting on them. A light hanging from the ceiling does not move because the force of gravity pulling down on the light is balanced by the force of the cord pulling upward.

One of these dogs is pulling with more force on the toy. The toy will move in the direction of the larger dog.

Unbalanced Forces Combine to Produce Acceleration

When the net force is not 0 N, the forces on the object are unbalanced. Unbalanced forces produce a change in motion, such as a change in speed or direction. This change in motion is acceleration. The acceleration is always in the direction of the net force.

Net Force Is a Combination of Forces

When the forces on an object are unbalanced, the object will begin to move. But in which direction?

The forces on an object can be unbalanced, but not perfectly opposite in direction. When this occurs, the net force will be in a direction that is a combination of the directions of the individual forces. For example, when a dog walker experiences a 20 N force pulling her east and another 20 N force pulling her south, the resulting force will have a direction of southeast.

When the forces are not of equal strength, the direction will be closer to the direction of the stronger force.

The net force will have a direction that is a combination of the directions of the individual forces.

10 Illustrate Both players kick the ball with equal strength. Draw arrows to show the forces on the ball, and if the forces are unbalanced, draw an arrow to show which direction the ball will move.

How do forces act on objects?

You know that force and motion are related. When you exert a force on a baseball by hitting it with a bat, the ball will change its motion. In the 1680s, a British scientist named Sir Isaac Newton explained this relationship between force and motion with three laws of motion.

Newton's first law describes the motion of an object that has a net force of 0 N acting on it. The law states:

An object at rest remains at rest, and an object in motion maintains its velocity unless it experiences an unbalanced force.

This law may seem complicated when you first read it, but it is easy to understand in parts.

Even though the car has stopped moving, the test dummy does not stop until it hits the airbag and seat belt.

On the moon, there is no atmosphere and virtually no erosion to move the dust. With nothing to move it, this footprint left by an astronaut could remain unchanged for millions of years.

Forces Can Start Objects Moving

An object at rest remains at rest . . . unless it experiences an unbalanced force.

An object that is not moving is said to be at rest. A chair on the floor or a golf ball on a tee are examples of objects at rest. Newton's first law says that objects at rest will stay at rest unless acted on by an unbalanced force. An object will not start moving until a push or a pull is exerted upon it. So, a chair won't slide across the floor unless a force pushes the chair, and a golf ball won't move off the tee until a force pushes it off. Nothing at rest starts moving until a force makes it move.

Forces Can Bring Objects to Rest

An object in motion maintains its velocity unless it experiences an unbalanced force.

The second part of Newton's first law is about objects with a certain velocity. Such objects will continue to move forever with the same velocity unless an unbalanced force acts on them. Think about coming to a sudden stop while driving in a car. The car comes to a stop when the brakes are applied. But you continue to move forward until the force from your seat belt stops you.

These two parts of the law are really stating the same thing. After all, an object at rest has a velocity—its velocity is zero!

With little matter in space, there is nearly no friction or air resistance. Without a force to stop it, the satellite will stay in motion indefinitely.

Smooth ice does not have much friction, so a hockey puck can slide a long way without changing direction.

Forces Can Change the Motion of Objects

Newton's first law is also called the law of inertia. **Inertia** (ih•NER•shuh) is the tendency of all objects to resist any change in motion. Because of inertia, an object at rest will remain at rest until a force makes it move. Likewise, inertia is why a moving object will maintain its velocity until a force changes its speed or direction. Inertia is why it is impossible for a plane, a car, or a bicycle to stop immediately.

Active Reading **12 Identify** What is another name for Newton's first law?

Think Outside the Book (Inquiry)

11 Design Imagine that a scientist discovered a way to make a frictionless surface. What would be some useful applications for this discovery?

© Houghton Mifflin Harcourt Publishing Company • Image Credits: (bkgd) ©David Woods/Corbis; (tr) ©NASA; (cr) ©Richard Wolowicz/Getty Images Sport/Getty Images

Forces Can Accelerate Objects

When an unbalanced force acts on an object, the object moves with accelerated motion. Newton's second law describes the motion:

The acceleration of an object depends on the mass of the object and the amount of force applied.

This law links force, mass, and acceleration. This relationship can be expressed mathematically:

$$F = ma$$

From this equation, we see that a given force applied to a large mass will have only a small acceleration. When the same force is applied to a small mass, the acceleration will be large.

Imagine pushing a grocery cart. When the cart is empty, it has less mass. Your force accelerates the cart quickly. But when it is full, the same push accelerates the cart much more slowly.

13 Relate What three quantities does Newton's second law relate?

_____

_____

_____

$F_{net} = 150 \, N$

$F_{net} = 150 \, N$

Do the Math

Sample Problem

These players train by pushing a massive object. If the players produce a net force of 150 N, and the object has a mass of 75 kg, what is the object's acceleration?

You Try It!

14 Calculate For a more difficult training session, the mass to be pushed is increased to 300 kg. If the players still produce a net force of 150 N, what is the acceleration of the 300 kg mass?

Use Newton's law:

$F = ma$

$150 \, N = (75 \, kg)(a)$

$a = \dfrac{150 \, N}{75 \, kg}$

$a = 2 \, m/s^2$

Use Newton's law:

$F = ma$

$150 \, N =$

A Wearable Robot?

Scientists and engineers are working on developing powered exoskeletons for people to wear. These special suits have many useful applications.

Feats of Strength

The suits have sensors that detect a person's muscle movements, and they typically have an air pump that increases lifting force.

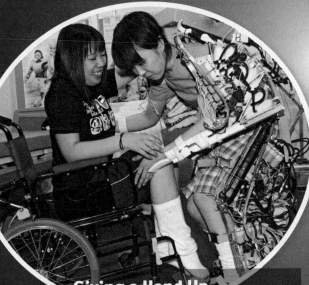

Giving a Hand Up

These suits were designed to help in nursing care. Here, the suit lets a nurse lift a patient out of a wheelchair with ease.

Extend

Inquiry

15 Analyze How does the extra force from a power suit make moving a mass easier?

16 Predict What do you think are some of the difficulties in making a power suit work?

17 Apply Think of some other tasks that could benefit from the development of a cheaper, more durable power suit. Make a drawing showing how much easier the task would be with a power suit.

A Matching Pair

How do force pairs act?

Newton also devised a third law of motion:

> *Whenever one object exerts a force on a second object, the second object exerts an equal and opposite force on the first.*

Newton's third law can be simply stated as follows: All forces act in pairs.

Forces Always Occur in Pairs

If a force is exerted, another force occurs that is equal in size and opposite in direction. The law itself addresses only forces. But the way that force pairs interact affects the motion of objects.

How do forces act in pairs? Action and reaction forces are present even when there is no motion. For example, you exert a force on a chair when you sit on it. Your weight pushing down on the chair is the action force. The reaction force is the force you feel exerted by the chair that pushes up on your body.

Active Reading

18 Identify What do we call the two forces in a force pair?

_____

_____

_____

The bear's paw exerts a force on the water.

The water exerts a force on the bear's paw.

Force Pairs Do Not Act on the Same Object

A force is always exerted on one object by another object. This rule is true for all forces, including action and reaction forces. However, action and reaction forces in a pair do not act on the same object. If they did, the net force would always be 0 N and nothing would ever move!

To understand how force pairs act on different objects, consider the act of swimming. When a bear swims, the action force is the bear's paw pushing on the water. The reaction force is the water pushing on the bear's paw. The action force pushes the water backward, and the reaction force moves the bear forward. Each object exerts a force on the other. Instead of neither moving, both the bear and the water move!

Force Pairs Can Have Unequal Effects

Even though both the action force and the reaction force are equal in size, their effects are often different. The force of gravity is a force pair between two objects. If you drop a ball, gravity pulls the ball toward Earth. This force is the action force exerted by Earth on the ball. But gravity also pulls Earth toward the ball! This is the reaction force. It's easy to see the action force in this example. Why don't you notice the effect of the reaction force—Earth being pulled upward? Think about Newton's second law. The force on the ball is the same size as the force on the Earth, but the Earth has much, much more mass than the ball. So the Earth's acceleration is much, much smaller than that of the ball!

It is difficult to observe the effect of this reaction force due to Earth's large mass.

Active Reading **19 Explain** Why don't force pairs have equal effects?

_____

_____

_____

Forces Can Occur in Several Pairs

An object can have multiple forces acting on it at once. When this happens, each force is part of a force pair. When a baseball bat hits a baseball, the bat does not fly backward, because the player's hand is exerting another force on the bat. What keeps the player's hand from flying back? A force exerted on the hand by the bones and muscles in the player's arm, and so on.

Visualize It!

20 Apply Name one force pair that has not been pointed out in the picture of the baseball player below.

_____

_____

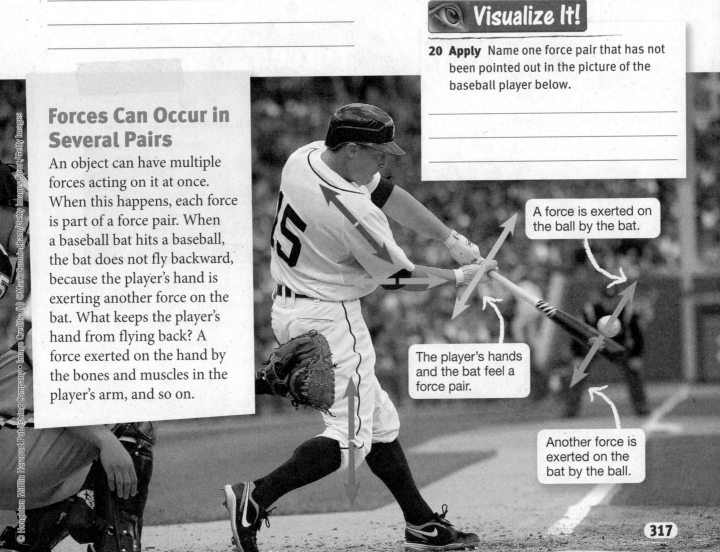

A force is exerted on the ball by the bat.

The player's hands and the bat feel a force pair.

Another force is exerted on the bat by the ball.

Visual Summary

To complete this summary, fill in the blanks with the correct word or phrase. Then use the key below to check your answers. You can use this page to review the main concepts of the lesson.

Balanced forces do not change motion. Unbalanced forces produce acceleration.

21 When the net force is not _____ N, the forces on the object are unbalanced, and the object will accelerate in the direction of the _____

Forces are required to change the motion of objects.

22 Newton's first law states that objects maintain their velocity unless

_____

_____

Forces

Forces accelerate objects.

F = 150N

23 Newton's second law states that force equals _____ times _____

Forces occur in action/reaction pairs.

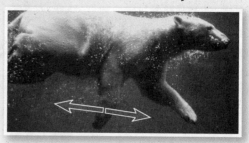

24 Newton's third law states that whenever one object exerts a force on a second object, the second object exerts an _____ and _____ force on the first.

25 Calculate A 6-kg ball and a 4-kg ball are acted on by forces of equal size. If the large ball accelerates at 2 m/s², what acceleration will the small ball undergo?

Lesson Review

Vocabulary

Draw a line to connect the following terms to their definitions.

1 force

2 inertia

3 net force

A a push or a pull exerted on an object

B the combination of all forces acting on an object

C the tendency of an object to resist a change in motion

Key Concepts

4 Identify Give an example of a contact force and an example of a force that acts at a distance.

_____

_____

_____

_____

5 Explain Two forces are applied on a soccer ball. Which of the following statements explains why the ball accelerates?

A The net force applied to the ball is 0 N.

B The ball resists one force but not the other.

C Newton's second law does not apply to round objects.

D The two forces are unbalanced.

6 Calculate What force is necessary to accelerate a 70-kg object at a rate of 4.2 m/s²? Show your work below.

Critical Thinking

Use this diagram to answer the following questions.

7 Explain When the mover pushes the box, two equal forces result. Explain why the box moves even though the forces are equal and opposite.

_____

_____

_____

_____

8 Apply When the box is moving, it experiences a friction force of 20 N to the left, or toward the mover. What force does the mover need to apply in order to keep the box moving to the right at 1 m/s?

_____

_____

9 Conclude Use Newton's first law of motion to explain why air bags in cars are important during head-on collisions.

_____

_____

_____

_____

_____

_____

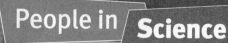

Steve Okamoto

ROLLER COASTER DESIGNER

A day in the life of a roller coaster designer is filled with twists and turns—just ask designer Steve Okamoto. As a kid, he became interested in roller coasters after a trip to Disneyland. To become a product designer, Steve studied subjects like math and science. He later earned a degree in product design that involved studying mechanical engineering and studio art.

Before he starts designing roller coasters, Steve has to think about all of the parts of a roller coaster and how it will fit in the amusement park. It's like putting together a huge puzzle. Different parts of the puzzle include the safety equipment needed, what the roller coaster will be made out of, and how the track will fit in next to other rides.

He also has to think about what visitors to the park will want to see and experience in a roller coaster ride.

As he is designing a roller coaster, Steve's math and science background comes in handy. For example, in order to make sure that a roller coaster's cars make it up each hill, he has to calculate the speed and acceleration of the cars on each part of the track. To create the curves, loops, and dips of the roller coaster track, he uses his knowledge of physics and geometry.

Acceleration from the downhill run provides the speed for the next climb.

JOB BOARD

Machinists

What You'll Do: Use machine tools, such as lathes, milling machines, and machining centers, to produce new metal parts.

Where You Might Work: Machine shops and manufacturing plants in industries including the automotive and aerospace industries.

Education: In high school, you should take math courses, especially trigonometry, and, if available, courses in blueprint reading, metalworking, and drafting. After high school, most people acquire their skills in an apprenticeship program. This gives a person a mix of classroom and on-the-job training.

Bicycle Mechanic

What You'll Do: Repair and maintain different kinds of bikes, from children's bikes to expensive road bikes.

Where You Might Work: Independent bicycle shops or large chain stores that carry bicycles; certain sporting events like Olympic and national trials.

Education: Some high schools and trade schools have shop classes that teach bicycle repair. Most bicycle mechanics get on-the-job training. To work as a mechanic at national and international cycling events, you will have to earn a bicycle mechanic's license.

PEOPLE IN SCIENCE NEWS

Mike Hensler

The Surf Chair

As a Daytona Beach lifeguard, Mike Hensler realized that the beach was almost impossible for someone in a wheelchair. Although he had never invented a machine before, Hensler decided to build a wheelchair that could be driven across sand without getting stuck. He began spending many evenings in his driveway with a pile of lawn-chair parts, designing the chair by trial and error.

The result looks very different from a conventional wheelchair. With huge rubber wheels and a thick frame of white PVC pipe, the Surf Chair not only moves easily over sandy terrain but also is weather resistant and easy to clean. The newest models of the Surf Chair come with optional attachments, such as a variety of umbrellas, detachable armrests and footrests, and even places to attach fishing rods.

© Houghton Mifflin Harcourt Publishing Company • Image Credits: (bkgd) ©David R. Frazier Photolibrary, Inc./Alamy; (tr) ©Mika/Corbis; (br) AP Photo/Jacksonville Daily News, Chuck Beckley

Gravity and Motion

ESSENTIAL QUESTION

How do objects move under the influence of gravity?

By the end of this lesson, you should be able to describe the effect that gravity, including Earth's gravity, has on matter.

Overcoming the force of gravity is hard to do for very long!

Sunshine State Standards

SC.6.P.13.1 Investigate and describe types of forces including contact forces and forces acting at a distance, such as electrical, magnetic, and gravitational.

SC.6.P.13.2 Explore the Law of Gravity by recognizing that every object exerts gravitational force on every other object and that the force depends on how much mass the objects have and how far apart they are.

Engage Your Brain

1 Predict Check *T* or *F* to show whether you think each statement is true or false.

T	F	
☐	☐	Earth's gravity makes heavy objects fall faster than light objects.
☐	☐	A person would weigh the same on other planets as on Earth.
☐	☐	Planets are round because of gravity.

2 Infer List some ways houses would be built differently if gravity were much stronger or much weaker.

_____

_____

_____

_____

_____

Active Reading

3 Predict What do you think the phrase *free fall* might mean? Write your own definition. After reading the lesson, see how close you were!

_____

_____

_____

_____

Vocabulary Terms

- gravity
- free fall
- orbit

4 Apply This list contains the key terms you'll learn in this section. As you read, underline the definition of each term.

Down to EARTH

Gravity pulls the skydiver, his clothes, and his parachute toward the Earth, all with the same acceleration.

This stop-action photo shows that when there is no air resistance, a feather and a billiard ball fall at the same rate.

Active Reading

5 Analyze What has to happen for a feather and a ball to fall at the same rate?

_____

_____

What is gravity?

If you watch video of astronauts on the moon, you see them wearing big, bulky spacesuits and yet jumping lightly. Why is leaping on the moon easier than on Earth? The answer is gravity. **Gravity** is a force of attraction between objects due to their mass. Gravity is a noncontact force that acts between two objects at any distance apart. Even when a skydiver is far above the ground, Earth's gravity acts to pull him downward.

Gravity Is An Attractive Force

Earth's gravity pulls everything toward Earth's center. It pulls, but it does not push, so it is called an attractive force.

You feel the force due to Earth's gravity as the heaviness of your body, or your weight. Weight is a force, and it depends on mass. Greater mass results in greater weight. This force of gravity between Earth and an object is equal to the mass of the object m multiplied by a factor due to gravity g.

$$F = mg$$

On Earth, g is about 9.8 m/s^2. The units are the same as the units for acceleration. Does this mean that Earth's gravity accelerates all objects in the same way? The surprising answer is yes.

Suppose you dropped a heavy object and a light object at the same time. Which would hit the ground first? Sometimes an object experiences a lot of air resistance and falls slowly or flutters to the ground. But if you could take away air resistance, all objects would fall with the same acceleration. When gravity is the only force affecting the fall, a light object and a heavy object hit the ground at the same time.

Acceleration depends on both force and mass. The heavier object experiences a greater force, or weight. But the heavier object is also harder to accelerate, because it has more mass. The two effects cancel, and the acceleration due to gravity is the same for all masses.

Gravity Affects Mass Equally

All matter has mass. Gravity is a result of mass, so all matter is affected by gravity. Every object exerts a gravitational pull on every other object. Your pencil and shoes are gravitationally attracted to each other, each to your textbook, all three to your chair, and so on. So why don't objects pull each other into a big pile? The gravitational forces between these objects are too small. Other forces, such as friction, are strong enough to balance the gravitational pulls and prevent changes in motion. Gravity is not a very powerful force—you overcome the attraction of Earth's entire mass on your body every time you stand up!

However, when enough mass gathers together, its effect can be large. Gravity caused Earth and other planets to become round. All parts of the planet pulled each other toward the center of mass, resulting in a sphere.

Some astronomical bodies do not have enough mass to pull themselves into spheres. Small moons and asteroids can maintain a lumpy shape, but larger moons such as Earth's have enough mass to form a sphere.

Gravity also acts over great distances. It determines the motion of celestial bodies. The paths of planets, the sun, and other stars are determined by gravity. Even the motion of our galaxy through the universe is due to gravity.

Galaxies, made up of billions of stars, have characteristic shapes and motions that are due to gravity.

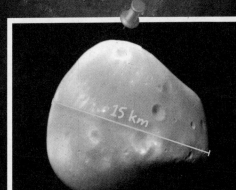

Deimos, one of the moons of Mars, is only about 15 km at its longest stretch. Deimos does not have enough mass to form a sphere.

Earth's moon has a diameter of more than 3,400 km. It has more than enough mass to pull itself into a sphere.

3,400 km

Think Outside the Book

6 **Incorporate** Write a short story about a time when you had to overcome the force of gravity to get something done.

A WEIGHTY Issue

What determines the force of gravity?

The law of universal gravitation relates gravitational force, mass, and distance. It states that all objects attract each other through gravitational force. The strength of the force depends on the masses involved and distance between them.

Gravity Depends on Distance

The gravitational force between two objects increases as the distance between their centers decreases. This means that objects far apart have a weaker attraction than objects close together.

If two objects move closer, the attraction between them increases. For example, you can't feel the sun's gravity because it is so far away, but if you were able to stand on the surface of the sun, you would find it impossible to move due to the gravity!

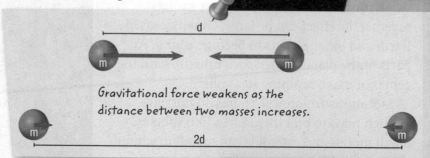

Gravitational force weakens as the distance between two masses increases.

Active Reading **7 Explain** How does distance affect gravitational force?

_____

_____

Gravity Depends on Mass

The gravitational force between two objects increases with the mass of each object. This means that objects with greater mass have more attraction between them. A cow has more mass than a cat, so there is more attraction between the Earth and the cow, and the cow weighs more.

This part of the law of universal gravitation explains why astronauts on the moon bounce when they walk. The moon has less mass than Earth, so the astronauts weigh less. The force of each step pushes an astronaut higher than it would on Earth.

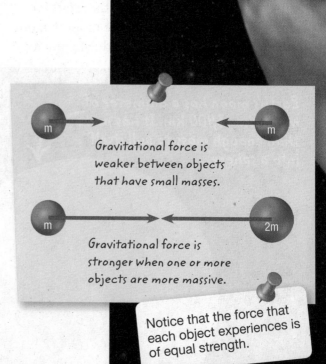

Gravitational force is weaker between objects that have small masses.

Gravitational force is stronger when one or more objects are more massive.

Active Reading **8 Explain** How does mass affect gravitational force?

_____

_____

Notice that the force that each object experiences is of equal strength.

Lesson Review

Vocabulary

Fill in the blanks with the term that best completes the following sentences.

1 _____ is a force that attracts all matter to each other.

2 When the only force affecting an object is gravity, that object is in _____.

3 An object traveling around another object in space is in _____.

Key Concepts

4 Relate The gravitational attraction between two objects will _____ if one object acquires more mass.

5 Relate The gravitational attraction between two objects will _____ if the objects move farther apart.

6 Explain Why are large astronomical bodies such as planets and stars round?

_____

_____

_____

7 Identify What two motions combine to produce an orbit?

_____

_____

_____

8 Distinguish Explain the difference between mass and weight.

_____

_____

_____

_____

Critical Thinking

9 Infer The weight of an object on a planet depends not only on its mass, but also on its distance from the planet's center. This table lists the weight of 80 kg on each planet in the solar system. Uranus has more than 14 times as much mass as Earth, yet the gravitational force is less. Explain how this could be.

_____

_____

_____

_____

Planet	Weight of 80 kg
Mercury	296 N
Venus	710 N
Earth	784 N
Mars	297 N
Jupiter	1983 N
Saturn	838 N
Uranus	708 N
Neptune	859 N

10 Apply Why don't satellites in orbit fall to the ground? Why don't they fly off into space?

_____

_____

_____

_____

_____

_____

_____

My Notes

Unit 5 **Summary**

Kinetic and Potential Energy

↓

Motion and Speed

↓

Acceleration ← **Forces** → **Gravity and Motion**

1 Interpret The Graphic Organizer above shows that force is related to acceleration and gravity. Explain.

_____

_____

_____

_____

2 Distinguish What is the difference between kinetic energy, potential energy, and mechanical energy?

_____

_____

_____

3 Judge "An object will only change its motion if a force is directly applied to it." Is this a true statement? Explain why or why not.

_____

_____

_____

4 Infer You are riding in a car that is traveling at a constant speed. Yet, the car is accelerating. Explain how this can be true.

_____

_____

_____

Name _____

Multiple Choice

Identify the choice that best completes the statement or answers the question.

1 In order for a space shuttle to leave Earth, it must produce a great amount of thrust. Its rocket boosters create this thrusting force by burning great amounts of fuel. However, once in space, the shuttle needs very little fuel. It circles Earth while gravity pulls it toward Earth. What term describes the circular path the shuttle makes in space?

    A. orbit

    B. gravity

    C. free fall

    D. weight

2 A weather station records the wind as blowing from the northeast at 12 km/h. Which statement explains why northeast at 12 km/h is a vector?

    F. The speed is given in km/h.

    G. The speed is a constant value.

    H. An average speed is reported.

    I. Speed and direction are given.

3 One ball rolls along a shelf at a steady rate. A second ball rolls off the shelf and gains speed as it falls in a curved path. Which must have an unbalanced force acting on it?

    A. the ball that rolls along the shelf

    B. the ball that falls

    C. both balls

    D. neither ball

4 Penny says that there is no gravitational force between dust particles because they have too little mass. Ella says that dust particles do pull on each other gravitationally and would move toward each other if they were in outer space instead of in air. Who has the better argument, and why?

    F. Penny, because objects with only a little mass are not affected by gravity.

    G. Penny, because any force on a dust particle would change its motion.

    H. Ella, because any two objects exert a gravitational force on each other.

    I. Ella, because objects with smaller mass have more gravity acting on them.

5 Luis is trying to push a box of new soccer balls across the floor. In the illustration, the arrow on the box represents the force that Luis exerts.

If the box is not moving, which of the following must be true?

    A. The box is exerting a larger force on Luis than he is exerting on the box.

    B. There is another force acting on the box that balances Luis's force.

    C. Luis is applying a force that acts at a distance.

    D. There is no force of friction acting on the box.

6 Ignacio uses a hammer to hit a nail into a board on the floor. How does gravity make it easier to hammer the nail?

    F. Gravity pushes the board up to help the nail go in.

    G. Gravity pulls the board and the nail toward each other.

    H. Gravity pulls the hammer down so that it pushes on the nail.

    I. Gravity pulls the nail down but does not pull on the hammer.

7 Every moving object has kinetic energy. This illustration shows four vehicles. Assume that they are all traveling at the same speed on a highway.

What do you know about the kinetic energy of the vehicles?

A. The motorcycle has the most kinetic energy because it is the vehicle with the least mass.

B. All of the vehicles have the same kinetic energy because they are moving at the same speed.

C. The delivery van has the greatest kinetic energy because its mass is greater than that of the other vehicles.

D. The delivery van has the greatest kinetic energy because it has the most tires in contact with the pavement.

8 Andre boarded a train at Lincoln Station. The train left the station at 9:10 p.m. and traveled, without stopping, 6 miles to Union Station. What additional information does Andre need to find the average speed of the train from Lincoln Station to Union Station?

F. the direction the train traveled

G. the time the train left Union Station

H. the initial and maximum speeds of the train

I. the time the train arrived at Union Station

9 Measuring acceleration requires the appropriate units. Scientists measure acceleration using a standardized set of units that are part of the SI system. Which are SI units for acceleration?

A. N

B. m/s

C. m/s^2

D. kg·m/s

10 Two identical space probes are orbiting Jupiter. Scientists determine that one of the space probes has a larger gravitational force acting on it than the other. Which of the following is the most likely reason for the difference?

    F. One space probe reached Jupiter before the other.

    G. One space probe has more air resistance than the other.

    H. Only one space probe is exerting a gravitational force on the other.

    I. One space probe is closer to Jupiter than the other.

11 Blair and Aaron competed in a 400-m running race. Blair finished the race in 55 s and came in first. Aaron finished the race in 58 s and came in second. Which of the following must have been greater for Blair than for Aaron?

    A. maximum speed during the race

    B. average speed for the entire race

    C. speed for the last 100 m of the race

    D. initial speed for the first 100 m the race

12 When a pendulum is released, it swings back and forth. The speed and position change throughout each swing. The illustration identifies three positions of the pendulum during its swing.

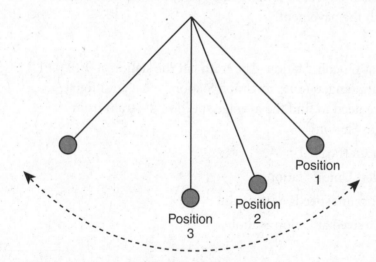

At which point does the pendulum weight have the greatest amount of mechanical energy?

    F. Position 1

    G. Position 2

    H. Position 3

    I. Mechanical energy does not change.

Look It Up!

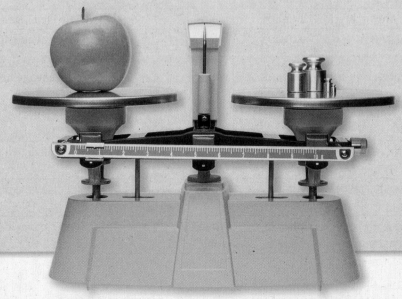

Reference Tables

Mineral Properties

Here are five steps to take in mineral identification:

1 Determine the color of the mineral. Is it light-colored, dark-colored, or a specific color?

2 Determine the luster of the mineral. Is it metallic or non-metallic?

3 Determine the color of any powder left by its streak.

4 Determine the hardness of your mineral. Is it soft, hard, or very hard? Using a glass plate, see if the mineral scratches it.

5 Determine whether your sample has cleavage or any special properties.

TERMS TO KNOW	DEFINITION
adamantine	a non-metallic luster like that of a diamond
cleavage	how a mineral breaks when subject to stress on a particular plane
luster	the state or quality of shining by reflecting light
streak	the color of a mineral when it is powdered
submetallic	between metallic and nonmetallic in luster
vitreous	glass-like type of luster

Silicate Minerals					
Mineral	**Color**	**Luster**	**Streak**	**Hardness**	**Cleavage and Special Properties**
Beryl	deep green, pink, white, bluish green, or yellow	vitreous	white	7.5–8	1 cleavage direction; some varieties fluoresce in ultraviolet light
Chlorite	green	vitreous to pearly	pale green	2–2.5	1 cleavage direction
Garnet	green, red, brown, black	vitreous	white	6.5–7.5	no cleavage
Hornblende	dark green, brown, or black	vitreous	none	5–6	2 cleavage directions
Muscovite	colorless, silvery white, or brown	vitreous or pearly	white	2–2.5	1 cleavage direction
Olivine	olive green, yellow	vitreous	white or none	6.5–7	no cleavage
Orthoclase	colorless, white, pink, or other colors	vitreous	white or none	6	2 cleavage directions
Plagioclase	colorless, white, yellow, pink, green	vitreous	white	6	2 cleavage directions
Quartz	colorless or white; any color when not pure	vitreous or waxy	white or none	7	no cleavage

| \multicolumn{6}{c}{**Nonsilicate Minerals**} | | | | | |
Mineral	**Color**	**Luster**	**Streak**	**Hardness**	**Cleavage and Special Properties**
\multicolumn{6}{c}{**Native Elements**}					
Copper	copper-red	metallic	copper-red	2.5–3	no cleavage
Diamond	pale yellow or colorless	adamantine	none	10	4 cleavage directions
Graphite	black to gray	submetallic	black	1–2	1 cleavage direction
\multicolumn{6}{c}{**Carbonates**}					
Aragonite	colorless, white, or pale yellow	vitreous	white	3.5–4	2 cleavage directions; reacts with hydrochloric acid
Calcite	colorless or white to tan	vitreous	white	3	3 cleavage directions; reacts with weak acid; double refraction
\multicolumn{6}{c}{**Halides**}					
Fluorite	light green, yellow, purple, bluish green, or other colors	vitreous	none	4	4 cleavage directions; some varieties fluoresce
Halite	white	vitreous	white	2.0–2.5	3 cleavage directions
\multicolumn{6}{c}{**Oxides**}					
Hematite	reddish brown to black	metallic to earthy	dark red to red-brown	5.6–6.5	no cleavage; magnetic when heated
Magnetite	iron-black	metallic	black	5.5–6.5	no cleavage; magnetic
\multicolumn{6}{c}{**Sulfates**}					
Anhydrite	colorless, bluish, or violet	vitreous to pearly	white	3–3.5	3 cleavage directions
Gypsum	white, pink, gray, or colorless	vitreous, pearly, or silky	white	2.0	3 cleavage directions
\multicolumn{6}{c}{**Sulfides**}					
Galena	lead-gray	metallic	lead-gray to black	2.5–2.8	3 cleavage directions
Pyrite	brassy yellow	metallic	greenish, brownish, or black	6–6.5	no cleavage

Reference Tables

Classification of Living Things

Domains and Kingdoms

All organisms belong to one of three domains: Domain Archaea, Domain Bacteria, or Domain Eukarya. Some of the groups within these domains are shown below. (Remember that genus names are italicized.)

Domain Archaea

The organisms in this domain are single-celled prokaryotes, many of which live in extreme environments.

Archaea		
Group	**Example**	**Characteristics**
Methanogens	*Methanococcus*	produce methane gas; can't live in oxygen
Thermophiles	*Sulpholobus*	require sulphur; can't live in oxygen
Halophiles	*Halococcus*	live in very salty environments; most can live in oxygen

Domain Bacteria

Organisms in this domain are single-celled prokaryotes and are found in almost every environment on Earth.

Bacteria		
Group	**Example**	**Characteristics**
Bacilli	*Escherichia*	rod shaped; some fix nitrogen; some cause disease
Cocci	*Streptococcus*	spherical shaped; cause diseases; can form spores
Spirilla	*Treponema*	spiral shaped; cause diseases, such as syphilis

Domain Eukarya

Organisms in this domain are single-celled or multicellular eukaryotes.

Kingdom Protista Many protists resemble fungi, plants, or animals, but are smaller and simpler in structure. Most are single-celled.

Protists		
Group	**Example**	**Characteristics**
Sarcodines	*Amoeba*	radiolarians; single-celled consumers
Ciliates	*Paramecium*	single-celled consumers
Flagellates	*Trypanosoma*	single-celled parasites
Sporozoans	*Plasmodium*	single-celled parasites
Euglenas	*Euglena*	single celled; photosynthesize
Diatoms	*Pinnularia*	most are single celled; photosynthesize
Dinoflagellates	*Gymnodinium*	single celled; some photosynthesize
Algae	*Volvox*	single celled or multicellular; photosynthesize
Slime molds	*Physarum*	single celled or multicellular; consumers or decomposers
Water molds	powdery mildew	single celled or multicellular; parasites or decomposers

Kingdom Fungi Most fungi are multicellular. Their cells have thick cell walls. Fungi absorb food from their environment.

Fungi		
Group	**Examples**	**Characteristics**
Bread molds	black bread mold	decomposers
Sac fungi	yeast; morels	saclike; parasites and decomposers
Club fungi	mushrooms; rusts; smuts	club shaped; parasites and decomposers
Chytrids	chytrid frog fungus	usually aquatic; can be decomposers or parasites

Kingdom Plantae Plants are multicellular and have cell walls made of cellulose. Plants make their own food through photosynthesis. Plants are classified into divisions instead of phyla.

Plants		
Group	**Examples**	**Characteristics**
Bryophytes	mosses, peat moss	no vascular tissue; reproduce by spores
Anthocerotophytes	hornworts	no vascular tissue; reproduce using horn-like structures
Hepatophytes	liverworts	no vascular tissue; live in moist environments
Lycophytes	*Lycopodium;* ground pine	grow in wooded areas; reproduce by spores
Pterophytes	horsetails; ferns	seedless, vascular tissue; reproduce by spores
Conifers	pines; spruces; firs	needlelike leaves; reproduce by seeds made in cones
Cycads	*Zamia*	slow-growing; reproduce by seeds made in large cones
Ginkgoes	*Ginkgo*	only one living species; reproduce by seeds
Angiosperms	all flowering plants	reproduce by seeds made in flowers; fruit

Kingdom Animalia Animals are multicellular. Their cells do not have cell walls. Most animals have specialized tissues and complex organ systems. Animals get food by eating other organisms.

Animals		
Group	**Examples**	**Characteristics**
Sponges	glass sponges	no symmetry or true segmentation; aquatic
Cnidarians	jellyfish; coral	radial symmetry; aquatic
Flatworms	planaria; tapeworms; flukes	bilateral symmetry; organ systems
Roundworms	*Trichina;* hookworms	bilateral symmetry; organ systems
Annelids	earthworms; leeches	bilateral symmetry; organ systems
Mollusks	snails; octopuses	bilateral symmetry; organ systems
Echinoderms	sea stars; sand dollars	radial symmetry; organ systems
Arthropods	insects; spiders; lobsters	bilateral symmetry; organ systems
Chordates	fish; amphibians; reptiles; birds; mammals	bilateral symmetry; complex organ systems

Reference Tables

Periodic Table of the Elements

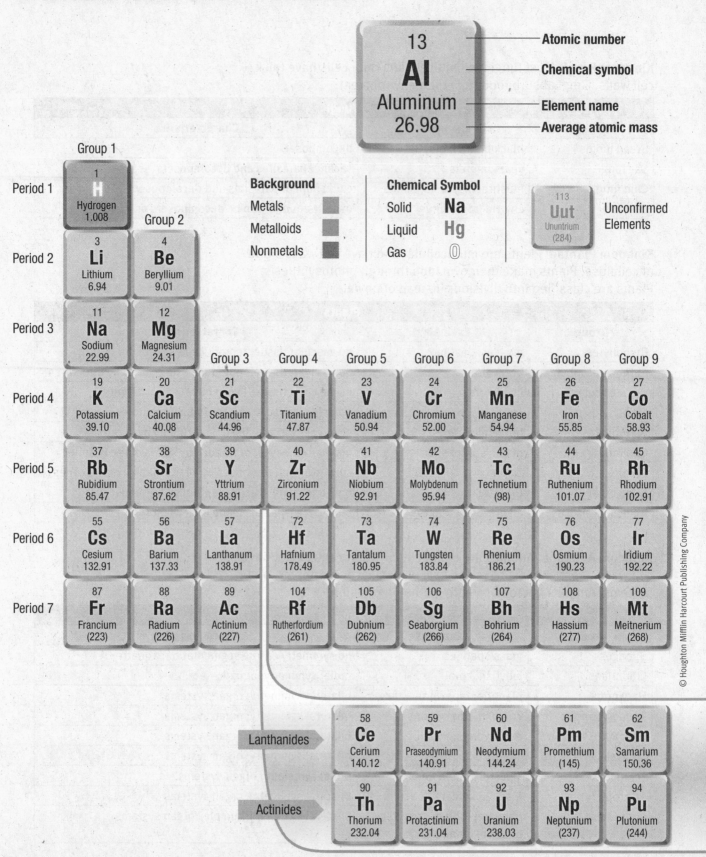

	13
	Al
	Aluminum
	26.98

- Atomic number
- Chemical symbol
- Element name
- Average atomic mass

Background
- Metals
- Metalloids
- Nonmetals

Chemical Symbol
- Solid **Na**
- Liquid **Hg**
- Gas 0

113 **Uut** Ununtrium (284) — Unconfirmed Elements

Group 1

Period 1 — 1 **H** Hydrogen 1.008

Group 2

Period 2 — 3 **Li** Lithium 6.94 | 4 **Be** Beryllium 9.01

Period 3 — 11 **Na** Sodium 22.99 | 12 **Mg** Magnesium 24.31

	Group 3	Group 4	Group 5	Group 6	Group 7	Group 8	Group 9
Period 4	21 **Sc** Scandium 44.96	22 **Ti** Titanium 47.87	23 **V** Vanadium 50.94	24 **Cr** Chromium 52.00	25 **Mn** Manganese 54.94	26 **Fe** Iron 55.85	27 **Co** Cobalt 58.93
Period 5	39 **Y** Yttrium 88.91	40 **Zr** Zirconium 91.22	41 **Nb** Niobium 92.91	42 **Mo** Molybdenum 95.94	43 **Tc** Technetium (98)	44 **Ru** Ruthenium 101.07	45 **Rh** Rhodium 102.91
Period 6	57 **La** Lanthanum 138.91	72 **Hf** Hafnium 178.49	73 **Ta** Tantalum 180.95	74 **W** Tungsten 183.84	75 **Re** Rhenium 186.21	76 **Os** Osmium 190.23	77 **Ir** Iridium 192.22
Period 7	89 **Ac** Actinium (227)	104 **Rf** Rutherfordium (261)	105 **Db** Dubnium (262)	106 **Sg** Seaborgium (266)	107 **Bh** Bohrium (264)	108 **Hs** Hassium (277)	109 **Mt** Meitnerium (268)

Period 4 — 19 **K** Potassium 39.10 | 20 **Ca** Calcium 40.08

Period 5 — 37 **Rb** Rubidium 85.47 | 38 **Sr** Strontium 87.62

Period 6 — 55 **Cs** Cesium 132.91 | 56 **Ba** Barium 137.33

Period 7 — 87 **Fr** Francium (223) | 88 **Ra** Radium (226)

Lanthanides ▶

58 **Ce** Cerium 140.12	59 **Pr** Praseodymium 140.91	60 **Nd** Neodymium 144.24	61 **Pm** Promethium (145)	62 **Sm** Samarium 150.36

Actinides ▶

90 **Th** Thorium 232.04	91 **Pa** Protactinium 231.04	92 **U** Uranium 238.03	93 **Np** Neptunium (237)	94 **Pu** Plutonium (244)

							Group 18
							2 **He** Helium 4.003

			Group 13	Group 14	Group 15	Group 16	Group 17	
			5 **B** Boron 10.81	6 **C** Carbon 12.01	7 **N** Nitrogen 14.01	8 **O** Oxygen 16.00	9 **F** Fluorine 19.00	10 **Ne** Neon 20.18
Group 10	Group 11	Group 12	13 **Al** Aluminum 26.98	14 **Si** Silicon 28.09	15 **P** Phosphorus 30.97	16 **S** Sulfur 32.07	17 **Cl** Chlorine 35.45	18 **Ar** Argon 39.95
28 **Ni** Nickel 58.69	29 **Cu** Copper 63.55	30 **Zn** Zinc 65.41	31 **Ga** Gallium 69.72	32 **Ge** Germanium 72.64	33 **As** Arsenic 74.92	34 **Se** Selenium 78.96	35 **Br** Bromine 79.90	36 **Kr** Krypton 83.80
46 **Pd** Palladium 106.42	47 **Ag** Silver 107.87	48 **Cd** Cadmium 112.41	49 **In** Indium 114.82	50 **Sn** Tin 118.71	51 **Sb** Antimony 121.76	52 **Te** Tellurium 127.6	53 **I** Iodine 126.9	54 **Xe** Xenon 131.29
78 **Pt** Platinum 195.08	79 **Au** Gold 196.97	80 **Hg** Mercury 200.59	81 **Tl** Thallium 204.38	82 **Pb** Lead 207.2	83 **Bi** Bismuth 208.98	84 **Po** Polonium (209)	85 **At** Astatine (210)	86 **Rn** Radon (222)
110 **Ds** Darmstadtium (271)	111 **Rg** Roentgenium (272)	112 **Cn** Copernicium (285)	113 **Uut** Ununtrium (284)	114 **Uuq** Ununquadium (289)	115 **Uup** Ununpentium (288)	116 **Uuh** Ununhexium (292)		118 **Uuo** Ununoctium (294)

63 **Eu** Europium 151.96	64 **Gd** Gadolinium 157.25	65 **Tb** Terbium 158.93	66 **Dy** Dysprosium 162.5	67 **Ho** Holmium 164.93	68 **Er** Erbium 167.26	69 **Tm** Thulium 168.93	70 **Yb** Ytterbium 173.04	71 **Lu** Lutetium 174.97
95 **Am** Americium (243)	96 **Cm** Curium (247)	97 **Bk** Berkelium (247)	98 **Cf** Californium (251)	99 **Es** Einsteinium (252)	100 **Fm** Fermium (257)	101 **Md** Mendelevium (258)	102 **No** Nobelium (259)	103 **Lr** Lawrencium (262)

Reading and Study Skills

A How-To Manual for Active Reading

This book belongs to you, and you are invited to write in it. In fact, the book won't be complete until you do. Sometimes you'll answer a question or follow directions to mark up the text. Other times you'll write down your own thoughts. And when you're done reading and writing in the book, the book will be ready to help you review what you learned and prepare for the Sunshine State Benchmark tests.

Active Reading Annotations

Before you read, you'll often come upon an Active Reading prompt that asks you to underline certain words or number the steps in a process. Here's an example.

Marking the text this way is called **annotating,** and your marks

> **Active Reading**
>
> **12 Identify** In this paragraph, number the sequence of sentences that describe replication.

are called **annotations.** Annotating the text can help you identify important concepts while you read.

There are other ways that you can annotate the text. You can draw an asterisk (*) by vocabulary terms, mark unfamiliar or confusing terms and information with a question mark (?), and mark main ideas with a double underline. And you can even invent your own marks to annotate the text!

Other Annotating Opportunities

Keep your pencil, pen, or highlighter nearby as you read, so you can make a note or highlight an important point at any time. Here are a few ideas to get you started.

- Notice the headings in red and blue. The blue headings are questions that point to the main idea of what you're reading. The red headings are answers to the questions in the blue ones. Together these headings outline the content of the lesson. After reading a lesson, you could write your own answers to the questions.

- Notice the bold-faced words that are highlighted in yellow. They are highlighted so that you can easily find them again on the page where they are defined. As you read or as you review, challenge yourself to write your own sentence using the bold-faced term.

- Make a note in the margin at any time. You might
  - Ask a "What if" question
  - Comment on what you read
  - Make a connection to something you read elsewhere
  - Make a logical conclusion from the text

Use your own language and abbreviations. Invent a code, such as using circles and boxes around words to remind you of their importance or relation to each other. Your annotations will help you remember your questions for class discussions, and when you go back to the lesson later, you may be able to fill in what you didn't understand the first time you read it. Like a scientist in the field or in a lab, you will be recording your questions and observations for analysis later.

Active Reading Questions

After you read, you'll often come upon Active Reading questions that ask you to think about what you've just read. You'll write your answer underneath the question. Here's an example.

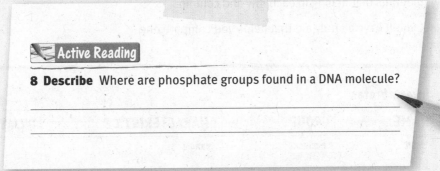

Active Reading

8 Describe Where are phosphate groups found in a DNA molecule?

_____

_____

This type of question helps you sum up what you've just read and pull out the most important ideas from the passage. In this case the question asks you to **describe** the structure of a DNA molecule that you have just read about. Other times you may be asked to do such things as **apply** a concept, **compare** two concepts, **summarize** a process, or **identify a cause-and-effect** relationship. You'll be strengthening those critical thinking skills that you'll use often in learning about science.

Reading and Study Skills

Using Graphic Organizers to Take Notes

Graphic organizers help you remember information as you read it for the first time and as you study it later. There are dozens of graphic organizers to choose from, so the first trick is to choose the one that's best suited to your purpose. Following are some graphic organizers to use for different purposes.

To remember lots of information	To relate a central idea to subordinate details	To describe a process	To make a comparison
• Arrange data in a Content Frame • Use Combination Notes to describe a concept in words and pictures	• Show relationships with a Mind Map or a Main Idea Web • Sum up relationships among many things with a Concept Map	• Use a Process Diagram to explain a procedure • Show a chain of events and results in a Cause-and-Effect Chart	• Compare two or more closely related things in a Venn Diagram

Content Frame

1 Make a four-column chart.

2 Fill the first column with categories (e.g., snail, ant, earthworm) and the first row with descriptive information (e.g., group, characteristic, appearance).

3 Fill the chart with details that belong in each row and column.

4 When you finish, you'll have a study aid that helps you compare one category to another.

Invertebrates

NAME	GROUP	CHARACTERISTICS	DRAWING
snail	mollusks	mangle	
ant	arthropods	six legs, exoskeleton	
earthworm	segmented worms	segmented body, circulatory and digestive systems	
heartworm	roundworms	digestive system	
sea star	echinoderms	spiny skin, tube feet	
jellyfish	cnidarians	stinging cells	

Combination Notes

1 Make a two-column chart.

2 Write descriptive words and definitions in the first column.

3 Draw a simple sketch that helps you remember the meaning of the term in the second column.

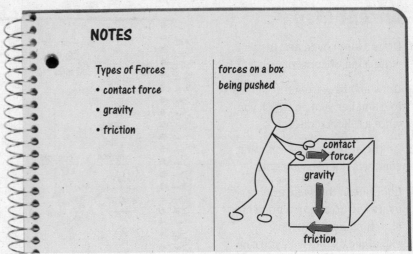

Mind Map

1 Draw an oval, and inside it write a topic to analyze.

2 Draw two or more arms extending from the oval. Each arm represents a main idea about the topic.

3 Draw lines from the arms on which to write details about each of the main ideas.

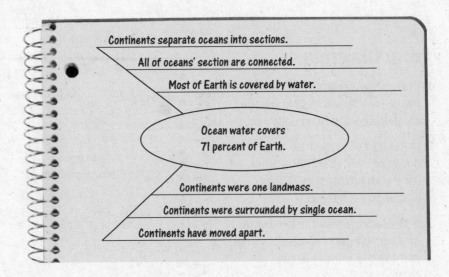

Main Idea Web

1 Make a box and write a concept you want to remember inside it.

2 Draw boxes around the central box, and label each one with a category of information about the concept (e.g., definition, formula, descriptive details)

3 Fill in the boxes with relevant details as you read.

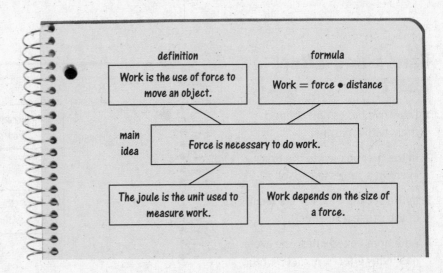

Reading and Study Skills

Concept Map

1 Draw a large oval, and inside it write a major concept.

2 Draw an arrow from the concept to a smaller oval, in which you write a related concept.

3 On the arrow, write a verb that connects the two concepts.

4 Continue in this way, adding ovals and arrows in a branching structure, until you have explained as much as you can about the main concept.

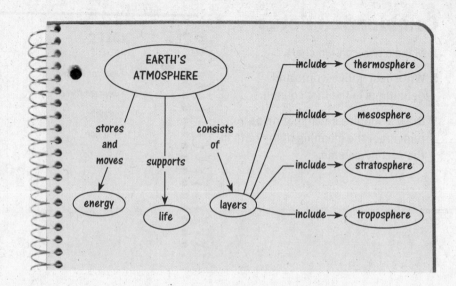

Venn Diagram

1 Draw two overlapping circles or ovals—one for each topic you are comparing—and label each one.

2 In the part of each circle that does not overlap with the other, list the characteristics that are unique to each topic.

3 In the space where the two circles overlap, list the characteristics that the two topics have in common.

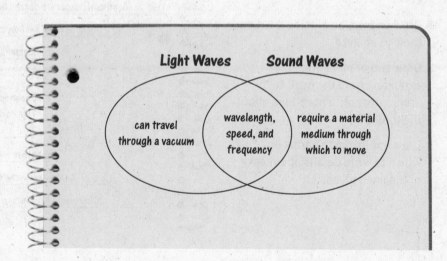

Cause-and-Effect Chart

1 Draw two boxes and connect them with an arrow.

2 In the first box, write the first event in a series (a cause).

3 In the second box, write a result of the cause (the effect).

4 Add more boxes when one event has many effects, or vice versa.

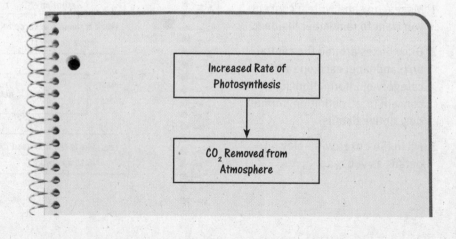

Process Diagram

A process can be a never-ending cycle. As you can see in this technology design process, engineers may backtrack and repeat steps, they may skip steps entirely, or they may repeat the entire process before a useable design is achieved.

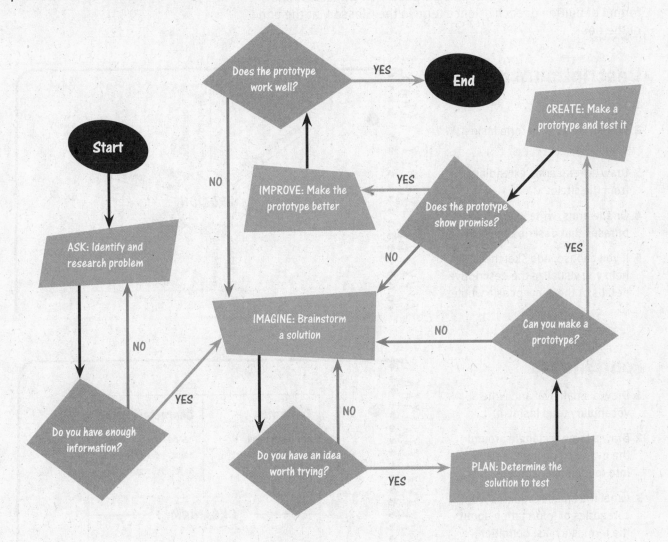

Reading and Study Skills

Using Vocabulary Strategies

Important science terms are highlighted where they are first defined in this book. One way to remember these terms is to take notes and make sketches when you come to them. Use the strategies on this page and the next for this purpose. You will also find a formal definition of each science term in the Glossary at the end of the book.

Description Wheel

1 Draw a small circle.

2 Write a vocabulary term inside the circle.

3 Draw several arms extending from the circle.

4 On the arms, write words and phrases that describe the term.

5 If you choose, add sketches that help you visualize the descriptive details or the concept as a whole.

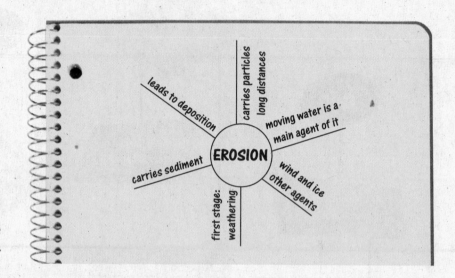

Four Square

1 Draw a small oval and write a vocabulary term inside it.

2 Draw a large rectangle around the oval, and divide the rectangle into four smaller squares.

3 Label the smaller squares with categories of information about the term, such as: definition, characteristics, examples, non-examples, appearance, and root words.

4 Fill the squares with descriptive words and drawings that will help you remember the overall meaning of the term and its essential details.

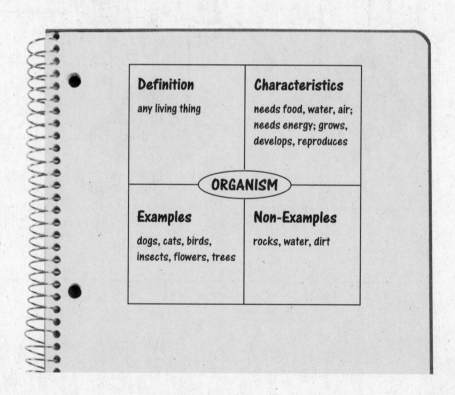

Frame Game

1 Draw a small rectangle, and write a vocabulary term inside it.

2 Draw a larger rectangle around the smaller one. Connect the corners of the larger rectangle to the corners of the smaller one, creating four spaces that frame the word.

3 In each of the four parts of the frame, draw or write details that help define the term. Consider including a definition, essential characteristics, an equation, examples, and a sentence using the term.

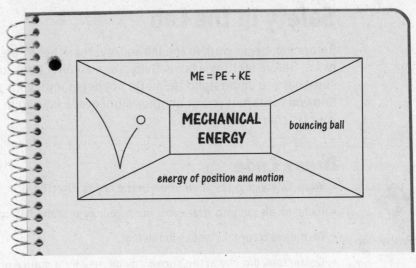

Magnet Word

1 Draw horseshoe magnet, and write a vocabulary term inside it.

2 Add lines that extend from the sides of the magnet.

3 Brainstorm words and phrases that come to mind when you think about the term.

4 On the lines, write the words and phrases that describe something essential about the term.

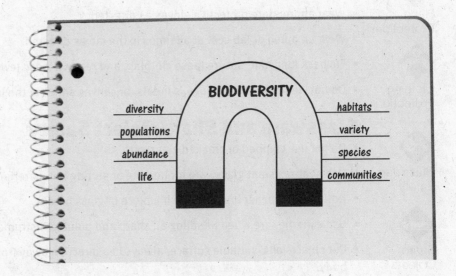

Word Triangle

1 Draw a triangle, and add lines to divide it into three parts.

2 Write a term and its definition in the bottom section of the triangle.

3 In the middle section, write a sentence in which the term is used correctly.

4 In the top section, draw a small picture to illustrate the term.

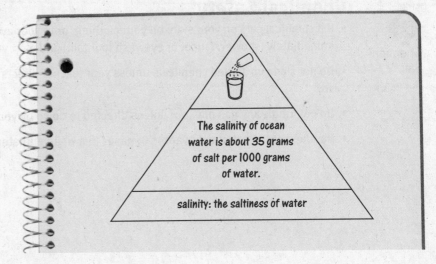

Science Skills

Safety in the Lab

Before you begin work in the laboratory, read these safety rules twice. Before starting a lab activity, read all directions and make sure that you understand them. Do not begin until your teacher has told you to start. If you or another student are injured in any way, tell your teacher immediately.

Dress Code

Eye Protection

Hand Protection

Clothing Protection

- Wear safety goggles at all times in the lab as directed.
- If chemicals get into your eyes, flush your eyes immediately.
- Do not wear contact lenses in the lab.
- Do not look directly at the sun or any intense light source or laser.
- Do not cut an object while holding the object in your hand.
- Wear appropriate protective gloves as directed.
- Wear an apron or lab coat at all times in the lab as directed.
- Tie back long hair, secure loose clothing, and remove loose jewelry.
- Do not wear open-toed shoes, sandals, or canvas shoes in the lab.

Glassware and Sharp Object Safety

Glassware Safety

Sharp Objects Safety

- Do not use chipped or cracked glassware.
- Use heat-resistant glassware for heating or storing hot materials.
- Notify your teacher immediately if a piece of glass breaks.
- Use extreme care when handling all sharp and pointed instruments.
- Cut objects on a suitable surface, always in a direction away from your body.

Chemical Safety

Chemical Safety

- If a chemical gets on your skin, on your clothing, or in your eyes, rinse it immediately (shower, faucet or eyewash fountain) and alert your teacher.
- Do not clean up spilled chemicals unless your teacher directs you to do so.
- Do not inhale any gas or vapor unless directed to do so by your teacher.
- Handle materials that emit vapors or gases in a well-ventilated area.

Electrical Safety

Electrical Safety

- Do not use equipment with frayed electrical cords or loose plugs.
- Do not use electrical equipment near water or when clothing or hands are wet.
- Hold the plug housing when you plug in or unplug equipment.

Heating Safety

Heating and Fire Safety

- Be aware of any source of flames, sparks, or heat (such as flames, heating coils, or hot plates) before working with any flammable substances.
- Know the location of lab fire extinguishers and fire-safety blankets.
- Know your school's fire-evacuation routes.
- If your clothing catches on fire, walk to the lab shower to put out the fire.
- Never leave a hot plate unattended while it is turned on or while it is cooling.
- Use tongs or appropriate insulated holders when handling heated objects.
- Allow all equipment to cool before storing it.

Wafting

Plant Safety

Animal Safety

Plant and Animal Safety

- Do not eat any part of a plant.
- Do not pick any wild plants unless your teacher instructs you to do so.
- Handle animals only as your teacher directs.
- Treat animals carefully and respectfully.
- Wash your hands thoroughly after handling any plant or animal.

Proper Waste Disposal

Hygienic Care

Cleanup

- Clean all work surfaces and protective equipment as directed by your teacher.
- Dispose of hazardous materials or sharp objects only as directed by your teacher.
- Keep your hands away from your face while you are working on any activity.
- Wash your hands thoroughly before you leave the lab or after any activity.

Science Skills

Designing an Experiment

An **experiment** is an organized procedure to study something under controlled conditions. Use the following steps of the scientific method when designing or conducting an experiment.

1 Identify a Research Problem

Every day you make **observations** by using your senses to gather information. Careful observations lead to good **questions,** and good questions can lead you to a purpose, or problem, for an experiment.

Imagine, for example, that you pass a pond every day on your way to school, and you notice green scum beginning to form on top of it. You wonder what it is and why it seems to be growing. You list your questions, and then you do a little preliminary research to find out what is already known.

You talk to others about your observations, learn that the scum is algae, and look for relvant information in books, journals, and online. You are especially interested in the data and conclusions from earlier experiments. Finally, you write the problem that you want to investigate. Your notes might look like these.

Area of Interest	Research Questions	Research Problem
Algae growth in lakes and ponds	• How do algae grow? • How do people measure algae? • What kind of fertilizer would affect the growth of algae? • Can fertilizer and algae be used safely in a lab? How?	How does fertilizer affect the presence of algae in a pond?

2 Make a Prediction

A **prediction** is a statement of what you expect will happen in your experiment. Before making a prediction, you need to decide in a general way what you will do in your procedure. You may state your prediction in an if-then format.

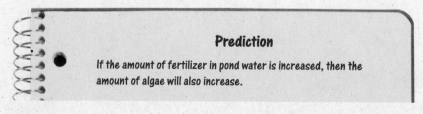

Prediction

If the amount of fertilizer in pond water is increased, then the amount of algae will also increase.

3 Form a Hypothesis

Many experiments are designed to test a hypothesis. A **hypothesis** is a tentative explanation for an expected result. You have predicted that additional fertilizer will cause additional algae growth in pond water; your hypothesis goes beyond your prediction to explain why fertilizer has that effect.

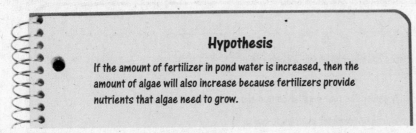

Hypothesis

If the amount of fertilizer in pond water is increased, then the amount of algae will also increase because fertilizers provide nutrients that algae need to grow.

4 Identify Variables to Test the Hypothesis

The next step is to design an experiment to test the hypothesis. The experiment may or may not support the hypothesis. Either way, the information that results from the experiment may be useful for future investigations.

Experimental Group and Control Group

An experiment to determine how two factors are related has a control group and an experimental group. The two groups are the same, except that the experimenter changes a single factor in the experimental group and does not change it in the control group.

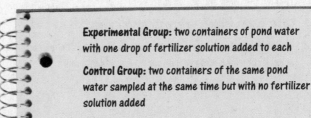

Experimental Group: two containers of pond water with one drop of fertilizer solution added to each

Control Group: two containers of the same pond water sampled at the same time but with no fertilizer solution added

Variables and Constants

In a controlled experiment, a **variable** is any factor that can change. **Constants** are all of the variables that are kept the same in both the experimental group and the control group.

The **independent variable** is the factor that is manipulated or changed in order to test the effect of the change on another variable. The **dependent variable** is the factor that the experimenter measures to gather data about the effect.

Independent Variable	Dependent Variable	Constants
Amount of fertilizer in pond water	Amount of algae that grow	• Where and when the pond water is obtained • The type of container used • Light and temperature conditions where the water is stored

Science Skills

5 Write a Procedure

Write each step of your procedure. Start each step with a verb, or action word, and keep the steps short. Your procedure should be clear enough for someone else to use as instructions for repeating your experiment.

Procedure

1. Put on your gloves. Use the large container to obtain a sample of pond water.

2. Divide the water sample equally among the four smaller containers.

3. Use the eyedropper to add one drop of fertilizer solution to two of the containers.

4. Use the masking tape and the marker to label the containers with your initials, the date, and the identifiers "Jar 1 with Fertilizer," "Jar 2 with Fertilizer," "Jar 1 without Fertilizer," and "Jar 2 without Fertilizer."

5. Cover the containers with clear plastic wrap. Use the scissors to punch ten holes in each of the covers.

6. Place all four containers on a window ledge. Make sure that they all receive the same amount of light.

7. Observe the containers every day for one week.

8. Use the ruler to measure the diameter of the largest clump of algae in each container, and record your measurements daily.

6 Experiment and Collect Data

Once you have all of your materials and your procedure has been approved, you can begin to experiment and collect data. Record both quantitative data (measurements) and qualitative data (observations), as shown below.

Fertilizer and Algae Growth

Date and Time	Experimental Group		Control Group		Observations
	Jar 1 with Fertilizer (diameter of algae in mm)	Jar 2 with Fertilizer (diameter of algae in mm)	Jar 1 without Fertilizer (diameter of algae in mm)	Jar 2 without Fertilizer (diameter of algae in mm)	
5/3 4:00 P.M.	0	0	0	0	condensation in all containers
5/4 4:00 P.M.	0	3	0	0	tiny green blobs in jar 2 with fertilizer
5/5 4:15 P.M.	4	5	0	3	green blobs in jars 1 and 2 with fertilizer and jar 2 without fertilizer
5/6 4:00 P.M.	5	6	0	4	water light green in jar 2 with fertilizer
5/7 4:00 P.M.	8	10	0	6	water light green in jars 1 and 2 with fertilizer and jar 2 without fertilizer
5/8 3:30 P.M.	10	18	0	6	cover off jar 2 with fertilizer
5/9 3:30 P.M.	14	23	0	8	drew sketches of each container

Drawings of Samples Viewed Under Microscope on 5/9 at 100x

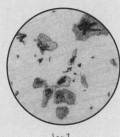
Jar 1 with Fertilizer

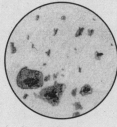
Jar 2 with Fertilizer

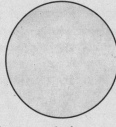
Jar 1 without Fertilizer

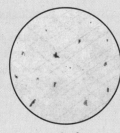
Jar 2 without Fertilizer

Science Skills

7 Analyze Data

After you have completed your experiments, made your observations, and collected your data, you must analyze all the information you have gathered. Tables, statistics, and graphs are often used in this step to organize and analyze the data.

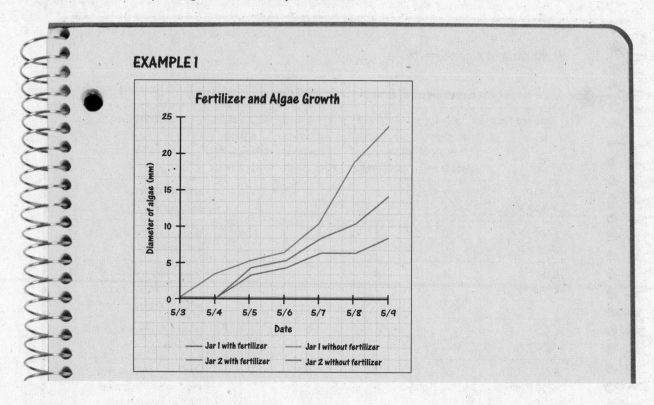

EXAMPLE 1

Fertilizer and Algae Growth

Jar 1 with fertilizer   Jar 1 without fertilizer
Jar 2 with fertilizer   Jar 2 without fertilizer

8 Make Conclusions

To draw conclusions from your experiment, first write your results. Then compare your results with your hypothesis. Do your results support your hypothesis?

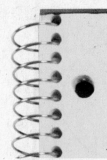

Conclusion

More algae grew in pond water to which fertilizer had been added than in pond water to which no fertilizer had been added. My hypothesis was supported. I conclude that it is possible that the growth of algae in ponds can be influenced by introduced fertilizer.

Graduated Cylinders

How to Measure the Volume of a Liquid with a Graduated Cylinder

- Be sure that the graduated cylinder is on a flat surface so that your measurement will be accurate.

- When reading the scale on a graduated cylinder, be sure to have your eyes at the level of the surface of the liquid.

- The surface of the liquid will be curved in the graduated cylinder. Read the volume of the liquid at the bottom of the curve, or meniscus (muh-NIHS-kuhs).

- You can use a graduated cylinder to find the volume of a solid object by measuring the increase in a liquid's level after you add the object to the cylinder.

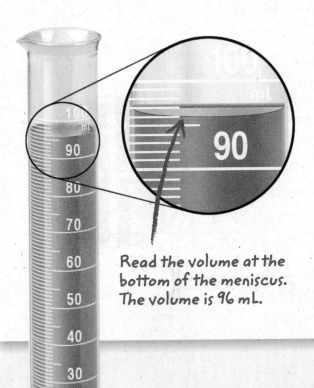

Read the volume at the bottom of the meniscus. The volume is 96 mL.

Metric Rulers

How to Measure the Length of a Leaf with a Metric Ruler

1 Lay a ruler flat on top of the leaf so that the 1-centimeter mark lines up with one end. Make sure the ruler and the leaf do not move between the time you line them up and the time you take the measurement.

2 Look straight down on the ruler so that you can see exactly how the marks line up with the other end of the leaf.

3 Estimate the length by which the leaf extends beyond a marking. For example, the leaf below extends about halfway between the 4.2-centimeter and 4.3-centimeter marks, so the apparent measurement is about 4.25 centimeters.

4 Remember to subtract 1 centimeter from your apparent measurement, since you started at the 1-centimeter mark on the ruler and not at the end. The leaf is about 3.25 centimeters long (4.25 cm − 1 cm = 3.25 cm).

Science Skills

Triple Beam Balance

This balance has a pan and three beams with sliding masses, called riders. At one end of the beams is a pointer that indicates whether the mass on the pan is equal to the masses shown on the beams.

How to Measure the Mass of an Object

1 Make sure the balance is zeroed before measuring the mass of an object. The balance is zeroed if the pointer is at zero when nothing is on the pan and the riders are at their zero points. Use the adjustment knob at the base of the balance to zero it.

2 Place the object to be measured on the pan.

3 Move the riders one notch at a time away from the pan. Begin with the largest rider. If moving the largest rider one notch brings the pointer below zero, begin measuring the mass of the object with the next smaller rider.

4 Change the positions of the riders until they balance the mass on the pan and the pointer is at zero. Then add the readings from the three beams to determine the mass of the object.

300 g	position of largest rider
90 g	position of middle rider
+ 3 g	position of smallest rider
393 g	mass of beaker and water

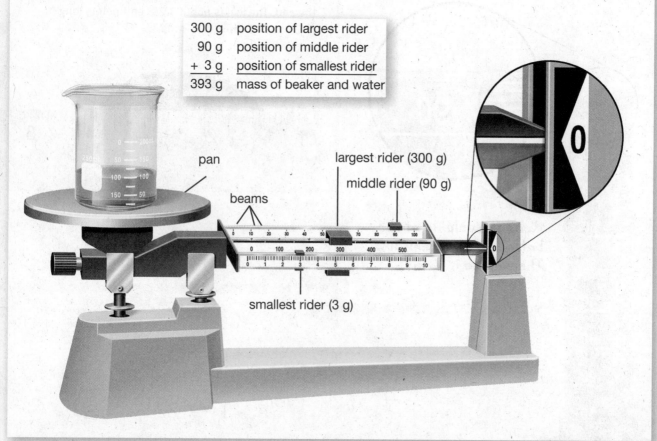

pan

beams

largest rider (300 g)

middle rider (90 g)

smallest rider (3 g)

Using the Metric System and SI Units

Scientists use International System (SI) units for measurements of distance, volume, mass, and temperature. The International System is based on powers of ten and the metric system of measurement.

Basic SI Units		
Quantity	**Name**	**Symbol**
length	meter	m
volume	liter	L
mass	gram	g
temperature	kelvin	K

SI Prefixes		
Prefix	**Symbol**	**Power of 10**
kilo-	k	1000
hecto-	h	100
deca-	da	10
deci-	d	0.1 or $\frac{1}{10}$
centi-	c	0.01 or $\frac{1}{100}$
milli-	m	0.001 or $\frac{1}{1000}$

Changing Metric Units

You can change from one unit to another in the metric system by multiplying or dividing by a power of 10.

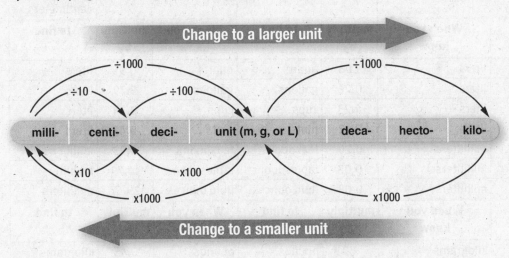

Example

Change 0.64 liters to milliliters.
1 Decide whether to multiply or divide.
2 Select the power of 10.

Change to a smaller unit by multiplying

mL ◄——— x 1000 ——— L

0.64 x 1000 = 640.

ANSWER 0.64 L = 640 mL

Example

Change 23.6 grams to kilograms.
1 Decide whether to multiply or divide.
2 Select the power of 10.

Change to a larger unit by dividing

g ——— ÷ 1000 ———► kg

26.3 ÷ 1000 = 0.0263

ANSWER 23.6 g = 0.0236 kg

Science Skills

Converting Between SI and U.S. Customary Units

Use the chart below when you need to convert between SI units and U.S. customary units.

SI Unit	From SI to U.S. Customary			From U.S. Customary to SI		
Length	**When you know**	**multiply by**	**to find**	**When you know**	**multiply by**	**to find**
kilometer (km) = 1000 m	kilometers	0.62	miles	miles	1.61	kilometers
meter (m) = 100 cm	meters	3.28	feet	feet	0.3048	meters
centimeter (cm) = 10 mm	centimeters	0.39	inches	inches	2.54	centimeters
millimeter (mm) = 0.1 cm	millimeters	0.04	inches	inches	25.4	millimeters
Area	**When you know**	**multiply by**	**to find**	**When you know**	**multiply by**	**to find**
square kilometer (km²)	square kilometers	0.39	square miles	square miles	2.59	square kilometers
square meter (m²)	square meters	1.2	square yards	square yards	0.84	square meters
square centimeter (cm²)	square centimeters	0.155	square inches	square inches	6.45	square centimeters
Volume	**When you know**	**multiply by**	**to find**	**When you know**	**multiply by**	**to find**
liter (L) = 1000 mL	liters	1.06	quarts	quarts	0.95	liters
	liters	0.26	gallons	gallons	3.79	liters
	liters	4.23	cups	cups	0.24	liters
	liters	2.12	pints	pints	0.47	liters
milliliter (mL) = 0.001 L	milliliters	0.20	teaspoons	teaspoons	4.93	milliliters
	milliliters	0.07	tablespoons	tablespoons	14.79	milliliters
	milliliters	0.03	fluid ounces	fluid ounces	29.57	milliliters
Mass	**When you know**	**multiply by**	**to find**	**When you know**	**multiply by**	**to find**
kilogram (kg) = 1000 g	kilograms	2.2	pounds	pounds	0.45	kilograms
gram (g) = 1000 mg	grams	0.035	ounces	ounces	28.35	grams

Temperature Conversions

Even though the kelvin is the SI base unit of temperature, the degree Celsius will be the unit you use most often in your science studies. The formulas below show the relationships between temperatures in degrees Fahrenheit (°F), degrees Celsius (°C), and kelvins (K).

$$°C = \frac{5}{9} \ (°F - 32) \qquad °F = \frac{9}{5} \ °C + 32 \qquad K = °C + 273$$

Examples of Temperature Conversions		
Condition	**Degrees Celsius**	**Degrees Fahrenheit**
Freezing point of water	0	32
Cool day	10	50
Mild day	20	68
Warm day	30	86
Normal body temperature	37	98.6
Very hot day	40	104
Boiling point of water	100	212

Math Refresher

Performing Calculations

Science requires an understanding of many math concepts. The following pages will help you review some important math skills.

Mean

The mean is the sum of all values in a data set divided by the total number of values in the data set. The mean is also called the *average*.

Example

Find the mean of the following set of numbers: 5, 4, 7, and 8.

Step 1   Find the sum.

$5 + 4 + 7 + 8 = 24$

Step 1   Divide the sum by the number of numbers in your set. Because there are four numbers in this example, divide the sum by 4.

$24 \div 4 = 6$

Answer The average, or mean, is 6.

Median

The median of a data set is the middle value when the values are written in numerical order. If a data set has an even number of values, the median is the mean of the two middle values.

Example

To find the median of a set of measurements, arrange the values in order from least to greatest. The median is the middle value.

13 mm   14 mm   16 mm   21 mm   23 mm

Answer The median is 16 mm.

Mode

The mode of a data set is the value that occurs most often.

Example

To find the mode of a set of measurements, arrange the values in order from least to greatest and determine the value that occurs most often.

13 mm, 14 mm, 14 mm, 16 mm,
21 mm, 23 mm, 25 mm

Answer The mode is 14 mm.

A data set can have more than one mode or no mode. For example, the following data set has modes of 2 mm and 4 mm:

2 mm   2 mm   3 mm   4 mm   4 mm

The data set below has no mode, because no value occurs more often than any other.

2 mm   3 mm   4 mm   5 mm

Math Refresher

Ratios

A **ratio** is a comparison between numbers, and it is usually written as a fraction.

Example

Find the ratio of thermometers to students if you have 36 thermometers and 48 students in your class.

Step 1   Write the ratio.

$$\frac{36 \text{ thermometers}}{48 \text{ students}}$$

Step 2   Simplify the fraction to its simplest form.

$$\frac{36}{48} = \frac{36 \div 12}{48 \div 12} = \frac{3}{4}$$

The ratio of thermometers to students is 3 to 4 or 3:4.

Proportions

A **proportion** is an equation that states that two ratios are equal.

$$\frac{3}{1} = \frac{12}{4}$$

To solve a proportion, you can use cross-multiplication. If you know three of the quantities in a proportion, you can use cross-multiplication to find the fourth.

Example

Imagine that you are making a scale model of the solar system for your science project. The diameter of Jupiter is 11.2 times the diameter of the Earth. If you are using a plastic-foam ball that has a diameter of 2 cm to represent the Earth, what must the diameter of the ball representing Jupiter be?

$$\frac{11.2}{1} = \frac{x}{2 \text{ cm}}$$

Step 1   Cross-multiply.

$$\frac{11.2}{1} = \frac{x}{2}$$

$$11.2 \times 2 = x \times 1$$

Step 2   Multiply.

$$22.4 = x \times 1$$

$$x = 22.4 \text{ cm}$$

You will need to use a ball that has a diameter of 22.4 cm to represent Jupiter.

Rates

A **rate** is a ratio of two values expressed in different units. A unit rate is a rate with a denominator of 1 unit.

Example

A plant grew 6 centimeters in 2 days. The plant's rate of growth was $\frac{6 \text{ cm}}{2 \text{ days}}$. To describe the plant's growth in centimeters per day, write a unit rate.

Divide numerator and denominator by 2:

$$\frac{6 \text{ cm}}{2 \text{ days}} = \frac{6 \text{ cm} \div 2}{2 \text{ days} \div 2}$$

Simplify: $= \frac{3 \text{ cm}}{1 \text{ day}}$

Answer The plant's rate of growth is 3 centimeters per day.

Percent

A **percent** is a ratio of a given number to 100. For example, 85% = 85/100. You can use percent to find part of a whole.

Example
What is 85% of 40?

Step 1 Rewrite the percent as a decimal by moving the decimal point two places to the left.

$$0.85$$

Step 2 Multiply the decimal by the number that you are calculating the percentage of.

$$0.85 \times 40 = 34$$

85% of 40 is 34.

Decimals

To **add** or **subtract decimals**, line up the digits vertically so that the decimal points line up. Then, add or subtract the columns from right to left. Carry or borrow numbers as necessary.

Example
Add the following numbers: 3.1415 and 2.96.

Step 1 Line up the digits vertically so that the decimal points line up.

$$
\begin{array}{r}
3.1415 \\
+ 2.96 \\
\hline
\end{array}
$$

Step 2 Add the columns from right to left, and carry when necessary.

$$
\begin{array}{r}
3.1415 \\
+ 2.96 \\
\hline
6.1015 \\
\end{array}
$$

The sum is 6.1015.

Fractions

A **fraction** is a ratio of two nonzero whole numbers.

Example
Your class has 24 plants. Your teacher instructs you to put 6 plants in a shady spot. What fraction of the plants in your class will you put in a shady spot?

Step 1 In the denominator, write the total number of parts in the whole.

$$\frac{?}{24}$$

Step 2 In the numerator, write the number of parts of the whole that are being considered.

$$\frac{6}{24}$$

So, $\frac{6}{24}$ of the plants will be in the shade.

Math Refresher

Simplifying Fractions

It is usually best to express a fraction in its simplest form. Expressing a fraction in its simplest form is called **simplifying a fraction**.

Example

Simplify the fraction $\frac{30}{45}$ to its simplest form.

Step 1 Find the largest whole number that will divide evenly into both the numerator and denominator. This number is called the greatest common factor (GCF).

Factors of the numerator 30:
1, 2, 3, 5, 6, 10, **15**, 30

Factors of the denominator 45:
1, 3, 5, 9, **15**, 45

Step 2 Divide both the numerator and the denominator by the GCF, which in this case is 15.

$$\frac{30}{45} = \frac{30 \div 15}{45 \div 15} = \frac{2}{3}$$

Thus, $\frac{30}{45}$ written in its simplest form is $\frac{2}{3}$.

Adding and Subtracting Fractions

To **add** or **subtract fractions** that have the same denominator, simply add or subtract the numerators.

Examples

$\frac{3}{5} + \frac{1}{5} = ?$ and $\frac{3}{4} - \frac{1}{4} = ?$

Step 1 Add or subtract the numerators.

$$\frac{3}{5} + \frac{1}{5} = \frac{4}{}\ \text{and}\ \frac{3}{4} - \frac{1}{4} = \frac{2}{}$$

Step 2 Write the sum or difference over the denominator.

$$\frac{3}{5} + \frac{1}{5} = \frac{4}{5}\ \text{and}\ \frac{3}{4} - \frac{1}{4} = \frac{2}{4}$$

Step 3 If necessary, write the fraction in its simplest form.

$\frac{4}{5}$ cannot be simplified, and $\frac{2}{4} = \frac{1}{2}$.

To **add** or **subtract fractions** that have **different denominators,** first find the least common denominator (LCD)

Examples

$\frac{1}{2} + \frac{1}{6} = ?$ and $\frac{3}{4} - \frac{2}{3} = ?$

Step 1 Write the equivalent fractions that have a common denominator.

$$\frac{3}{6} + \frac{1}{6} = ?\ \text{and}\ \frac{9}{12} - \frac{8}{12} = ?$$

Step 2 Add or subtract the fractions.

$$\frac{3}{6} + \frac{1}{6} = \frac{4}{6}\ \text{and}\ \frac{9}{12} - \frac{8}{12} = \frac{1}{12}$$

Step 3 If necessary, write the fraction in its simplest form.

$\frac{4}{6} = \frac{2}{3}$, and $\frac{1}{12}$ cannot be simplified.

Multiplying Fractions

To **multiply fractions,** multiply the numerators and the denominators together, and then change the fraction to its simplest form.

Example

$\frac{5}{9} \times \frac{7}{10} = ?$

Step 1 Multiply the numerators and denominators.

$$\frac{5}{9} \times \frac{7}{10} = \frac{5 \times 7}{9 \times 10} = \frac{35}{90}$$

Step 2 Simplify the fraction.

$$\frac{35}{90} = \frac{35 \div 5}{90 \div 5} = \frac{7}{18}$$

Dividing Fractions

To **divide fractions**, first exchange the numerator and the denominator of the divisor (the number you divide by). This number is called the reciprocal of the divisor. Then multiply and simplify if necessary.

Example

$$\frac{5}{8} \div \frac{3}{2} = ?$$

Step 1   Rewrite the divisor as its reciprocal.

$$\frac{3}{2} \rightarrow \frac{2}{3}$$

Step 2   Multiply the fractions.

$$\frac{5}{8} \times \frac{2}{3} = \frac{5 \times 2}{8 \times 3} = \frac{10}{24}$$

Step 3   Simplify the fraction.

$$\frac{10}{24} = \frac{10 \div 2}{24 \div 2} = \frac{5}{12}$$

Using Significant Figures

The **significant figures** in a decimal are the digits that are warranted by the accuracy of a measuring device.

When you perform a calculation with measurements, the number of significant figures to include in the result depends in part on the number of significant figures in the measurements. When you multiply or divide measurements, your answer should have only as many significant figures as the measurement with the fewest significant figures.

Examples

Using a balance and a graduated cylinder filled with water, you determined that a marble has a mass of 8.0 grams and a volume of 3.5 cubic centimeters. To calculate the density of the marble, divide the mass by the volume.

Write the formula for density: $\text{Density} = \dfrac{\text{mass}}{\text{volume}}$

Substitute measurements: $= \dfrac{8.0\ g}{3.5\ cm^3}$

Use a calculator to divide: $\approx 2.285714286\ g/cm^3$

Answer Because the mass and the volume have two significant figures each, give the density to two significant figures. The marble has a density of 2.3 grams per cubic centimeter.

Using Scientific Notation

Scientific notation is a shorthand way to write very large or very small numbers. For example, 73,500,000,000,000,000,000,000 kg is the mass of the Moon. In scientific notation, it is 7.35×10^{22} kg. A value written as a number between 1 and 10, times a power of 10, is in scientific notation.

Examples

You can convert from standard form to scientific notation.

Standard Form	Scientific Notation
720,000	7.2×10^5
5 decimal places left	Exponent is 5.
0.000291	2.91×10^{-4}
4 decimal places right	Exponent is −4.

You can convert from scientific notation to standard form.

Scientific Notation	Standard Form
4.63×10^7	46,300,000
Exponent is 7.	7 decimal places right
1.08×10^{-6}	0.00000108
Exponent is −6.	6 decimal places left

Math Refresher

Making and Interpreting Graphs

Circle Graph

A circle graph, or pie chart, shows how each group of data relates to all of the data. Each part of the circle represents a category of the data. The entire circle represents all of the data. For example, a biologist studying a hardwood forest in Wisconsin found that there were five different types of trees. The data table at right summarizes the biologist's findings.

Wisconsin Hardwood Trees	
Type of tree	**Number found**
Oak	600
Maple	750
Beech	300
Birch	1,200
Hickory	150
Total	3,000

How to Make a Circle Graph

1 To make a circle graph of these data, first find the percentage of each type of tree. Divide the number of trees of each type by the total number of trees, and multiply by 100%.

$$\frac{600 \text{ oak}}{3,000 \text{ trees}} \times 100\% = 20\%$$

$$\frac{750 \text{ maple}}{3,000 \text{ trees}} \times 100\% = 25\%$$

$$\frac{300 \text{ beech}}{3,000 \text{ trees}} \times 100\% = 10\%$$

$$\frac{1,200 \text{ birch}}{3,000 \text{ trees}} \times 100\% = 40\%$$

$$\frac{150 \text{ hickory}}{3,000 \text{ trees}} \times 100\% = 5\%$$

2 Now, determine the size of the wedges that make up the graph. Multiply each percentage by 360°. Remember that a circle contains 360°.

$20\% \times 360° = 72°$ $25\% \times 360° = 90°$

$10\% \times 360° = 36°$ $40\% \times 360° = 144°$

$5\% \times 360° = 18°$

3 Check that the sum of the percentages is 100 and the sum of the degrees is 360.

$20\% + 25\% + 10\% + 40\% + 5\% = 100\%$

$72° + 90° + 36° + 144° + 18° = 360°$

4 Use a compass to draw a circle and mark the center of the circle.

5 Then, use a protractor to draw angles of 72°, 90°, 36°, 144°, and 18° in the circle.

6 Finally, label each part of the graph, and choose an appropriate title.

A Community of Wisconsin Hardwood Trees

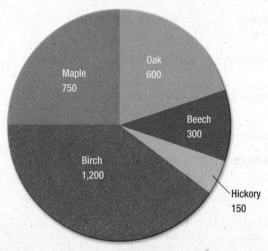

Line Graphs

Line graphs are most often used to demonstrate continuous change. For example, Mr. Smith's students analyzed the population records for their hometown, Appleton, between 1910 and 2010. Examine the data at right.

Because the year and the population change, they are the variables. The population is determined by, or dependent on, the year. Therefore, the population is called the **dependent variable,** and the year is called the **independent variable**. Each year and its population make a **data pair**. To prepare a line graph, you must first organize data pairs into a table like the one at right.

Population of Appleton, 1910–2010	
Year	**Population**
1910	1,800
1930	2,500
1950	3,200
1970	3,900
1990	4,600
2010	5,300

How to Make a Line Graph

1 Place the independent variable along the horizontal (x) axis. Place the dependent variable along the vertical (y) axis.

2 Label the x-axis "Year" and the y-axis "Population." Look at your greatest and least values for the population. For the y-axis, determine a scale that will provide enough space to show these values. You must use the same scale for the entire length of the axis. Next, find an appropriate scale for the x-axis.

3 Choose reasonable starting points for each axis.

4 Plot the data pairs as accurately as possible.

5 Choose a title that accurately represents the data.

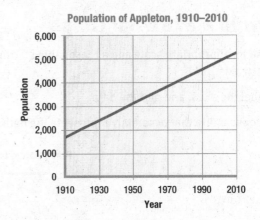

How to Determine Slope

Slope is the ratio of the change in the y-value to the change in the x-value, or "rise over run."

1 Choose two points on the line graph. For example, the population of Appleton in 2010 was 5,300 people. Therefore, you can define point A as (2010, 5,300). In 1910, the population was 1,800 people. You can define point B as (1910, 1,800).

2 Find the change in the y-value. (y at point A) − (y at point B) = 5,300 people − 1,800 people = 3,500 people

3 Find the change in the x-value. (x at point A) − (x at point B) = 2010 − 1910 = 100 years

4 Calculate the slope of the graph by dividing the change in y by the change in x.

$$slope = \frac{change\ in\ y}{change\ in\ x}$$

$$slope = \frac{3,500\ people}{100\ years}$$

$$slope = 35\ people\ per\ year$$

In this example, the population in Appleton increased by a fixed amount each year. The graph of these data is a straight line. Therefore, the relationship is **linear**. When the graph of a set of data is not a straight line, the relationship is **nonlinear**.

Math Refresher

Bar Graphs

Bar graphs can be used to demonstrate change that is not continuous. These graphs can be used to indicate trends when the data cover a long period of time. A meteorologist gathered the precipitation data shown here for Summerville for April 1–15 and used a bar graph to represent the data.

	Precipitation in Summerville, April 1–15		
Date	Precipitation (cm)	Date	Precipitation (cm)
April 1	0.5	April 9	0.25
April 2	1.25	April 10	0.0
April 3	0.0	April 11	1.0
April 4	0.0	April 12	0.0
April 5	0.0	April 13	0.25
April 6	0.0	April 14	0.0
April 7	0.0	April 15	6.50
April 8	1.75		

How to Make a Bar Graph

1 Use an appropriate scale and a reasonable starting point for each axis.

2 Label the axes, and plot the data.

3 Choose a title that accurately represents the data.

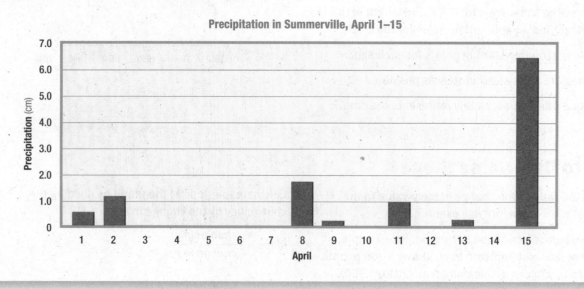

Precipitation in Summerville, April 1–15

Glossary

Sound	Symbol	Example	Respelling
ă	a	pat	PAT
ā	ay	pay	PAY
âr	air	care	KAIR
ä	ah	father	FAH•ther
är	ar	argue	AR•gyoo
ch	ch	chase	CHAYS
ĕ	e	pet	PET
ĕ (at end of a syllable)	eh	settee lessee	seh•TEE leh•SEE
ĕr	ehr	merry	MEHR•ee
ē	ee	beach	BEECH
g	g	gas	GAS
ĭ	i	pit	PIT
ĭ (at end of a syllable)	ih	guitar	gih•TAR
ī	y eye (only for a complete syllable)	pie island	PY EYE•luhnd
îr	ir	hear	HIR
j	j	germ	JERM
k	k	kick	KIK
ng	ng	thing	THING
ngk	ngk	bank	BANGK

Sound	Symbol	Example	Respelling
ŏ	ah	bottle	BAHT'l
ō	oh	toe	TOH
ô	aw	caught	KAWT
ôr	ohr	roar	ROHR
oi	oy	noisy	NOYZ•ee
o͝o	u	book	BUK
o͞o	oo	boot	BOOT
ou	ow	pound	POWND
s	s	center	SEN•ter
sh	sh	cache	CASH
ŭ	uh	flood	FLUHD
ûr	er	bird	BERD
z	z	xylophone	ZY•luh•fohn
z	z	bags	BAGZ
zh	zh	decision	dih•SIZH•uhn
ə	uh	around broken focus	uh•ROWND BROH•kuhn FOH•kuhs
ər	er	winner	WIN•er
th	th	thin they	THIN THAY
w	w	one	WUHN
wh	hw	whether	HWETH•er

absorption in optics, the transfer of light energy to particles of matter (213)

absorción en la óptica, la transferencia de energía luminosa a las partículas de materia

acceleration (ack•SELL•uh•ray•shuhn) the rate at which velocity changes over time; an object accelerates if its speed, direction, or both change (300)

aceleración la tasa a la que la velocidad cambia con el tiempo; un objeto acelera si su rapidez cambia, si su dirección cambia, o si tanto su rapidez como su dirección cambian

amplitude the maximum distance that the particles of a wave's medium vibrate from their rest position (186)

amplitud la distancia máxima a la que vibran las partículas del medio de una onda a partir de su posición de reposo

atom the smallest unit of an element that maintains the properties of that element (126, 141)

átomo la unidad más pequeña de un elemento que conserva las propiedades de ese elemento

atomic number the number of protons in the nucleus of an atom; the atomic number is the same for all atoms of an element (144)

número atómico el número de protones en el núcleo de un átomo; el número atómico es el mismo para todos los átomos de un elemento

average atomic mass the weighted average of the masses of all naturally occurring isotopes of an element (156)

masa atómica promedio el promedio ponderado de las masas de todos los isótopos de un elemento que se encuentran en la naturaleza

calorie the amount of energy needed to raise the temperature of 1 g of water 1 °C; the Calorie used to indicate the energy content of food is a kilocalorie (255)

caloría la cantidad de energía que se requiere para aumentar la temperatura de 1 g de agua en 1 °C; la Caloría que se usa para indicar el contenido energético de los alimentos es la kilocaloría

centripetal acceleration (sehn•TRIP•ih•tahl ack•SELL•uh•ray•shuhn) the acceleration directed toward the center of a circular path (303)

aceleración centrípeta la aceleración que se dirige hacia el centro de un camino circular

chemical change a change that occurs when one or more substances change into entirely new substances with different properties (106)

cambio químico un cambio que ocurre cuando una o más sustancias se transforman en sustancias totalmente nuevas con propiedades diferentes

chemical property a property of matter that describes a substance's ability to participate in chemical reactions (92)

propiedad química una propiedad de la materia que describe la capacidad de una sustancia de participar en reacciones químicas

chemical symbol a one-, two-, or three-letter abbreviation of the name of an element (156)

compound a substance made up of atoms or ions of two or more different elements joined by chemical bonds (127)

compuesto una sustancia formada por átomos de dos o más elementos diferentes unidos por enlaces químicos

conduction (kuhn•DUHK•shuhn) the transfer of energy as heat through a material (257)

conducción calor la transferencia de energía en forma de calor a través del contacto directo

conductor (kuhn•DUHK•ter) a material that transfers energy easily (257)

conductor un material a través del cual se transfiere energía

convection (kuhn•VECK•shuhn) the movement of matter due to differences in density that are caused by temperature variations; can result in the transfer of energy as heat (258)

convección el movimiento de la materia debido a diferencias en la densidad que se producen por variaciones en la temperatura; puede resultar en la transferencia de energía en forma de calor

data (DAY•tuh) information gathered by observation or experimentation that can be used in calculating or reasoning (29)

datos la información recopilada por medio de la observación o experimentación que puede usarse para hacer cálculos o razonar

degree (dih•GREE) the units of a temperature scale (244)

grado la unidad de una escala de temperatura

density the ratio of the mass of a substance to the volume of the substance (79)

densidad la relación entre la masa de una sustancia y su volumen

efficiency (ih•FISH•uhn•see) a quantity, usually expressed as a percentage, that measures the ratio of work output to work input (236)
eficiencia una cantidad, generalmente expresada como un porcentaje, que mide la relación entre el trabajo de entrada y el trabajo de salida

electromagnetic spectrum all of the frequencies or wavelengths of electromagnetic radiation (200)
espectro electromagnético todas las frecuencias o longitudes de onda de la radiación electromagnética

electromagnetic wave a wave that consists of electric and magnetic fields that vibrate at right angles to each other (180)
onda electromagnética una onda que está formada por campos eléctricos y magnéticos que vibran formando un ángulo recto unos con otros

electron a subatomic particle that has a negative charge (143)
electrón una partícula subatómica que tiene carga negativa

electron cloud a region around the nucleus of an atom where electrons are likely to be found (143)
nube de electrones una región que rodea al núcleo de un átomo en la cual es probable encontrar a los electrones

element a substance that cannot be separated or broken down into simpler substances by chemical means; all atoms of an element have the same atomic number (127)
elemento una sustancia que no se puede separar o descomponer en sustancias más simples por medio de métodos químicos; todos los átomos de un elemento tienen el mismo número atómico

empirical evidence (em•PIR•ih•kuhl EV•ih•duhns) the observations, measurements, and other types of data that people gather and test to support and evaluate scientific explanations (8)
evidencia empírica las observaciones, mediciones y demás tipos de datos que se recopilan y examinan para apoyar y evaluar explicaciones científicas

energy (EN•er•jee) the ability to do work or to cause a change (274)
energía la capacidad para trabajar o causar un cambio

energy transformation the process of energy changing from one form into another (234)
transformación de energía el proceso de cambio de un tipo de energía a otro

experiment (ik•SPEHR•uh•muhnt) an organized procedure to study something under controlled conditions (26)
experimento un procedimiento organizado que se lleva a cabo bajo condiciones controladas para estudiar algo

force a push or a pull; something that changes the motion of an object (308)
fuerza un empuje o un jalón; algo que cambia el movimiento de un objeto

free fall the motion of a body when only the force of gravity is acting on the body (328)
caída libre el movimiento de un cuerpo cuando la única fuerza que actúa sobre él es la fuerza de gravedad

frequency (FRE•kwuhn•see) the number of waves produced in a given amount of time, such as a second (187)
frecuencia el número de ondas producidas en una cantidad de tiempo determinada, como por ejemplo, un segundo

gas a form of matter that does not have a definite volume or shape (117)
gas un estado de la materia que no tiene volumen ni forma definidos

gravity a force of attraction between objects that is due to their masses (324)
gravedad una fuerza de atracción entre dos objetos debido a sus masas

group a vertical column of elements in the periodic table; elements in a group share chemical properties (158)
grupo una columna vertical de elementos de la tabla periódica; los elementos de un grupo comparten propiedades químicas

H

heat the energy transferred between objects that are at different temperatures (254)
calor la transferencia de energía entre objetos que están a temperaturas diferentes

Hertz (HERTS) a unit of frequency equal to one cycle per second (187)
hertz una unidad de frecuencia que representa un ciclo por segundo

heterogeneous (het•uhr•uh•JEE•nee•uhs) describes something that does not have a uniform structure or composition throughout (134)
heterogéneo término que describe algo que no tiene una estructura o composición totalmente uniforme

homogeneous (hoh•muh•JEE•nee•uhs) describes something that has a uniform structure or composition throughout (134)
homogéneo término que describe a algo que tiene una estructura o composición global uniforme

hypothesis (hy•PAHTH•eh•sys) a testable idea or explanation that leads to scientific investigation (28)
hipótesis una idea o explicación que conlleva a la investigación científica y que se puede probar

inertia (ih•NER•shuh) the resistance of an object to change in the speed or direction of its motion (313)
inercia la resistencia de un objeto al cambio de la velocidad o de la direccio'n de su movimiento

infrared (in•fruh•RED) electromagnetic wavelengths immediatley outside the red end of the visible spectrum (200)
infrarrojo longitudes de onda electromagnéticas inmediatamente adyacentes al color rojo en el espectro visible

insulator (IN•suh•lay•ter) a material that reduces or prevents the transfer of energy (257)
aislante un material que reduce o evita la transferencia de energía

kinetic energy (kuh•NET•ik) the energy of an object that is due to the object's motion (275)
energía cinética la energía de un objeto debido al movimiento del objeto

kinetic theory of matter (kuh•NET•ik THEE•uh•ree UHV MAT•er) a theory that states that all of the particles that make up matter are constantly in motion (242)
teoría cinética de la materia una teoría que establece que todas las partículas que forman la materia están en movimiento constante

L

law a descriptive statement or equation that reliably predicts events under certain conditions (18)
ley una ecuación o afirmación descriptiva que predice sucesos de manera confiable en determinadas condiciones

law of conservation of energy the law that states that energy cannot be created or destroyed but can be changed from one form to another (235, 279)
ley de la conservación de la energía la ley que establece que la energía ni se crea ni se destruye, sólo se transforma de una forma a otra

law of conservation of mass the law that states that mass cannot be created or destroyed in ordinary chemical and physical changes (110)
ley de la conservación de la masa la ley que establece que la masa no se crea ni se destruye por cambios químicos o físicos comunes

liquid the state of matter that has a definite volume but not a definite shape (117)
líquido el estado de la materia que tiene un volumen definido, pero no una forma definida

longitudinal wave (lawn•ji•TOOD• ehn•uhl) a wave in which the particles of the medium vibrate parallel to the direction of wave motion (178)
onda longitudinal una onda en la que las partículas del medio vibran paralelamente a la dirección del movimiento de la onda

mass a measure of the amount of matter in an object (73)
masa una medida de la cantidad de materia que tiene un objeto

mass number the sum of the numbers of protons and neutrons in the nucleus of an atom (145)
número de masa la suma de los números de protones y neutrones que hay en el núcleo de un átomo

matter anything that has mass and takes up space (72)
materia cualquier cosa que tiene masa y ocupa un lugar en el espacio

mechanical energy (meh•KAN•ih•kuhl) the amount of work an object can do because of the object's kinetic and potential energies (278)
energía mecánica la cantidad de trabajo que un objeto realiza debido a las energías cinética y potencial del objeto

mechanical wave a wave that requires a medium through which to travel (180)
onda mecánica una onda que requiere un medio para desplazarse

medium a physical environment in which phenomena occur (176)
medio un ambiente físico en el que ocurren fenómenos

metal an element that is shiny and that conducts heat and electricity well (157)
metal un elemento que es brillante y conduce bien el calor y la electricidad

metalloid an element that has properties of both metals and nonmetals (157)
metaloide un elemento que tiene propiedades tanto de metal como de no metal

mixture a combination of two or more substances that are not chemically combined (127)
mezcla una combinación de dos o más sustancias que no están combinadas químicamente

model a pattern, plan, representation, or description designed to show the structure or workings of an object, system, or concept (17, 44)

modelo un diseño, plan, representación o descripción cuyo objetivo es mostrar la estructura o funcionamiento de un objeto, sistema o concepto

motion (MOH•shuhn) a change in position over time (288)

movimiento un cambio de posición en el tiempo

net force the combination of all of the forces acting on an object (310)

fuerza neta la combinación de todas las fuerzas que actúan sobre un objeto

neutron a subatomic particle that has no charge and that is located in the nucleus of an atom (142)

neutrón una partícula subatómica que no tiene carga y que está ubicada en el núcleo de un átomo

nonmetal an element that conducts heat and electricity poorly (157)

no metal un elemento que es mal conductor del calor y la electricidad

nucleus 1. in a eukaryotic cell, a membrane-bound organelle that contains the cell's DNA and that has a role in processes such as growth, metabolism, and reproduction, 2. in physical science, an atom's central region, which is made up of protons and neutrons (142)

núcleo 1. en una célula eucariótica, un organelo cubierto por una membrana, el cual contiene el ADN de la célula y participa en procesos tales como el crecimiento, metabolismo y reproducción, 2. en ciencias físicas, la región central de un átomo, la cual está constituida por protones y neutrones

observation the process of obtaining information by using the senses; the information obtained by using the senses (27)

observación el proceso de obtener información por medio de los sentidos; la información que se obtiene al usar los sentidos

opaque (oh•PAYK) describes an object that is not transparent or translucent; a material through which light cannot pass (213)

opaco término que describe un objeto que no es transparente ni translúcido

orbit the path that a body follows as it travels around another body in space (328)

órbita la trayectoria que sigue un cuerpo al desplazarse alrededor de otro cuerpo en el espacio

P-Q

period in chemistry, a horizontal row of elements in the periodic table (159)

período en química, una hilera horizontal de elementos en la tabla periódica

periodic table an arrangement of the elements in order of their atomic numbers such that elements with similar properties fall in the same column, or group (153)

tabla periódica un arreglo de los elementos ordenados en función de su número atómico, de modo que los elementos que tienen propiedades similares se encuentran en la misma columna, o grupo

physical change a change of matter from one form to another without a change in chemical properties (104)

cambio físico un cambio de materia de una forma a otra sin que ocurra un cambio en sus propiedades químicas

physical property a characteristic of a substance that does not involve a chemical change, such as density, color, or hardness (88)

propiedad física una característica de una sustancia que no implica un cambio químico, tal como la densidad, el color o la dureza

position (puh•ZISH•uhn) the location of an object (286)

posición la ubicación de un objeto

potential energy the energy that an object has because of the position, shape, or condition of the object (276)

energía potencial la energía que tiene un objeto debido a su posición, forma o condición

proton a subatomic particle that has a positive charge and that is located in the nucleus of an atom; the number of protons in the nucleus is the atomic number, which determines the identity of an element (142)

protón una partícula subatómica que tiene una carga positiva y que está ubicada en el núcleo de un átomo; el número de protones que hay en el núcleo es el número atómico, y éste determina la identidad del elemento

pure substance a sample of matter, either a single element or a single compound, that has definite chemical and physical properties (128)

sustancia pura una muestra de materia, ya sea un solo elemento o un solo compuesto, que tiene propiedades químicas y físicas definidas

R

radiation (ray•dee•AY•shuhn) the transfer of energy as electromagnetic waves (198, 258)
radiación la transferencia de energía en forma de ondas electromagnéticas

reference point (REF•uhr•uhns POYNT) a location to which another location is compared (286)
punto de referencia una ubicación con la que se compara otra ubicación

reflection the bouncing back of a ray of light, sound, or heat when the ray hits a surface that it does not go through (213)
reflexión el rebote de un rayo de luz, sonido o calor cuando el rayo golpea una superficie pero no la atraviesa

refraction (ri•FRAK•shuhn) the bending of a wave as it passes between two substances in which the speed of the wave differs (216)
refracción el curvamiento de una onda a medida que pasa entre dos sustancias en el que la velocidad de la onda difiere

S

scattering (SKAT•er•ing) the spreading out of light rays in all directions (217)
dispersión la dissipacio'n de los rayos de luz en todas las direcciones

science the knowledge obtained by observing natural events and conditions in order to discover facts and formulate laws or principles that can be verified or tested (6)
ciencia el conocimiento que se obtiene por medio de la observación natural de acontecimientos y condiciones con el fin de descubrir hechos y formular leyes o principios que puedan ser verificados o probados

solid the state of matter in which the volume and shape of a substance are fixed (116)
sólido el estado de la materia en el cual el volumen y la forma de una sustancia están fijos

speed the distance traveled divided by the time interval during which the motion occurred (289)
rapidez la distancia que un objeto se desplaza dividida entre el intervalo de tiempo durante el cual ocurrió el movimiento

T

temperature (TEM•per•uh•chur) a measure of how hot or cold something is; specifically, a measure of the average kinetic energy of the particles in an object (244)
temperatura una medida de qué tan caliente o frío está algo; específicamente, una medida de la energía cinética promedio de las partículas de un objeto

theory the explanation for some phenomenon that is based on observation, experimentation, and reasoning; that is supported by a large quantity of evidence; and that does not conflict with any existing experimental results or observations (16)
teoría una explicación sobre algún fenómeno que está basada en la observación, experimentación y razonamiento; que está respaldada por una gran cantidad de pruebas; y que no contradice ningún resultado experimental ni observación existente

thermal energy the total kinetic energy of a substance's atoms (252)
energía térmica la energía cinética de los átomos de una sustancia

thermometer an instrument that measures and indicates temperature (244)
termómetro un instrumento que mide e indica la temperatura

translucent (tranz•LOO•suhnt) describes matter that transmits light but that does not transmit an image (212)
traslúcido término que describe la materia que transmite luz, pero que no transmite una imagen

transparent (tranz•PAHR•uhnt) describes matter that allows light to pass through with little interference (212)
transparente término que describe materia que permite el paso de la luz con poca interferencia

transverse wave a wave in which the particles of the medium move perpendicularly to the direction the wave is traveling (179)
onda transversal una onda en la que las partículas del medio se mueven perpendicularmente respecto a la dirección en la que se desplaza la onda

ultraviolet (uhl•truh•VY•uh•lit) electromagnetic wavelengths immediately outside the violet end of the visible range (200)
ultravioleta longitudes de onda electromagnéticas inmediatamente adyacentes al color violeta en el espectro visible

variable (VAIR•ee•uh•buhl) any factor that can change in an experiment, observation, or model (29)
variable cualquier factor que puede modificarse en un experimento, observación o modelo

vector (VEK•ter) a quantity that has both size and direction (295)
vector una cantidad que tiene tanto magnitud como dirección

velocity the speed of an object in a particular direction (295)
velocidad la rapidez de un objeto en una dirección dada

volume (VAHL•yoom) the amount of space that an object takes up, or occupies (75)
volumen la cantidad de espacio que ocupa un objeto

wave a disturbance that transfers energy from one place to another without requiring matter to move the entire distance (176)
onda una perturbacio'n que transfiere energi'a de un lugar a otro sin que sea necesario que la materia se mueva toda la distancia

wavefront the collection of points that are reached at the same instant by a wave propagating through a medium (189)

wave period the time required for one wavelength to pass a given point (187)
período de onda el tiempo que se requiere para que una longitud de onda pase por un punto dado

wave speed the speed at which a wave travels through a medium (190)
rapidez de onda la rapidez a la cual viaja una onda a través de un medio

wavelength the distance between two adjacent crests or troughs of a wave (186)
longitud de onda la distancia entre dos crestas o senos adyacentes de una onda

weight (WAYT) a measure of the gravitational force exerted on an object; its value can change with the location of the object in the universe (73)
peso una medida de la fuerza gravitacional ejercida sobre un objeto; su valor puede cambiar en función de la ubicación del objeto en el universo

Index

Page numbers for definitions are printed in **boldface** type.
Page numbers for illustrations, maps, and charts are printed in *italics*.

© Houghton Mifflin Harcourt Publishing Company